# WORLD CINEMA AND THE ESSAY FILM

# WORLD CINEMA AND THE ESSAY FILM
*Transnational Perspectives on a Global Practice*

Edited by Brenda Hollweg and
Igor Krstić

EDINBURGH
University Press

Edinburgh University Press is one of the leading university presses in the UK.
We publish academic books and journals in our selected subject areas across the
humanities and social sciences, combining cutting-edge scholarship with high editorial
and production values to produce academic works of lasting importance. For more
information visit our website: edinburghuniversitypress.com

© editorial matter and organisation Brenda Hollweg and Igor Krstić, 2019, 2021
© the chapters their several authors, 2019, 2021

Edinburgh University Press Ltd
The Tun – Holyrood Road
12 (2f) Jackson's Entry
Edinburgh EH8 8PJ

First published in hardback by Edinburgh University Press 2019

Typeset in 10/12.5 pt Sabon by
Servis Filmsetting Ltd, Stockport, Cheshire

A CIP record for this book is available from the British Library

ISBN 978 1 4744 2924 5 (hardback)
ISBN 978 1 4744 2925 2 (paperback)
ISBN 978 1 4744 2926 9 (webready PDF)
ISBN 978 1 4744 2927 6 (epub)

The right of the contributors to be identified as authors of this work has been asserted
in accordance with the Copyright, Designs and Patents Act 1988 and the Copyright
and Related Rights Regulations 2003 (SI No. 2498).

Chapter 13: all stills are from the film *Forgetting Vietnam*, Trinh T. Minh-ha,
2015–16. © Moongift Films.

# CONTENTS

List of Figures   vii
Acknowledgements   ix
Notes on the Contributors   x

    Introduction   1
    *Brenda Hollweg and Igor Krstić*

## PART ONE   CINEPHILIC DIALOGUES

1. The Essay Film and its Global Contexts: Conversations on Forms and Practices   21
   *Laura Rascaroli, Nguyen Trinh Thi, Bo Wang and Susana Barriga*

2. Essay Films about Film: The 'Filmed Correspondence' between José Luis Guerin and Jonas Mekas   36
   *Fernando Canet*

## PART TWO   MOBILITIES AND MOVEMENTS

3. Accented Essay Films: The Politics and Poetics of the Essay Film in the Age of Migration   55
   *Igor Krstić*

CONTENTS

4. *Cottonopolis*: Experimenting with the Cinematographic, the Ethnographic and the Essayistic  70
   Cathy Greenhalgh

5. The World Essay Film and the Politics of Traceability  89
   Giorgio Avezzù and Giuseppe Fidotta

## PART THREE   LABORATORY OF MEMORIES

6. Memory as a Motor of Images: The Essayistic Mode in Apichatpong Weerasethakul's Variations of *Uncle Boonmee*  107
   Christa Blümlinger

7. 'Time Turning into Space': *Innocence of Memories*' Prismatic Istanbul  122
   Tim O'Farrell

8. *Lovers in Time*: An Essay Film of Contested Memories  138
   Thomas Elsaesser and Agnieszka Piotrowska

## PART FOUR   LANDSCAPES OF TRAUMA

9. *No Man's Zone*: The Essay Film in the Aftermath of the Tsunami in Japan  159
   Marco Bohr

10. 'Image-writing': The Essayistic/*Sanwen* in Chinese Nonfiction Cinema and Zhao Liang's *Behemoth*  172
    Kiki Tianqi Yu

## PART FIVE   ARCHIVAL EFFECTS

11. Indigenous Australia and the Archive Effect: Frances Calvert's *Talking Broken* as Essay Film  193
    Peter Kilroy

12. Between Autobiography, Personal Archive and Mourning: David Perlov's *Diary 1973–1983* in Tel Aviv  211
    Ilana Feldman

## AFTERIMAGES: A PHOTO-ESSAY

Strangely Real: A Reassemblage from the Film *Forgetting Vietnam*  226
Trinh T. Minh-ha

Index  238

# FIGURES

| | | |
|---|---|---|
| 1.1 | *Letters from Panduranga* | 23 |
| 1.2 | *China Concerto* | 29 |
| 1.3 | *The Illusion* | 33 |
| 2.1 | *The Complete Letters: Filmed Correspondence* | 37 |
| 2.2 | Guerin and Mekas's shadows | 45 |
| 2.3 | Guerin's fourth letter | 48 |
| 3.1 | Homesickness in *Lost, Lost, Lost* | 58 |
| 3.2 | Arctic landscapes in *The Nine Muses* | 66 |
| 4.1 | Appliquéd and animated title panel in *Cottonopolis* | 71 |
| 4.2 | Mise-en-abyme, the loom like a camera | 77 |
| 4.3 | Implicating the camerawoman in the essay | 84 |
| 5.1 | *World of Plenty* | 94 |
| 5.2 | *Ananas* | 95 |
| 5.3 | *Genèse d'un repas* | 96 |
| 5.4 | *The Forgotten Space* | 96 |
| 6.1 | *A Letter to Uncle Boonmee* | 112 |
| 6.2 | *Primitive* | 114 |
| 6.3 | *Uncle Boonmee Who Can Recall His Past Lives* | 117 |
| 7.1 | The wall of cigarette butts in *Innocence of Memories* | 131 |
| 7.2 | Condemnatory photographs of women in Turkish media in *Innocence of Memories* | 134 |
| 7.3 | Istanbul street dogs in *Innocence of Memories* | 135 |
| 8.1 | Company of *Lovers in Time* | 140 |

| | | |
|---|---|---|
| 8.2 | Performance of *Lovers in Time* | 144 |
| 8.3 | Co-directors and co-producers Agnieszka Piotrowska and Joe Njagu | 148 |
| 8.4 | Writer and co-director Agnieszka Piotrowska with musicians Pauline Gungidza and Discord Makalanga | 152 |
| 9.1 | Opening sequence of *No Man's Zone* | 161 |
| 9.2 | The framing of natural beauty in *No Man's Zone* | 167 |
| 10.1 | Man curled up in a foetal position in *Behemoth* | 181 |
| 10.2 | Guide carrying a mirror on his back in *Behemoth* | 182 |
| 10.3 | Faces of three workers covered by dust in *Behemoth* | 183 |
| 10.4 | Sheep running down a scarred hillside in *Behemoth* | 185 |
| 11.1 | The politics of space in *Talking Broken* | 200 |
| 11.2 | The language of power in *Talking Broken* | 201 |
| 11.3 | 'Contrapuntal' voices in *Talking Broken* | 203 |
| 12.1 | Chapter 1, São Paulo, 1973, in *Diary 1973–1983* | 213 |
| 12.2 | Letter by David Feldman, from Israel to Brazil | 215 |
| 12.3 | Chapter 3, Julio and Fela at Perlov's home, Tel Aviv, 1981–2, in *Diary 1973–1983* | 216 |
| 12.4 | Chapter 3, still of *Passion of Joan of Arc*, Carl Dreyer, 1928, in *Diary 1973–1983* | 217 |
| 12.5 | David Perlov's notebooks | 219 |
| 12.6 | Rue de l'Aqueduc, Paris, David Perlov | 222 |
| 12.7 | Chapter 5, Rue de l'Aqueduc, Paris, 1983, in *Diary 1973–1983* | 222 |

# ACKNOWLEDGEMENTS

We are very grateful to the authors for their thoughtful contributions, which have given shape to this collaborative project across borders.

We wish to thank Lúcia Nagib and the Department of Film, Theatre and Television at the University of Reading for their hospitality and for providing the institutional framework for the 'World Cinema and the Essay Film' conference in May 2015, which inspired this volume. We thank the DAAD (German Academic Exchange Service) for financing Igor Krstić's postdoctoral research on essay films. We are also grateful to Laura Rascaroli for her support and sustained interest in our project. To Gillian Leslie, Richard Strachan and the rest of the team at Edinburgh University Press, thank you for your professionalism that made this volume possible.

Finally, our thanks go to our respective families for their enduring support and patience. Roman Lennard and Monroe Sternberg, this book that always got in the way when you would rather have played with us is dedicated to you.

# NOTES ON THE CONTRIBUTORS

**Giorgio Avezzù** is Postdoctoral Researcher at the University of Bologna, with a research project about data for audio-visual content analysis and recommendation. He has published on VOD recommender systems, film aesthetics, semiotics and narratology, media archaeology, the cinematic 'representability' of the globe and related questions of film historiography and cartography. He co-edited the special issue 'Mapping' for *Necsus: European Journal of Media Studies* (Autumn 2018), on the intersections between media, geography and mapping, and a special issue of *Cinergie* on geography, film and visual culture. His book *L'evidenza del mondo. Cinema contemporaneo e angoscia geografica* (2017) is currently being translated into English.

**Susana Barriga** is a filmmaker and theorist interested in film essays rooted in reality. She holds a BA in Social Communication, a Master's in Psychoanalysis and Cultural Theory as well as an MA in Contemporary Art History and Visual Culture. Her films have screened at over fifty international film festivals and academic institutions around the world. She was a recipient of the DAAD Artist Residency Fellowship awarded at the Berlinale in 2009 for her film *The Illusion*. She has taught at the EICTV and other film schools and institutions in Spain, Portugal and Latin America. She also developed the theoretical foundations for the MA programme in Essay Filmmaking at the EICTV, which she co-directed and coordinated in 2016. Currently, she is a PhD candidate in Philosophy at the Complutense University of Madrid.

# NOTES ON THE CONTRIBUTORS

**Christa Blümlinger** is Professor in Film Studies at the University Vincennes-Saint-Denis (Paris 8). She formerly taught at the University Sorbonne Nouvelle and at the Free University Berlin. She has published widely on the essay film, media art, film aesthetics and Austrian cinema, including the edition of writings of Harun Farocki (in French) and of Serge Daney (in German). She is a founding member of the French research group *Théâtres de la mémoire* and of the Austrian film distributor *Sixpack Film*. She is also known for her multiple curatorial and critical activities in Vienna, Berlin and Paris. She guest- and co-edited *Paysage et mémoire. Photographie, Cinéma, Dispositifs audiovisuels* (2014), *Attrait de l'archive* (*Cinémas*, 2014), *Morgan Fisher, Off-Screen Cinema* (2017) and *Geste filmé, gestes filmiques* (2018). She is currently working on a book about Harun Farocki.

**Marco Bohr** is the Postgraduate Programme Director for the Arts at Loughborough University. He holds a BFA in Image Arts, a Master's of Photography, a Master's in the History of Art with specialism in early Japanese photography and a PhD from the University of Westminster for a theoretical thesis that investigates contemporary Japanese photography. In 2016, he was awarded a Postdoctoral Fellowship from the Japan Society for the Promotion of Science (JSPS) for his ongoing research on the photographic representation of post-tsunami landscapes. He co-edited *The Evolution of the Image: Political Action and the Digital Self* (2018). He also contributed to *On Perfection*, *Films on Ice: Cinemas of the Arctic* (Edinburgh University Press, 2015), *Directory of World Cinema* and *World Film Locations*. He is on the editorial board for the journal *East Asian Journal of Popular Culture*.

**Fernando Canet** is Associate Professor in Media and Film Studies at the Fine Arts College, Polytechnic University of Valencia. He authored and co-authored several books and is the co-editor of *(Re)viewing Creative, Critical and Commercial Practices in Contemporary Spanish Cinema* (2014). He was guest editor of a special issue of *Hispanic Research Journal* on contemporary Spanish cinema and a special issue of *L'Atalante. International Film Studies Journal* on cinephile directors in modern times. He has published articles in *Communication & Society*, *Studies in European Cinema*, *Studies in Documentary Films*, *The Journal of Popular Culture*, *Popular Communication*, *Bulletin of Spanish Studies* and *Journal of Film and Video*.

**Thomas Elsaesser** is Professor Emeritus at the Department of Media and Culture of the University of Amsterdam. Since 2013, he is also Visiting Professor at Columbia University. Among his recent books are *German Cinema – Terror and Trauma: Cultural Memory Since 1945* (2013), *Film Theory – An Introduction Through the Senses* (with Malte Hagener, 2nd revised edn, 2015), *Körper, Tod und Technik* (with Michael Wedel, 2016) and *Film History as Media Archaeology* (2016). His latest book is *European Cinema and Continental Thought* (2018).

**Ilana Feldman** has a PhD in Film Studies from the School of Communications and Arts at the University of São Paulo, with an internship in the Department of Philosophy, Arts and Aesthetics at the University Paris 8, where she developed research about the contemporary Brazilian documentary. In 2011, she curated the exhibition 'David Perlov: Epiphanies of the Everyday' held in the Brazilian Cinematheque, which resulted in a publication with the same title published by the Jewish Cultural Center of São Paulo. This work was followed by postdoctoral research in Literary Theory at UNICAMP, titled 'David Perlov's Film Diaries: From the Private Sphere to Politics'. Currently, she is Postdoctoral Fellow in Film and Media Studies at the University of São Paulo, with a special interest in the relations between trauma, mourning and autobiography in cinema and literature.

**Giuseppe Fidotta** holds a PhD from the University of Udine and is currently enrolled as PhD student in Film and Moving Image Studies at the Mel Hoppenheim School of Cinema, Concordia University, where he is conducting a media-ethnographic project on media ecology, alternative culture industry and globalisation in Western Sicily. He has published in *Necsus*, *Journal of Italian Cinema and Media Studies*, *Immagine: note di storia del cinema*, *Fata Morgana*, *Il cinema come disciplina* (2017) and in *Cine-Ethiopia: The History and Politics of Film in the Horn of Africa* (2018). He co-edited *At the Borders of (Film) History: Temporality, Archaeology, Theories* (2015), an anthology in Italian on media archaeology (2018) and a special issue for *Necsus* on mapping and the media (2018). He is editor-in-chief of *Synoptique*.

**Cathy Greenhalgh** is a filmmaker, lecturer, media anthropologist and writer. She directs and shoots ethnographic essay documentaries and art film shorts for cinema, gallery and museum spaces. Her films have been screened in film festivals worldwide. *Aftermath* (2006) won first prize Best Experimental Film at Strange Screen Film Festival, Greece; *Switch* (2013) is distributed by the Royal Anthropological Institute. Her research interests and publications centre on sensory ethnography and material culture of light, landscape and textiles, the anthropology of media and visual anthropology, collaborative and interdisciplinary creativity, filmmaking practices and communities of practice as well as cinematographic phenomena and aesthetics. Most recently, she taught as Principal Lecturer in Film and Television at the London College of Communication, University of the Arts London.

## NOTES ON THE CONTRIBUTORS

**Brenda Hollweg** is Research Fellow in the School of Fine Art, History of Art and Cultural Studies at the University of Leeds. A specialist in American literature and a scholar of the essay as literary and expanded cultural form, she worked on two major research collaborations that addressed questions of gender, genre and the essay (DFG, Humboldt University Berlin, 2000–3) as well as the aesthetic and affective dimensions of democratic participation (AHRC, University of Leeds, 2009–11). She has published on contemporary documentary and the cinematic essay and, in 2010, made the video essay *The Road to Voting*.

**Peter Kilroy** is Lecturer in the Department of Sociology at City, University of London. He works across the fields of British and Australian cultural and media studies, postcolonial studies and political theory, deconstruction and Indigenous studies. He has special research interests in the relationship between Australian First Nations politics and media strategies, and is currently working on a comparative analysis of decolonisation discourse in Australia and the UK. Recent publications include 'Postcolonial Justice? Recognition, Redistribution and the Mabo Legacy' in *Postcolonial Justice in Australia: Reassessing the 'Fair Go'* (2016) and 'Screening Indigenous Australia: Space, Place and Media in Frances Calvert's *Talking Broken*' in *Ilha do Desterro* (2016). A former co-editor of *parallax* and *Ex plus Ultra* journals, he is now co-editing a book on Australian screen media.

**Igor Krstić** lectures in the American Studies Department at the University of Stuttgart and in the Centre for Cultural and General Studies at the Karlsruhe Institute of Technology (KIT). From 2014 to 2016, he was DAAD-Postdoctoral Researcher at the University of Reading, where he worked on the research project 'Accented Essay Films' and organised the 'World Cinema and the Essay Film' conference. He has published articles, book chapters and reviews, and co-edited collections on film philosophy, national and transnational cinema, documentary and the essay film in, among others, *New Cinemas, Historical Journal of Film, Radio and Television, Mediapolis* and *Aniki*. He is the author of two monographs, most recently *Slums on Screen: World Cinema and the Planet of Slums* (Edinburgh University Press, 2016).

**Trinh T. Minh-ha** is a Vietnam-born filmmaker, writer and composer. Best known perhaps for her essay film *Surname Viet Given Name Nam* (1989), she has formed and co-defined the field of film essayistic practice for over thirty years. Her award-winning works include *Forgetting Vietnam* (2015), *Night Passage* (2004), *The Fourth Dimension* (2001), *A Tale of Love* (1995), *Naked Spaces – Living is Round* (1985) and *Reassemblage* (1982). She is the recipient of the Trailblazers Award at MIPDOC, Cannes, and the AFI National Independent Filmmaker Maya Deren Award. Her films have been shown widely and have been given over fifty retrospectives in countries across the world. She has also travelled and lectured extensively on film, art, feminism and cultural politics. She is currently Professor of Gender and Women's Studies and of Rhetoric at the University of California, Berkeley.

**Tim O'Farrell** teaches in the School of Film and Television at the Victorian College of the Arts, University of Melbourne. He has a PhD in Cinema Studies, which focuses on the Direct Cinema Celebrity Documentary cycle. He also curates the film programme for the Melbourne International Film Festival. Otherwise, he works as a lawyer.

**Agnieszka Piotrowska** is a filmmaker and theorist. She has written extensively on psychoanalysis and culture. She is best known for her documentary *Married to the Eiffel Tower* (2008). Her current work focuses on asymmetrical power relationships in culture and cinema. She is the author of *Psychoanalysis and Ethics in Documentary Film* (Edinburgh University Press, 2014) and *Black and White: Cinema, Politics and the Arts in Zimbabwe* (2016), the editor of *Embodied Encounters: New Approaches to Psychoanalysis and Cinema* (2015) and co-editor of *Psychoanalysis and the Unrepresentable: From Culture to the Clinic* (2016).

**Laura Rascaroli** is Professor of Film and Screen Media at University College Cork, Ireland. She is the author and editor of a number of volumes, including *How the Essay Film Thinks* (2017), *The Personal Camera: Subjective Cinema and the Essay Film* (2009), *Crossing New Europe: Postmodern Travel and the European Road Movie* (2006), co-written with Ewa Mazierska, and *Antonioni: Centenary Essays* (2011), co-edited with John David Rhodes. Her work has been translated into several languages, including Chinese, Italian, French, German, Polish, Spanish and Taiwanese. She is the General Editor of *Alphaville: Journal of Film and Screen Media*.

**Nguyen Trinh Thi** is a Hanoi-based filmmaker/moving image artist. Her moving image works engage with memory and history and reflect on the role and position of artists in society. Her materials are diverse, from self-produced video and photographs to images she appropriates from sources such as press photos, corporate videos and classic films. Her practice crosses the boundaries between film and video art, installation and performance. Her video works have been shown at international festivals and exhibitions, including Jeu de Paume (Paris), CAPC musée d'art contemporain de Bordeaux, the Lyon Biennale 2015, Asian Art Biennial 2015 (Taiwan), Fukuoka Asian Art Triennial 2014 and Singapore Biennale 2013. In 2009, she founded DOCLAB, an independent centre for documentary and the moving image in Hanoi.

## NOTES ON THE CONTRIBUTORS

**Bo Wang** is an artist and filmmaker based in Brooklyn, New York. His works have been exhibited internationally, including the Museum of Modern Art and Guggenheim Museum in New York, CPH: DOX in Copenhagen, Garage Museum of Contemporary Art in Moscow, Shanghai Biennale, Bi-city Biennale of Urbanism/Architecture in Shenzhen, Asia Society Texas Center, DMZ Docs in South Korea and DOKUARTS at the German Historical Museum in Berlin. He was a fellow at the Robert Flaherty Film Seminar in 2013. He is also a faculty member at the Visual and Critical Studies programme at the School of Visual Arts, New York.

**Kiki Tianqi Yu** is a filmmaker, film curator and lecturer in the Department of Film Studies, Queen Mary University of London. Her research focuses on first person documentary, essayistic nonfiction, non-western cinemas and the documentary industry. She is the author of *'My' Self On Camera: First Person Documentary Practice in an Individualising China* (Edinburgh University Press, 2018) and co-editor of *China's iGeneration: Cinema and Moving Image Culture for the Twenty-First Century* (2014). Her films include *Photographing Shenzhen* (2007), the essay film *Memory of Home* (2009) and the award-winning documentary feature *China's van Goghs* (2016). She curated *Polyphonic China*, the first Chinese independent documentary screening series in the UK, at Regent Cinema London (2008–9), and *Memory Talks*, a series of personal nonfiction films in Shanghai in 2017.

# INTRODUCTION

## Brenda Hollweg and Igor Krstić

Whether in analogue or digital form, as single- or multi-channel projection, an increasing number of essay films are currently exhibited at museums, art shows or film festivals around the world. Thomas Elsaesser has called this phenomenon, borrowing this phrase from Christy Wampole, the 'essayfication of everything' (2017: 241).[1] But why has this performative documentary practice gained such currency lately? Obviously, the digital technologies have made it possible for small, independent and malleable forms like the essay film to be produced, disseminated and consumed widely. More important, however, as both Laura Rascaroli (2017: 5) and Nora Alter (2018: 15) have argued, is the tendency of the essay film to proliferate in times of crisis. Both theorists refer us to the second half of the twentieth century when international events such as the Vietnam War (1955–75) not only elicited strong reactions, but also were conducive to the production of essay films. These films were used as a means for a more personalised audio-visual expression or, as Alter observes, 'as a medium for protest, resistance, witness, or commentary' (2018: 148).[2]

Today, roughly sixty years later, essay films have not lost their radical potential. In times of accelerated globalisation – or 'liquid modernity', as Zygmunt Bauman (2000) has called it – artists and filmmakers around the world, once again, exploit the essay film for purposes of socio-political critique. This potential of the essay film as a critical mode of enquiry and vehicle for resistance rests with its form. Essays are, according to Theodor W. Adorno (2017), border-crossers *par excellence*; they borrow freely from seemingly more established genres such as letter, pamphlet or poetry.[3] They also provoke resistance because of their inherently heretic and anachronistic (that is, against their time) character, as he argues. For Rascaroli, this untimeliness of the essay – and, consequently, the essay film – 'accounts for its political value' (2017: 5). Politics and ethics are thereby closely connected. She writes: 'To say "I" or "we" is, first, a gesture of responsibility and accountability, in filmmaking too. The moment of the essay film is, therefore, politically inflected' (5).[4] With reference to an argument that Michelle Boulous Walker makes about the ability of the essay to keep alive 'the hope for a slow engagement with the complexity and ambiguity of the world' (2011: 274), Rascaroli also attests to the essay film a strong utopian potential: it is 'the future film, the film of tomorrow' (2017: 6).

With the current omnipresence of the essay film in a continuously evolving media environment, whether on- or offline, this mode of documentary practice 'has necessarily become an object of intensified critical interest' (Papazian and Eades 2016: 1). Not co-incidentally, *World Cinema and the Essay Film* has an academic conference with the same title in its background. In May 2015, more than one hundred international essay film practitioners as well as senior and early career researchers – alongside keynote speakers Thomas Elsaesser, Timothy Corrigan and Walter Salles – gathered at the University of Reading (UK) to discuss what was at that time fast becoming one of the most debated film genres in film studies. In the same year, the Birkbeck Institute of the Moving Image, headed by Laura Mulvey – herself an ardent admirer and practitioner of the essay film – inaugurated the first *Essay Film Festival* in London. Further conferences, workshops and symposia on the essay film were held at Columbia University (2015), Florida State University (2015), the University of York (2017) and the American University of Beirut (2019), as well as in less academic spaces of intellectual debate, including Zeughauskino and Denkerei in Berlin (2016, 2018) or Foundation Perdu in Amsterdam (2018).

The same period also saw the publication of a series of volumes on the essay film (Alter 2018; Alter and Corrigan 2017; Rascaroli 2017; Papazian and Eades 2016). *World Cinema and the Essay Film* complements these volumes. Unlike previous books, which situate the essay film and, by extension, first person documentaries largely within the socio-political contexts, theoretic frameworks and aesthetic traditions of European and North American avant-garde, experimental and abstract cinema,[5] this volume draws attention to the essay film as a highly reflective worldwide as well as 'world-ing' practice. First, essay filmmaking in a global context is still underexplored, although more recent collections and monographs (Alter 2018; Rascaroli 2017; Papazian and Eades 2016) have broadened the field by including in-depth analyses of non-western filmmakers and their essayistic productions.[6] In bringing the generic term 'essay film' together with the category of 'world cinema', we hope to inspire future researchers to regard the essay film as a global counter-practice that has evolved from different, potentially uneven centres of moving image-making around the world. Historically, as we shall see in more detail, essay films were also made and consumed beyond the world's 'old' and traditional economic power centres (London, Paris, Berlin or New York), in cities such as Moscow or Buenos Aires. Today, their points of departure are just as well the large urban centres of Beijing, Beirut, Istanbul, Rio de Janeiro or Tokyo, which are all marked by lively and diverse independent media production scenes.

Second, essay films encourage us 'to rethink the complex relationship between specificity and generality' (Silverman 2013: 20). These films provide their audiences with a form of philosophical thinking that seeks its object of enquiry in the most specific and concrete. For this purpose, film essayists usually adopt a mundane perspective and practise a 'down-to-earth' grip of things, which can be likened to other embedded modes of critical enquiry such as the ethnographic or the journalistic. In the last instance, however, essays/ essayists are less interested in individual stories *per se* than what they allow us to 'apprehend' on a more abstract, philosophical, conceptual or affective level, with regards to a specific collective, a *Weltanschauung*, a larger question that might develop from these materials or their own conditions of possibility.

Studies in this book focus on the essayistic practices of John Akomfrah, Susana Barriga, Noël Burch and Allan Sekula, Frances Calvert, Toshi Fujiwara, Grant Gee, Amos Gitai, Cathy Greenhalgh, José Luis Guerín, Jonas Mekas, Angela Melitopoulos, Luc Moullet, Nguyen Trinh Thi, David Perlov, Agnieszka Piotrowska, Trinh T. Minh-ha, Bo Wang, Apichatpong Weerasethakul and Zhao Liang. These artists and film essayists, like many of their kind, are concerned with questions that result from the planetary effects of more abstract phenomena such as globalisation, but also brought about by the (often unpredictable) consequences of environmental disasters, war or ethnic conflicts. These are questions of universal concern, but they usually have their source in very specific local or regional events. While film essayists address these questions, they typically find themselves 'grappling with, rather than generalizing from' (Haraway 2008: 3) the situation in front of them, probing and testing it from different angles and aligning themselves in the (research) process with 'the voices of many peoples, knowledges, and earthly practices' (Stengers 2015: 50).

To a large extent, artists and filmmakers investigated in this book were born in one place but live and work in exilic, diasporic or transnational contexts. This is typically reflected in their thematic choice and the transnational perspective that is developed in their works. Conceptually, 'the transnational' not only takes account of mobility and movement across national/geographical borders and time zones, but also implies, as Nataša Ďurovičová and Kathleen Newman argue, 'relations of unevenness' (2010: x) between different nations. It is these relations that, arguably, provoke artists and filmmakers to make use of the essay as a mode of critical enquiry and politico-aesthetic intervention, generating a disposition favourable to what Nelly Richard calls 'peripheral operations': operations of the fragment, citation, montage or collage (1996: 82). As works that operate in the gaps and cracks of diverse global image economies, across different genre and media, and often also explore one particular moment in time through the (historical/memory) traces of another, essay films embrace the prefix 'trans' on many different levels. They point us to multiply entangled yet also divergent local, regional and global forces, some of which are capable of traversing the limits of specific systems of cultural distribution to expose its arbitrary and vulnerable condition. Seemingly stable or fixed entities such as 'national' identity, cinema, culture, and so on, in these films, become sites of (often unresolved) conflict and tension but also politico-aesthetic contestation.

The emphasis that is placed in this book on essay film practice as a worldwide phenomenon does not imply that *World Cinema and the Essay Film* provides readers with a representative collection of such practice. Rather, exemplary studies illuminate the capacity of the essay film to exist, even thrive, as a tool or medium for unorthodox and dialectical modes of thinking, storytelling and political intervention, some of which might be located in Africa or Latin America – but not necessarily so. This corresponds with our notion of 'world cinema' as both a critical *and* inclusive or 'positive' (cf. Nagib 2006) category. Following Andrew Higson's influential 1989 essay 'The Concept of National Cinema', 'world cinema' has been re-evaluated by numerous scholars and from different angles. The term has been heavily criticised for being too slippery, too general or for its lack of heuristic value.[7] It was often deployed as a term to designate all film productions that are either 'non-Hollywood' or non-western (cf. Nagib 2006). The old concept of 'world cinema' has been (rather non-theoretically) used as a category to describe an amalgam of more or less separately evolving national (Japanese, Argentine, Iranian, etc.) or regional (Southeast Asian, Francophone African, Latin American, etc.) non-western cinemas, centred around art and/or fictional cinema as the dominant form(s). However, with scholars like Lúcia Nagib (2006), Nataša Ďurovičová (2010), Rosalind Galt (2010), Dudley Andrew (2006), Chris Berry (2010) or Paul Cooke (2007), world cinema is now seen as a polycentric (developing from different centres around the world), polyvalent (ascribed with various meanings, depending on the point of view and the cultural or geographical context from which one looks at its productions etc.) and polymorphic (involving various forms, from fictional to avant-garde and documentary) phenomenon, as Shekhar Deshpande and Meta Mazaj have most recently proposed in their book *World Cinema: A Critical Introduction* (2018). They argue that even though the term is slippery and contentious, world cinema of such kind 'is a reality, at the very least denoting that cinema is a global phenomenon that is produced around the world and circulates in nearly all its corners' (2).

As we shall see, contributors to this volume explore the manifold implications that the essay film as a critical and independent media practice has for engendering change in different places and socio-political contexts around the world. Studies in this volume investigate the filmed correspondence between exilic filmmakers; or they explore the strategies film essayists deploy to think 'with' or 'alongside' the more or less visible flows of migrants, goods and finance capital to build an argument about the dehumanising effects of accelerated globalisation. Authors further examine how film essayists that work, among others, with traditions of African theatre, Indian music and myth, Buddhist fables, Thai soap operas, Chinese 'image writing', the landscape theory of 1960s Japanese experimental films or the visual archive of distinct Indigenous populations provoke questions about a nation's colonial history, race, gender or class conceptions, collective memory or traumatic pasts. Contributors investigate how these often multilingual works stage critical encounters between divergent (narrative, aesthetic, performative) conventions and cine-essayistic traditions, for instance of the vernacular, the ritualistic or the international avant-garde from Asia, Africa or Europe, and thereby allow the essay film's argumentative structure to become 'visible'. This structure enables its creators to address forms of injustice, oppression, exclusion, silencing, invisibility, subjugation or abuse, just as well as to mobilise forces of resistance against such forms. Characteristically, this is done in oblique, imaginative and affectively charged ways, creating an interstitial or 'third space' through the use of formal and narrative techniques such as the palimpsest, diachronic gaze, montage, analogy, allegory, intertextuality or 'slow' cinematography. As individual chapters show in more detail, the essay film here forms a distinct medium of cine-aesthetic heresy or, to put it with Jacques Rancière (2010, 2004), *dissensus*. It gives voice to a politics of aesthetics that engenders new legibilities and new modes of apprehension: 'new modes of individuality and new connections between those modes, new forms of perception of the given and new plots of temporality' (Rancière 2010: 141).

An account of global film essayistic production as counter-practice – one that, from a typically marginalised position, is critical of mainstream ideologies, production modes and film formats and has been, almost from the beginning, carried by a transnational perspective – first requires us to look more closely into the specific conditions that have nurtured this cinematic form in different places and regions around the world. In doing so, we are, to speak with Morgan Adamson, 'less interested in defining the history and formal characteristics of a cinematic genre than in understanding how [. . . these films] became a vehicle to imagine new political possibilities, modes of social organization, and affective forms of communication' (2018: Introduction, para. 5).[8]

## Times of Crisis: A Polycentric Genealogy of the Essay Film

One influential conception of the essay film can be traced back to the notion (or dream) of merging the medium of writing with that of cinema. This notion becomes first visible in *auteur* theory – a theory originating from French film criticism of the 1940s, in particular the enormously influential film journal *Cahiers du Cinéma* with its leading figures François Truffaut and André Bazin (who was, with Hans Richter, among the first to coin the term 'essay film'). Alexandre Astruc's notion of the 'caméra-stylo' ('camera-pen') as well as his idea that film is a language in itself and filmmakers therefore not only able to 'depict' the visible reality, but also to express abstract (or invisible) concepts, thoughts and ideas via mastering the art of cinematography and editing, also emerge during that time. This idea of the *caméra-stylo* (and by extension, that of the *auteur*) directly links to the notion of the essay film as a filmic 'adaptation' of a literary-philosophical style or form. It may thus not come as a surprise that the essay film in Europe prospers and thrives, for the first time, in the intellectually stimulating and vibrant atmosphere of 1950s Paris. The form is embraced by emerging avant-garde filmmakers such as Chris Marker (*Letter from Siberia*, 1957) or Alain Resnais (*Night and Fog*, 1955) and soon becomes a prominent feature of French *ciné-club* culture. Here the *Nouvelle Vague* meets Michel de Montaigne, existentialism the *Nouveau Roman*, and in dialogue and mutual exchange with one another's literary, philosophical or cinematic works a culture of *cinécriture* as well as an audience of educated spectators is generated, which appreciate challenging (essayistic) films as equally demanding (essayistic) prose. In this regard, the late 1940s and early 1950s certainly become 'watershed years for the essay film' (Corrigan 2011: 63), with Paris at their centre.

But are the origins of the essay film solely to be found in *auteur* theory and in French film culture of the 1950s? In fact, one can easily question this story. While there is no doubt that French film (and, by extension, literary and philosophical) culture had a strong affinity with the essayistic mode of expression – from Michel de Montaigne to Chris Marker, as the subtitle of Timothy Corrigan's monograph (2011) suggests – there is also little doubt that there are multiple, international trajectories, rather than a single, national strand, that lead to the evolvement of the essay film as a distinct mode of critical enquiry and documentary practice. With the transnational turn in film studies it has become *en vogue* to point out how film movements or genres seldom develop gradually from a centre to the various peripheries (of world cinema), but rather evolve 'polycentrically', involving many, rather than few, centres of production as well as reciprocal, albeit potentially uneven, interaction and interdependence between these centres. A polycentric, multidirectional genealogy can be attested to almost any kind of genre, whether popular or not, from *film noir* to documentary *as well as* the essay film.

For the formation of the essay film as global counter-practice, more specifically, the international 1920s avant-garde that emerges within very diverse socio-political contexts in metropolises such as Amsterdam, Paris, Berlin, Vienna or Moscow at about the same time is crucial. Because of the central role of cities for the avant-garde (cf. Hagener 2007: 33), it is also no coincidence that the city symphony emerges as this era's most vibrant (and most transnational) experimental documentary genre. Apart from *Berlin, Symphony of a Great City* (Walter Ruttmann, 1927), *À Propos de Nice* (Jean Vigo, 1930) and *Nothing But Time* (Alberto Cavalcanti, 1926), it is first and foremost Dziga Vertov's *Man with a Movie Camera* (1929) that needs to be mentioned here, as it is often regarded as an essay film on modern urban life and documentary cinema itself. If one considers the art of montage as a non-verbal 'authorial voice' (cf. Rascaroli 2017: 47–67), city symphonies as well as Soviet montage cinema form essay films proper.

Apart from non-verbal essayism, Russian montage theorists were also interested in the relation between images and words (or in cinema as 'linguistic' medium, capable of expressing thoughts in a language-like manner). Sergei Eisenstein, for instance, not only thought of turning Karl Marx's *Das Kapital* (1867) into an essay film – famously, the subject of a more contemporary essay film, Alexander Kluge's *News from Ideological Antiquity: Marx/Eisenstein/ Capital* (2008–15) – he also compared images to Egyptian hieroglyphs, while his montage theory included the technique of intellectual montage, which ought, according to Eisenstein, to create ideas, thoughts or concepts rather than just impressions or stories in the mind of the spectator. Another early essayistic approach, related with but still distinct from the idea of montage, is visible in Esfir Shub's *Fall of the Romanov Empire* (1927), which is a found footage or compilation film. These developments throw a different light on the genealogy of the essay film, not only as a kind of 'literary cinema' with a strong authorial voice and roots in the *ciné-club* culture of 1950s Paris, but also as a form of montage that makes basic principles of cinematic essayism visible for the first time, namely that of fragmented heterogeneity (of materials, topics, moods and stories).

Until very recently, this Soviet or Russian and therefore distinctly non-western influence was sidelined (or simply ignored) by contemporary essay film theorists and scholars – even though the experimental documentaries of the 1920s, including those from outside the Soviet Union, were readily accepted as either essay films or essayistic in spirit as well as in practice.[9] Because of this heritage, the essay film has especially strong ties to Marxist thought and to political (both propagandist and non-propagandist) film practice. The historical key year of the twentieth century, 1968 – the year in which Jean-Luc Godard and Jean-Pierre Gorin founded the *Dziga Vertov Group* in Paris, and Fernando Solanas and Octavio Getino released their masterpiece *The Hour of the Furnaces* – constitutes a significant year for the 'world essay film', too.

In fact, the decade leading up to 1968 can be regarded as the globalisation decade of the essay film. It is the decade in which 'world cinema' – spurred and inspired by its new world cinema *auteurs*, such as Glauber Rocha, Satyajit Ray or Nagisa Oshima, and the accompanying waves of 1960s new cinemas, including *Cinema Novo* in Brazil, Parallel Cinema in India and *Nuberu Bagu* in Japan – collides and colludes with the global spread of essay film practices. Rascaroli (2017: 3), among others, has shown that essay films start to appear outside of Europe (and, by extension, the Soviet Union) in polycentric fashion in the 1960s. This is the case in the USA with *Walden* (Jonas Mekas, 1969), in Iran with *The House is Black* (Forough Farrokhzad, 1963), in Mexico with *The Secret Formula* (Rúben Gámez, 1965), in Japan with *Yungbogi's Diary* (Nagisa Oshima, 1966) or in Armenia with *We* (Atavazad Peleshian, 1969). Obviously, not all of these films were inspired by Marxist thought, but many of them are the result of the 1960s revolutionary spirit that also kickstarted the numerous new waves, from the French *Nouvelle Vague* to the New American Cinema.

In this context, the largely Latin America-based and explicitly 'revolutionary' Third Cinema movement played a pivotal role in the evolution of the 'world essay film'. *The Hour of the Furnaces* is not only central here, because it was released in 1968. For Solanas and Getino, the essay film was (just as the essay for Adorno) a heresy to more (ideologically or economically) dominant forms, since for them the essay film was one 'of the privileged forms for the realization of a revolutionary, anticolonialist, anticapitalist filmmaking practice' (Rascaroli 2017: 4). Solanas and Getino's manifesto-essay 'Toward a Third Cinema', first published in 1969, as well as their radically critical – and therefore heretical – essay film show how this mode of documentary collides not only with world cinema, but also with critical (Marxist) theory. The spread of Critical Theory on university campuses across the world in the 1960s – that is, via Adorno, Herbert Marcuse and Walter Benjamin, who were all devoted to the essayistic form – corresponded directly with the spread of the essay film across the world of cinema.

Essay films, since the early 1920s, were not produced in a social and historical bubble but in close interaction with – and often in explicit resistance to – other cinematic, technological, social or political developments, such as the international spread of commercialised cinema, the arrival of sound in cinema, the modernisation of cities or the rise of totalitarian ideologies. In the 1960s, essay films thrive for the first time globally when portable sync sound cameras become widely used by documentary filmmakers, but they also thrive during a time in which the (partly violent) struggles between ideologies and political systems (Communism vs Capitalism) as well as progressive and conservative forces (the Left vs the Right) reach a peak. It is also a time of anti-colonialist struggle and upheaval in what was then called the 'Third World', but also a time in which gender and racial relations as well as workers' rights become hotly contested issues in the 'First World'. The many and diverse conflicts in the 1960s provide the fertile soil for essays in literary and visual form to be produced and circulated. They speak with or alongside dissidents, the homeless, the exiled or those that associate as black, feminist, bisexual, gay or lesbian. It is therefore no coincidence that essay films prosper and flourish internationally in a decade in which a new generation searched and fought for freedoms previously denied to them, among them also and most importantly the freedom of thought and expression.

Astruc's idea of a personalised *cinécriture* provided by a camera-pen has now, with desktop editing, *Vimeo* and affordable DV cameras – hence, with the *media-stylo*, as Eric Faden has called it with reference to Astruc in a 2008 manifesto-essay called 'A Manifesto for Critical Media' – become a reality rather than a distant utopian goal. While 'inequality' has become the new buzzword in economic theory and Marx or Marx-inspired thought and analysis celebrates an unexpected comeback among intellectuals and scholars since the global financial crisis in 2008 (cf. Eagleton 2018; Piketty 2014; Badiou 2010), essayistic theory as global critique thrives both on- and off-screen, with eminent figures such as Hito Steyerl, Mark Fisher, Allan Sekula, Akram Zaatari or Ursula Biemann, among others. And are we not living, at least since 2008, if not since 2001, in times of global crises (or 'in the End Times', as Slavoj Žižek (2011) has put it)? Such times have seen a crisis of capitalism, a global refugee crisis, a crisis of democracy and the rise of the New Right in Europe and the USA, among others effected by social media and digitisation, a crisis of free speech in universities, phenomena like global warming and the looming ecological disaster. Essay films, more than ever, address these issues today, emerging once again as a dissident, nonconformist practice, a viable means of expression for those at the margins and fringes of mainstream (world) cinema.

THE BOOK: CRITICAL INTERESTS AND STRUCTURE

Reflecting a diversity of voices, *World Cinema and the Essay Film* includes contributions from film scholars, cultural theorists and film practitioners situated both in and beyond Europe. Likewise, the book covers a broad range of textual formats, including three interviews with non-western filmmakers, an impassioned yet critical dialogue between a film scholar and a filmmaker, a feminist essay in which a film scholar questions her own role as archivist, an essay in which a filmmaker explores her unfinished film project, a multiply refracted photo-essay and various more traditional academic film analyses. These contributions are structured along five thematic clusters. Part One ('Cinephilic Dialogues') opens with a collaborative piece from Laura Rascaroli that stages three separate conversations she conducted via email and Skype with non-western born, yet globally operating, artists and intellectuals Susana Barriga (Cuba), Nguyen Trinh Thi (Vietnam) and Bo Wang (China). Their varied responses to questions of the essay's place in-between western and eastern traditions sketch a picture of essayistic cinema as programmatically experimental, anti-authoritarian and political. Essay film practices are used here, among others, to circumvent censorship or work against the conventions of public television or mainstream cinema. Of appeal to these three filmmakers is, as Barriga (this volume) points out, the essay's anti-systemic nature, its 'radical contortion of form, to the point of its revocation'.

Rascaroli's virtual roundtable is matched with Fernando Canet's study on the epistle as transnational cinematic dialogue. His contribution looks into the filmed letters exchanged between exilic filmmakers José Luis Guerín and Jonas Mekas. These letters constitute, as he argues, essay films proper. As epistolarity and exile often mutually condition one another, Canet also investigates a larger tradition of filmed correspondence projects that form cinephilic dialogues as passionate and multilayered reflection on artistic creation across geographical and existential borders.

Part Two ('Mobilities and Movements') includes three studies that share an interest in world cinema traditions, the dimensions of post-colonial modernity, authorship, inscriptions of subjectivity and diaspora aesthetics. Igor Krstić explores how central elements of essay film practice coalesce with what Hamid Naficy, in 2001, identified as 'accented cinema': a cinema that is in a perpetual 'state of preformation and emergence in disparate and dispersed pockets across the globe' (4); that is not restricted to 'the accented speech of the diegetic characters' (4), but emanates more profoundly 'from the displacement of the filmmakers and their artisanal production modes' (4). Essay film practices – like accented cinema – are open-form, fragmented, multilingual and self-reflexive, and they often include 'subject matter and themes that involve journeying, historicity, identity, and displacements' (4). In applying Naficy's terminology to prominent essay films such as John Akomfrah's *The Nine Muses* (2009), as well as to lesser-known 'world cinema' examples such as Jeong-Hyun Mun's *Grandmother's Flower* (2007), Margareta Hruza's *Home* (2008) or Sandra Kogut's *A Hungarian Passport* (2001), Krstić provides new perspectives on an emerging transnational body of films produced by diasporic, exilic or interstitial documentary and/or essay filmmakers in the recent past. He is particularly interested in the ways experience of (first, second or third generation) migration can be worked through in the essayistic format and what role the filmmaker's subjectivity plays in this process.

Approaching questions of subjectivity and post-colonialism from a more practice-based perspective, filmmaker Cathy Greenhalgh provides her readers with valuable insights into the pre-production phase of her proposed full feature film *Cottonopolis* (90′, 2020). In juxtaposing filmed material of the textile cities Manchester (England), Ahmedabad (Gujarat, India) and Łódź (Poland) with archive shots from these places, *Cottonopolis* moves back and forth between the three 'Manchesters' and also different times. Inspired by the Indian 'Cinemā of Prayōga', Greenhalgh's essayistic practice thereby functions like a cinematic power loom, weaving a thick audio-visual texture that interlaces historical material with observations of contemporary cotton manufacture. In her film, Greenhalgh recurs to formal and narrative techniques such as essayistic reflexivity, sensory and material culture ethnography, oral historiography and experimental visual immersion.

With reference to Luc Moullet's *Genèse d'un repas* (*Origins of a Meal*, 1979), Amos Gitai's *Ananas* (*Pineapple*, 1983) and Noël Burch and Allan Sekula's *The Forgotten Space* (2010), Giorgio Avezzù and Giuseppe Fidotta address the global production and distribution networks of commodities in what they call the 'world essay film', that is, essay films that attempt to depict nothing less than the totality of the world. Avezzù and Fidotta explore the formal and aesthetic strategies film essayists deploy to visualise an increasingly interconnected world, as goods are carried, shipped or flown around the world. At the same time, however, these films reflect, as they argue, the widened gap that exists between the visible mesh of geographical routes and supply chains vis-à-vis the invisible globalised flows of finance capital. This poses an epistemological problem for world essay films that otherwise seek to offer the world as 'object lesson'.

In Part Three ('Laboratory of Memories'), the focus is on the transient and often difficult-to-grasp work of memory (and trauma). To invoke rather than, strictly speaking, 'represent' processes of remembrance, contemporary artists and filmmakers work across different media and also increasingly exhibit (at least parts of) their work at a preparatory stage. These transmedial constellations produce, as Christa Blümlinger writes in this volume, 'a laboratory situation that corresponds to the original meaning of the essay as "exagium", that is, both "thinking" form and experiment'. She thereby explores the varied essayistic work of Apichatpong Weerasethakul, which unfolds across cinematic and installation art, documentary film and fiction. In this way, the Thailand-born filmmaker creates 'fiction' in Rancière's sense of a reframing of the real, as Blümlinger argues. This enables Weerasethakul to provide the anonymous with a voice and enables them to become political subjects.

Tim O'Farrell investigates the palimpsest-like structure, entanglements and transmedial effects of two fictionalised works: Grant Gee's essay film *Innocence of Memories* (2015) and its literary forebear, Orhan Pamuk's novel *The Museum of Innocence* (2009). 'Both film and novel straddle a deep love of the past, a desire to preserve and understand it, and a fascination with the inexorability of time, transformation and notions of progress', as O'Farrell writes. Their relationship is further complicated with reference to the *Museum of Innocence*, which was envisioned by Pamuk as companion piece to his novel and is now located in the centre of Istanbul (Turkey). Each one of the over eighty display cases refers visitors to a chapter from the book, and together with Gee's film they work 'as an intricate project to conjure the environment and culture of Istanbul in the second half of the twentieth century' (O'Farrell, this volume).

Agnieszka Piotrowska's essay film *Lovers in Time or How We Didn't Get Arrested in Harare* (2015) and her complementary book *Black and White: Cinema, Politics and the Arts in Zimbabwe* (2016) are the focal points in a two-part piece on practice-based research in the essayistic form. In the first part, drawing on Piotrowska's performative documentary, Thomas Elsaesser provides his readership with critical insights, sourced from his personal notebooks, into the unstable form of the essay (itself reflecting the unstable position of the filmmaker/author/researcher) and the possibilities that such form opens for the production of new knowledge. Part Two consists of Piotrowska's reflections on the making of her film, on the nature of post-colonial trauma in psychoanalytical terms and to what extent it can be worked through or ameliorated by creative collaborations. Piotrowska offers some further 'behind the scenes' insights into the experience of making a film in a post-colonial, post-traumatic environment, and the knowledge gained through this experience. Through such transmedial work an imaginative and/or critical third space is created that can function as a 'motor of memory' (Blümlinger, this volume) and extends authorship to the audience (cf. Rascaroli 2017, 2009).

In the fourth part of the book ('Landscapes of Trauma') Marco Bohr draws attention to the special affinities that exist between Toshi Fujiwara's post-nuclear catastrophe essay film *No Man's Zone* (*Mujin Chitai*, 2012) and 'slow cinema'. Bohr relates Fujiwara's film to a form of cine-aesthetic minimalism that makes use of long takes and observational camera to invoke the past. Especially the film's extended figurative opening sequence is exemplary of this form of cinema. It resonates with a number of contemporary productions that use, in varied but similar ways, an aesthetics of ruins, minimalism and contemplation to remember the violations inflicted on certain landscapes as well as the people forced to live and/or work in these areas, such as Oliver Zuchuat's *Like Stone Lions at the Gateway into Night* (*Comme des lions de pierre à l'entrée de la nuit*, 2012), Steve McQueen's *Hunger* (2008), Jia Zhangke's *Still Life* (三峡好人, 2006) or Apichatpong Weerasethakul's *Syndromes and a Century* (*Sang sattawat*, 2006).

*No Man's Zone* also bears similarities to Zhao Liang's *Behemoth* (2015), an epic essay film on the dehumanising effects of coal mining in the sovereign state of Mongolia, East Asia. Its still-image character caused critics such as Wendy Ide (2016) to relate the film to a tradition of landscape photography, rather than cinema. Tianqi Yu is in her contribution, however, more interested in placing *Behemoth* in a tradition of *yingxiang xiezuo* (影像写作) or 'image writing': an independent nonfiction film practice of experimenting with, and 'writing' through, moving image as artistic expression and cultural intervention in contemporary China. *Yingxiang xiezuo*, as she argues, can be understood as 'essayistic' in the sense that it is influenced by a Chinese literary essay tradition, Chinese language expression and socio-political conditions in China. In *Behemoth* (2015), eastern and western models of essayism collude when narrative techniques such as *paibi* (排比), that is 'parallelism', or *hongtuo* (烘托), that is 'juxtaposition', are used.

*World Cinema and the Essay Film* also includes two studies exploring the multiple a/effects of the archive. In Part Five ('Archival Effects') Peter Kilroy looks at the ways non-Indigenous Australian documentary filmmaker Frances Calvert, in her debut film *Talking Broken* (1990), works the film archive to explore the complex relationship Torres Strait Islanders have to the past, present and future. Kilroy draws attention to the mise-en-scène and cinematographic elements of Calvert's essay film which create a sense, as he writes, 'that the material is being used against the grain of its originally intended use'. Through the use of 'archival tropes' this experience of 'temporal' and/or 'intentional disparity' and the existence of multi-layered marginalities become visible. *Talking Broken* is the first of a trilogy of documentaries, including *Cracks in the Mask* (1997) on the subject of cultural repatriation and *The Tombstone Opening* (2013) on mourning practices, which all seek to 'speak nearby', as Trinh T. Minh-ha proposes in *Reassemblage* (1982), or in collaboration with, rather than on behalf of their subjects.

From a personalised perspective, Ilana Feldman explores the cinematographic archives of Israeli-born Brazilian filmmaker David Perlov (1930–2003). These archives include *Diary 1973–1983* (1985), which covers his extensive travels between the cities of Tel Aviv, São Paulo, Paris, Belo Horizonte, Rio de Janeiro and Lisbon, and the sequel *Updated Diaries 1990–1999*. In her piece, Feldman foregrounds the important role affect has played in this research, most importantly as a vehicle for self-reflexively problematising her own impassioned and/or conflicted position as researcher. Feldman is particularly interested in the 'prolonged process "of becoming aware"', which can have, as she writes, 'direct implications for the research'.

*World Cinema and the Essay Film* concludes with a photo-essay from acclaimed Vietnam-born filmmaker, writer and composer Trinh T. Minh-ha. 'Strangely Real' is a reassemblage of still images from her lyrical essay film, *Forgetting Vietnam* (2016), made in commemoration of the fortieth anniversary of the end of the Vietnam War in 1975, and of its survivors.[10] Although of a different temporality than the film, this digitised photo-essay invokes a dialogue between the two elements land and water, which form Vietnam as a country. While solid land/the earth points us to 'the old', ancient time, memory and corresponding image traditions, 'the new', as in new technologies or new national histories, can be associated with the digital age in liquid modern times. Digital technology, in particular, offers, as Trinh beautifully states in her essay,

> the possibility of working intensely with time in its liquidity and with indefinitely coexisting layers of temporalities, as ancient and modern meet on the light canvas. But in times of coercive politics and transnational terror, slowing down so as to learn to listen anew is a necessity. This is particularly relevant as one turns to digital systems in filmmaking, for the digital is here a *way* (of living) rather than a mere technology and the question is not so much to produce a *new image* as to provoke, facilitate and solicit a *new seeing*.

To conclude, this collection of essays on global essay film practice from a transnational perspective supports the idea of 'world cinema as a world of cinemas' (cf. Martin-Jones 2011: 23–7). The 'methodologically unmethodical' (Adorno 2017: 70) way in which film essayists proceed and build an argument facilitates and solicits 'new seeing' (in Trinh's sense) across media and cultural borders. Essay films help us to understand that conceptualisations of this/our world are not restricted to one place, community, nation, people or culture but constantly unravel at their limits. In these films, diverse and divergent thought formations happen in the transitive 'contact zones' (Pratt 1992) of folding and unfolding, multilayered or overlapping phenomena of this/our world. Each one of the essay films explored in this book constitutes, to put it with globalisation critic Peter Osborne, 'a condensed fragment of a worlding of the globe' (2014: 26). In more general terms, contemporary essay film practice can also be seen as a modern/ist form of self-reflexive *theory building* that evolves – as most acts of theorisation and conceptualisation do, according to German historian Phillip Felsch (2015, 2011) – from outside, or at least the margins, of academia. In this way, different formal, narrative and cinematographic strategies can be mobilised that allow film essayists to develop arguments against modernity's drawbacks and grievances. In present times, such practice can at least keep the hope alive for 'a more just and peaceful other-globalization' (Haraway 2008: 3).

## Notes

1. In her *New York Times* article (2013), Wampole claims that the essay provides 'an alternative to the dogmatic thinking that dominates much of social and political life in contemporary America'. In fact, she argues, 'I would advocate a conscious and more reflective deployment of the essay's spirit in all aspects of life as a resistance against the zealous closed-endedness of the rigid mind. I'll call this deployment

"the essayification of everything"' (n.p.). By contrast, Elsaesser uses this phrase to underpin the commodification of the essay film (and therefore its loss of radicalness) within globalised forms of image circulation.
2. Feminist video production in North America (as well as Europe and Australia) of the 1970s was, as Laura U. Marks argues, a prime example of 'a kind of organic relationship between the materiality of the medium [video] and its expressive and political properties' (2003: 41).
3. See in this context Claire de Obaldia's excellent chapter on the essay as literature *in potentia* (1996: 1–64).
4. Max Norman argues along similar lines in 'What Essays Are and What Essayists Do': 'The essay is a marginal, even trivial form, yet it is also deeply and seriously engaged with the weightiest questions of how a philosophical and political subject can be constituted out of a particular body and mind. Essayistic writing – as opposed to strict autobiography, which may simplify and explain a life through narrative – shows what is at stake when we say "you": another "I"' (2019, n.p.).
5. Cf. here Warner (2018), Sayad (2013), Lebow (2012), Kramer and Tode (2011), Alter (2007), Renov (2004), Liandrat-Guigues and Gagnebin (2004), Scherer (2001).
6. Cf. also Rascaroli (2009: 150) who, in her afterword, already insists on the transnational character of essay film production, circulation and spectatorship.
7. Vinzenz Hediger (2013) lists, for example, at least three possible definitions of 'world cinema', all of which leave him unsatisfied. The recent attempts to establish world cinema as a research category in film studies is, according to Hediger, nothing more than 'an attempt to retain, or regain, the lost unity of the object "cinema"' (n.p.).
8. Morgan draws on a quote from Guy Debord in which he moves away from a notion of cinema as pure spectacle to an understanding of the image as critique. Cinematic medium and revolutionary critique of the Left are thereby cross-fertilising one another to produce what we here understand to be an essay film: 'As revolutionary critique engages in a battle on the very terrain of the cinematic spectacle, it must thus *turn the language of that medium against itself* and give itself a form that is itself revolutionary' (Debord, in Adamson 2018: Introduction, para. 2; original emphasis).
9. In their most recent monographs, however, both Rascaroli (2017: 2–3) and Alter (2018: 17, 50–4) trace the beginnings of the essay film in Eisenstein's project of turning an abstract, invisible concept such as capital into visible material through a new form of dialectical and dissonant cinema.
10. The film premiered at Tate Modern, London, parallel to the full retrospective of Trinh's films at the Institute of Contemporary Arts, London. For insights into the film, see Lucie Kim-Chi Mercier, '*Forgetting Vietnam*: Interview with Trinh T. Min-ha', 2018.

## References

Adamson, Morgan (2018), *Enduring Images: A Future History of the New Left Cinema*, Kindle edn, Minneapolis: University of Minnesota Press, <https://www.amazon.co.uk/Enduring-Images-Future-History-Cinema/dp/1517903092> (last accessed 19 December 2018).

Adorno, Theodor W. (2017), 'The Essay as Form' (1958), in Nora Alter and Timothy Corrigan (eds), *Essays on the Essay Film*, New York: Columbia University Press, pp. 60–85.

Alter, Nora (2007), 'Translating the Essay into Film and Installation', *Journal of Visual Culture*, 6:1, 44–57.
Alter, Nora (2018), *The Essay Film After Fact and Fiction*, New York: Columbia University Press.
Alter, Nora and Timothy Corrigan (eds) (2017), *Essays on the Essay Film*, New York: Columbia University Press.
Andrew, Dudley (2006), 'Time Zones and Jetlag: The Flows and Phases of World Cinema', in Stephanie Dennison and Song Hwee Lim (eds), *Remapping World Cinema: Identity, Culture and Politics in Film*, London: Wallflower Press, pp. 59–89.
Badiou, Alain (2010), *The Communist Hypothesis*, London: Verso.
Bauman, Zygmunt (2000), *Liquid Modernity*, Cambridge: Polity Press.
Berry, Chris (2010), 'What Is Transnational Cinema? Thinking from the Chinese Situation', *Transnational Cinemas*, 1:2, 111–27.
Cooke, Paul (ed.) (2007), *World Cinema's 'Dialogues' with Hollywood*, Basingstoke: Palgrave Macmillan.
Corrigan, Timothy (2011), *The Essay Film: From Montaigne, After Marker*, Oxford and New York: Oxford University Press.
De Obaldia, Claire (1996), *The Essayistic Spirit: Literature, Modern Criticism and the Essay*, Wotton-under-Edge: Clarendon Press.
Deshpande, Shekhar and Meta Mazaj (2018), *World Cinema: A Critical Introduction*, London and New York: Routledge.
Ďurovičová, Nataša and Kathleen Newman (eds) (2010), *World Cinemas, Transnational Perspectives*, New York and London: Routledge.
Eagleton, Terry (2018), *Why Marx Was Right*, New Haven: Yale University Press.
Elsaesser, Thomas (2017), 'The Essay Film: From Film Festival Favorite to Flexible Commodity Form?', in Nora Alter and Timothy Corrigan (eds), *Essays on the Essay Film*, New York: Columbia University Press, pp. 240–58.
Felsch, Philipp (2011), 'Der arktische Konjunktiv: Auf der Suche nach dem eisfreien Polarmeer', *Osteuropa*, 2:3, 9–20.
Felsch, Philipp (2015), *Der lange Sommer der Theorie: Geschichte einer Revolte*, Munich: C. H. Beck.
Galt, Rosalind and Karl Schoonover (eds) (2010), *Global Art Cinema: New Theories and Histories*, New York: Oxford University Press.
Hagener, Malte (2007), *Looking Forward, Moving Back: The European Avant-garde and the Invention of Film Culture (1919–1939)*, Amsterdam: Amsterdam University Press.
Haraway, Donna J. (2008), *When Species Meet*, Minneapolis and London: University of Minnesota Press.
Hediger, Vinzenz (2013), 'What Do We Know When We Know Where Something Is? World Cinema and the Question of Spatial Ordering', *Screening the Past*, <http://www.screeningthepast.com/2013/10/what-do-we-know-when-we-know-where-something-is-world-cinema-and-the-question-of-spatial-ordering/> (last accessed 28 August 2018).
Higson, Andrew (1989), 'The Concept of National Cinema', *Screen*, 30:4, 36–47.
Ide, Wendy (2016), 'Behemoth Review: A Paradise Lost to Profiteers', *The Guardian*, 21 August, <https://www.theguardian.com/film/2016/aug/21/behemoth-zhao-liang-review> (last accessed 10 September 2018).
Kramer, Sven and Thomas Tode (eds) (2011), *Der Essayfilm: Ästhetik und Aktualität*, Konstanz: UVK Verlagsgesellschaft.
Lebow, Alisa (ed.) (2012), *The Cinema of Me: The Self and Subjectivity in First Person Documentary*, New York and Chichester: Columbia University Press.

Liandrat-Guigues, Suzanne and Murielle Gagnebin (2004), *L'Essai et le cinéma*, Seyssel: Champ Vallon.
Marks, Laura U. (2003), 'What Is That *and* between Arab Women and Video? The Case of Beirut', *Camera Obscura*, 54:18 (3), 40–69.
Martin-Jones, David (2011), *Deleuze and World Cinemas*, London: Continuum.
Mercier, Lucie Kim-Chi (2018), '*Forgetting Vietnam*: Interview with Trinh T. Min-ha', *Radical Philosophy*, 2.03 (December), 78–89.
Naficy, Hamid (2001), *Accented Cinema: Exilic and Diasporic Filmmaking*, Princeton: Princeton University Press.
Nagib, Lúcia (2006), 'Towards a Positive Definition of World Cinema', in Stephanie Dennison and Song Hwee Lim (eds), *Remapping World Cinema: Identity, Culture and Politics in Film*, London: Wallflower Press, pp. 30–7.
Norman, Max (2019), 'What Essay Films Are, and What Essayists Do', *Public Books*, 8 January, <https://www.publicbooks.org/what-essays-are-and-what-essayists-do/> (last accessed 15 January 2019).
Osborne, Peter (2014), 'The Postconceptual Condition; Or, the Logic of High Capitalism Today', *Radical Philosophy*, 184 (March/April), 9–27.
Papazian, Elizabeth A. and Caroline Eades (eds) (2016), *The Essay Film: Dialogue, Politics, Utopia*, London and New York: Wallflower Press.
Piketty, Thomas (2014), *Capital in the Twenty-First Century*, trans. Arthur Goldhammer, Cambridge, MA: Harvard University Press.
Pratt, Mary Louise (1992), *Imperial Eyes: Travel Writing and Transculturation*, London and New York: Routledge.
Rancière, Jacques (2004) *The Politics of Aesthetics*, London and New York: Continuum.
Rancière, Jacques (2010), *Dissensus: On Politics and Aesthetics*, ed. and trans. Steven Corcoran, London and New York: Continuum.
Rascaroli, Laura (2009), *The Personal Camera: Subjective Cinema and the Essay Film*, London: Wallflower Press.
Rascaroli, Laura (2017), *How the Essay Film Thinks*, New York: Oxford University Press.
Renov, Michael (2004), *The Subject in Documentary*, Minneapolis: University of Minnesota Press.
Richard, Nelly (1996), 'The Cultural Periphery and Postmodern Decentring: Latin America's Reconversion of Borders', in John C. Welchman (ed.), *Rethinking Borders*, Basingstoke and London: Palgrave Macmillan, pp. 71–84.
Sayad, Cecilia (2013), *Performing Authorship: Self-Inscription and Corporeality in the Cinema*, London and New York: I. B. Tauris.
Scherer, Christina (2001), *Ivens, Marker, Godard, Jarman: Erinnerung im Essayfilm*, Paderborn: Wilhelm Fink.
Silverman, Max (2013), *Palimpsestic Memory: The Holocaust and Colonialism in French and Francophone Fiction and Film*, New York and Oxford: Berghahn.
Stengers, Isabelle (2015), *In Catastrophic Times: Resisting the Coming Barbarism*, Lüneburg: Meson Press and Open Humanities Press.
Walker, Michelle Boulous (2011), 'Becoming Slow: Philosophy, Reading and the Essay', in Graham Robert Oppy and Nick N. Trakakis (eds), *The Antipodean Philosopher*, Plymouth: Lexington Books, pp. 268–78.
Wampole, Christy (2013), 'The Essayification of Everything', *New York Times*, 26 May, <https://opinionator.blogs.nytimes.com/2013/05/26/the-essayification-of-everything/> (last accessed 10 September 2018).
Warner, Rick (2018), *Godard and the Essay Film: A Form That Thinks*, Evanston, IL: Northwestern University Press.
Žižek, Slavoj (2011), *Living in the End Times*, London and New York: Verso.

# PART ONE

# CINEPHILIC DIALOGUES

# 1. THE ESSAY FILM AND ITS GLOBAL CONTEXTS: CONVERSATIONS ON FORMS AND PRACTICES

Laura Rascaroli, Nguyen Trinh Thi, Bo Wang and Susana Barriga

At the beginning of the millennium the term 'essay film' was rarely encountered; today, its use is almost inflationary. At once generalised and polyvalent, the term is used in ways that constantly reopen and stretch the limits of a conceptual field which a wealth of recent scholarship has attempted to map and demarcate. Shaped by commentaries mostly originating in the west, and predominantly drawing on western ideas on the essay form and the literary essay in particular, this is a conceptual field that is put to the test today as it is brought to bear on a growing global artistic practice. Artists worldwide increasingly describe their films or installations as essayistic. Meanwhile, international film festivals and art galleries use the term to label work, present it to audiences, award it prizes and give it visibility, sometimes with an element of pragmatism that banks on the elusive, shapeshifting features of the form.

While observing this evolving landscape, I became interested in knowing more about how global artists who call their films essays, or whose work has been labelled as such by art institutions, think of their practice in light of this somewhat ambiguous term. Equally, it seemed worth asking how non-western-born artists in particular see and refer to the essay as a form that has been conceptualised by heavily drawing on western thought and according to Enlightenment categories (those of the Self, of the relationship between the human subject and the world/society, and of the role of the artist). In my own reflection on the essay film, I have become increasingly interested in issues of praxis and of functioning over definitions and terminology (Rascaroli 2017). The following conversations with three artists and intellectuals born in Vietnam, China and Cuba respectively, yet all operating in global contexts, stem from this enquiry. Needless to say, while being eager to debate their practices and ideas with three filmmakers whose work I much appreciate, it was never my intention to try to identify and delimit a non-western practice of the essay film, as distinct from a western one, a project that would be all at once conceptually ambiguous, historically flawed and ideologically suspect.

As a privileged meeting ground of different impulses, the essay film is naturally a field of hybrid influences, as these interviews only confirm. Nevertheless, a critical reflection on the encounter between different models and forms of conceptualisation is warranted now more than ever. My questions thus aimed to highlight some themes that seemed worth exploring in the context of today's global growth of the essay film, while offering these artists an opportunity to share their thoughts on the form, on theorisations of it, and on how it is used by their models and their contemporaries alike. What truly motivated these conversations, then, was the desire for a joint reflection on the current status of a cinema of research and experimentation, and on its facilitation of personal expression, intellectual engagement, philosophical analysis, and social and ideological critique in this age of globalisation, all within a diverse range of geopolitical backgrounds and contexts.

## Nguyen Trinh Thi

Born in 1973 in Hanoi, Vietnam

*Until recently, the term 'essay film' was rarely encountered; today, artists, filmmakers, critics and institutions increasingly use it to categorise a diverse range of films. What is the essay film to you, and in what way is it relevant to your practice? Is the label at all useful to you to think of your work, to present it to festivals and art galleries, or to reach your audiences?*

It would be difficult for me to generalise about how the essay film is relevant to my practice. I actually haven't made many essay films, although some say that even my non-essay films have the tendency of the essay in them – for example, in *Landscape Series no. 1* (2013), which is a slide show without any dialogues or texts. My films and projects are quite different from each other in format – ranging from experimental documentaries, to found-footage films, to video installations. I typically look for a suitable form for each project. Up until *Letters from Panduranga* (2015) I actually always tried to avoid using texts and commentaries in my films. I didn't want to tell the audience what to think, so I avoided the 'voice of God'; I thought that commentaries can make a film too didactic.

In *Letters from Panduranga*, after looking at many different forms, I decided on the essay film because I thought it'd help me talk about this complex story.

Figure 1.1 *Letters from Panduranga*, Nguyen Trinh Thi, 2015. Courtesy of Nguyen Trinh Thi.

For me, the essay film has the ability to follow a thought process and make it visible/audible; the ability to bring many different times and spaces together; the ability to facilitate the development of an argument with oneself; the ability to interface between the private and the public; and the ability to generate meanings and imaginations in-between the image and the sound/text. I don't believe I think of the essay film in a very strict way, and in using the essay film, I allow myself to freely combine it with other formats such as observational cinema, video art and performance. In that way, I think the label is useful to me to think of my work, and to a lesser extent to present it to festivals and art galleries, or to reach my audiences.

*Critics often connect the essay film to western literary, philosophical, and artistic traditions, though a form of literary essay was present in Japan as early as the 1990s, for instance. In your films, you openly draw on western essays – for example, in* Letters from Panduranga *you cite both Chris Marker's* Letter from Siberia *(Lettre de Sibérie, 1958) and Alain Resnais's* Statues Also Die *(Les Statues meurent aussi, 1953); and in* Eleven Men *(2016) you adapted a short story by Franz Kafka ([1917] 1995). On the other hand, Trinh T. Minh-ha's work between experimental ethnography and essay is probably also a reference point for a Hanoi-based artist like you. How do you think about your use of the essay in-between western and eastern traditions and models?*

I wouldn't say that I was influenced by Trinh T. Minh-ha, although I watched a couple of her films a long time ago. I can't really trace all my influences

– there are many of them. I had a background in journalism and studied international relations and politics. I also studied ethnographic film, but I never wanted to make ethnographic films *per se*, nor was I an anthropologist. My first films were in the realm of observational documentary. Then I found myself becoming increasingly subjective and experimental, although my works have always retained a strong documentary root. Although I never intend for it to be there, somehow I can see an ethnographic aspect in almost all of my work as well.

I was strongly influenced by Chris Marker and his essay films, especially *Sans Soleil* (1983). I borrowed from Marker his strategies and structures. What I borrowed from Kafka, very importantly, was also the simple and straightforward structure (of his short story *Eleven Sons*). But an important influence for me came from John Cage, who made me think of background and foreground, of chance and indeterminacy, and of the eastern traditions and philosophy. I also studied and practised photography for a while, which prompted reflections in me around photography and image-making.

In my diary film *Jo Ha Kyu* (2012), the essential concept of narrative structure in traditional Japanese temporal arts, *jo-ha-kyû*, is loosely interpreted against my subjective experience of Tokyo shortly after the 2011 Japanese earthquake. In a way, the piece is about the conflict and coexistence of the concrete and abstract worlds, between objective observations and subjective experience, narrative and non-narrative, documentary and fiction.

I think, in general, my work has always been guided by my curiosity to make sense of realities, first of all for myself. In my projects, I like to have different layers through which the audience can read the work – the historical, the ethnographic, the political, the poetic.

*I loved* Jo Ha Kyu *and how it powerfully engages with the Japanese concept of the rhythm of physical activity, of music, of dramatic structure, of the accelerating cycle of opening, break and rapid climax. It is a very creative take on the diary film, in-between stasis and motion, observation and creation, proximity and distance. In* Letters from Panduranga, *the two narrators discuss the problem of how to find the right distance from the portrayed people, issues and realities – somewhere in-between the closeness of documentary and the distance of fiction. Do you find yourself struggling with that balance in your projects? Do you feel that the essay film, with its great freedom and hybridity, and interface between the private and the public, provides you with a useful middle ground between your desire for objectiveness and your critical stance on the world?*

Thank you for your great description of *Jo Ha Kyu*. Yes, I think that, somehow, I keep coming back to this issue of distance between myself and the subject/issues/realities/the world outside. I think to figure out the relationship between things is important for me, for example the relationship between ourselves and history/memories/the past; between the individual and the community; between objectivity and subjectivity; and so on. An important issue for me has been to figure out how to retain one's individuality while being a part of a collective. As an artist, I also feel the tension of having seemingly contradictory desires – one is to engage/be engaged in the world/society, and the other to disappear; to be able to be at once clear and decisive, and ambiguous, elusive and indeterminate.

In the two films *Letters from Panduranga* and *Eleven Men* – the only ones I've made so far with voice-over – I found it important to read the voice-over myself. (I also found it important to read the text in Vietnamese, although a large part of my audience is international.) I think the text is not only important for its content, but also for how it is read, and its bodily connection – the voice. I'd like the audience to feel this intimacy also generated by this form of the essay film in which supposedly private letters are read in a public film. Sometimes I call this 'my performance' in the film. Maybe this 'presence' and physical connection of mine also contribute to my considering these films to be somewhat my self-portraits.

I find struggling with this balance in my projects can actually be positive and generative. It's the same as searching for my place in relation to the world, trying to have better and more nuanced understandings of realities. In that way, I am able to observe how my philosophical thinking evolves. And yes, I agree with what you said about the ability of the essay film to provide the middle ground for all these in-between states.

*Your reflective stance on the image and on image-making, and on their politics, is clearly visible in your works. It strikes me that two of the most famous political essays of the late 1960s to early 70s, which are also commentaries on images – the collective film* Far from Vietnam *(Loin du Vietnam, 1967) and Jean-Luc Godard and Jean-Pierre Gorin's* Letter to Jane *(1972) – were both about the Vietnam/American War, seen from a western, albeit anti-USA, perspective. In your* Vietnam the Movie *(2016), you assembled a vast range of clips depicting the War, from mainstream Hollywood to European art film and beyond, thus highlighting how this extraordinary abundance of filmic images, both fictional and documentary, completely replaced the reality of Vietnam and of the War. Do you consider* Vietnam the Movie *a political essay in how it makes an eloquent argument, even without the need for a spoken commentary? Personally, I see* Vietnam the Movie *as opposite but complementary to your* Landscape *series, a montage of pictures of Vietnamese people taken against apparently innocent landscapes, pointing to indicate a past event or something that is now missing. Too many images versus lacking/empty images: reality seems to always be at one remove from the image. It's like a form of censorship.*

I'm not sure that I can consider *Vietnam the Movie* a political essay. I think it's too diffuse and ambivalent to be as efficient and effective as a political essay probably should be. Relying on associations and gestures rather than hard facts and a straight line of argument, I think the film is suggestive and open-ended in its way of making meanings, rather than being specific and goal oriented. Again, here, I pulled back into the distance to look at the 'backgrounds' rather than focusing on the 'foregrounds' of the picture. And, again, I was trying to resist the comprehensibility and linearity of history. I'm quoting my own statement for the film here: 'Utilising this external view of Vietnam, the film attempts a re-reading of this composed archive while resisting the comprehensibility and linearity of history. The anticipation of perspective in this new narrative is illusive; there is the logic of form through which no overt conclusion can be reached. In the complex nature of this narrative, the multi-layered perspective of many can only permit a shifting and fragmented history which is full of gaps; unlike its authorised cousin, it is naturally incomplete.'

Maybe I just can't write a political essay because, for me, to have meaning and to have no meaning are perhaps equally important.

I really like what you said about the *Landscape* series as opposite but complementary to *Vietnam the Movie*. Actually, I think all of my works, separately or combined, could be seen as this. In making my works I always feel like being at once an outsider and an insider. And yes, my works coming out of Vietnam somehow always return to the issue of the suppressed voice/censorship. As an artist working with images, I also try to resist the power of the image. Power structures are a theme that I keep coming back to in my work. The underlying theme in *Letters from Panduranga* is the power structures in our everyday life – the image is one of them.

*Can you say something about your current projects? What are you working on?*

I have multiple projects I work on, some of which are on-going projects. The one I am working on right now is called *Everyday's the Seventies*. I am continuing to explore my interest in gaps, holes, disconnections in-between personal memories/history and other kinds of collective histories, such as those portrayed by the popular media (both cinema and the press). I mixed footage of an interview I shot recently in Hong Kong with the owner of Paul's Records (a Chinese migrant born in China Town in Saigon during the Vietnam War who escaped to Hong Kong in 1975 to evade the draft) with images appropriated from Hong Kong movies made in the 1980s and 90s (all with Tony-Leung Kafai as main character), and wire service footage (mainly the AP Archives) covering the Vietnam War (the 1960s and 70s) and the Vietnamese refugee crisis in Hong Kong from the late 1970s until 1997, when Hong Kong was handed over to China.

Because of these gaps/disconnections between different kinds of histories, I think it's crucial to play with separate sound sources, and to allow the audience to experience them directly. For the same image, the spectator can hear the story/narrative mainly coming out of the media channel vs the cinema or the personal story told by Paul himself, depending on where he/she sits (while other sound sources fall into the background).

The film can be described as different versions of the same history – one personal, another depicted by the cinema, while the third is described by the media – laid on top of each other and collapsed.

*It sounds fascinating and I look forward to seeing it. Are there many Vietnam-based filmmakers and artists who are making essay films today, and of what type? Is there a sense that the essay film is becoming increasingly central to artistic practices there, as in many regions worldwide?*

Unfortunately, the essay film is not yet popular in Vietnam at all. I think I might be the only one who is currently making essay films here.

## Bo Wang

Born in 1982 in Chongqing, China

*Your multiform artistic projects, spanning photography, film and installation, are informed by a distinctively conceptual, research-based approach. Is it because of this that the essay film comes into your practice? What is the essay film to you, and how does it facilitate your artistic expression?*

If there is a continuum between exploring external subject matters and the development of pure formalistic languages within these, most artists have pinned themselves somewhere in-between. For me, I'm always interested in the bigger picture of the existing social/political orders that shape our world, and my practice is a way for me to access new possibilities of understanding. So, I'm strongly motivated by the external world. But then it has become very necessary also to look at the internal world to become aware of how we view things and are affected by ever-changing reality. So, I guess, it is due to the dual possibility of being able to look both outwards and inwards that the essay film comes into my practice. Meanwhile, I don't think the essay film can be a chosen format. You can choose to make a sculpture, a print or a painting. But the essay film for me might be different than a format. It is a way to position the film practice between subjectivity and objectivity.

*You were born in Chongqing, China but are currently based in New York. Critics often connect the essay film to western literary, philosophical and artistic traditions. In* China Concerto *(2012), you openly reference Michelangelo Antonioni's* Chung Kuo, Cina *(1979) and, more indirectly, through the type of voice-over commentary and narrator, Chris Marker, especially his essay film* Sans Soleil. *How do you think about your use of the essay between western and eastern traditions and models?*

The defeat of the Opium Wars shook Qing China awake from its bubble of cultural superiority. Throughout the following long periods of dynastic decline, foreign occupation, civil war, revolution and Cultural Revolution, all fuelled by a sense of being left behind, Chinese intellectuals have always been looking to the west to anchor China's own position in the modern world. The making of Modern China has been through the reflection of the west. It was even more so during the economic reform of the 1980s and 90s, which reopened the country after two decades of Cultural Revolution and closed-door policy (the closed-door policy during the Cultural Revolution for me was more a radical self-negation rather than a rejection of the west). That was the time when I grew up.

I have been very fascinated by Michelangelo Antonioni's *Chung Kuo*. The film was made during the Cultural Revolution and is probably one of very few existing visual documentations that shows everyday life in China from that time, however manipulated the presentation may have been. After completion, the film was heavily criticised by the Chinese government, so it could not make it to Chinese audiences. And after the Cultural Revolution, nobody was interested in this film any more (its first public screening in China happened at Beijing Film Academy in 2005, almost thirty-three years later, even though it had been available on pirate DVD back in the 1990s). It seems that historical memories are not relevant enough to contemporary life unless they can be commodified. This was the case particularly in the contemporary art world, and the commodification demands were also mostly from the west. History has flipped the page and the earlier ones are no longer pertinent.

When I made *China Concerto*, I was in my late twenties and had lived in the States for a few years. Watching *Chung Kuo* again and again, amazed by the images from a past that I had believed to be long gone, I kept asking myself the question of how much I really understand my country. How much authenticity do I have, even though I have lived through certain decades there? Maybe my conundrum is mainly a struggle with the way of seeing, as, for a long time, the western gaze has been the only way we have adopted to look at ourselves. But I also doubt if there still exists an authentic cultural mode, an eastern, or traditional one.

And in terms of the format, I think, the appropriation of the Chris Marker

THE ESSAY FILM AND ITS GLOBAL CONTEXTS

Figure 1.2   *China Concerto*, Bo Wang, 2012. Courtesy of Bo Wang.

*Sans Soleil* letter format did provide me with an easy solution to play with the ambiguity of my point of view.

*Can you say more about this ambiguity? In* China Concerto *the voice-over narrator, based on her accent and perspective, appears to be a western woman who talks in the first person and delivers her personal thoughts and observations on China. Why did you choose this narrator to convey your views on your country in the era of globalisation? Earlier, you also talked about the need to position your film practice between subjectivity and objectivity, an inward and an outward gaze. Do you feel this narrator, who is doubly alien to you (as a woman and as a stranger), allowed you to find the right distance, and, if so, from what exactly?*

While making *China Concerto*, I started to question the truthfulness of my own experience growing up in the post-Tiananmen era. I felt it necessary to distance myself from it. So, I wanted to use a third person voice as the intermediary. I also wanted a voice with an accent. Like in those old Hollywood cartoons, sometimes you see villains speak in foreign accents. I wanted someone with an accent that would deviate from the perfect 'western' ones. I found my friend Gabriela Jaime who has a mixed accent, with Argentine Spanish and London elements, which makes it hard to trace where she's from exactly. And the 'he' in the film is also a bit ambiguous. I wanted this person to occupy a fluid position, shifting between both insider closeness and sensibility and outsider curiosity and reason. 'He' could be myself, but not necessarily.

*You spoke of the role of Antonioni's images of Cultural Revolution China in your film, which, however, also includes, and critiques, contemporary images produced in China, particularly from television and advertising. One of your other projects,* Brother Sharp Arrives Home *(2010), is a montage of found footage regarding a notorious Internet phenomenon in China, and an examination of the commercial exploitation of a personal tragedy, while* Picture Postcards from the Future *(an ongoing collaboration with Pan Lu commissioned by City Pavilion, Shanghai Biennale 2014) is a postcard-photography project on images of 'future monuments', capturing the transformation of landscape in contemporary China. In what distinctive ways do you feel the essay film supports an investigation into the status of the image today, compared with these or other formats you have used in your practice? How does it allow you to negotiate or critique the control of images channelled by forms of surveillance, propaganda and commercialisation?*

I think there is a common interest in my practice throughout different media. I want to examine the way images work under certain political/social/historical contexts. As an artist, I want to recontextualise the relationships of or between images, whether to expose the structures that support them, or to establish new meanings. If we simply consider the use of voice-over on top of images as its definition, the essay film seems to be a very natural choice. But I think that, in reality, the choice of using voice-over can be much more complicated. I recently finished a video essay, *Miasma, Plants, Export Paintings* (2017), for an exhibition. The work is about nature, imperialism, race and cultural production in nineteenth-century Canton. It deals largely with archival materials and aims to construct new connections between very different historical materials. It seems to me very difficult to come up with solutions without a voice to organise the historical materials.

*In my own thinking on the essay film, I have moved away from concerns with voice-over, as well as with literary models, and have become more interested in how the essay film thinks non-verbally, in-between images, sequences, sounds, the frame and the filmed object, and layers of narration and meaning; so, what you say about recontextualising the relationships of or between images, and complicating the use of voice-over, is very interesting to me.* Miasma, Plants, Export Painting *is a two-channel video installation. Do you feel the space of the gallery is better suited than the film screen to experiment with the in-between-ness and complexity that you are looking for?*

*Miasma, Plants, Export Paintings* is the first time I have tried to work with space and/in the essay format. Technically, the making was very different from my past experiences. The editing process also felt quite different, as I had to imagine images shown on two screens in space. In the installation, we set the two screens face to face. The audience would only be able to see one screen at a time. As in most exhibition settings, audiences just walk in, somewhere in the middle of the work. I think the experience then becomes more immersive with images. I feel in this setting I become less concerned about the verbal aspects of the flow. I think the scripts are a bit too straightforward if the work is played in a normal theatrical, single-channel setting, but under the two-channel exhibition conditions it is actually okay, or indeed better, that the audiences are not too overwhelmed by both images and words.

*The essay film, which is a rapidly growing practice throughout the world, is seen as the epitome of subjective and idiosyncratic expression in film. We know that in China, too, more personal forms of documentary, including autobiographical documentary, are currently spreading. What is the place of the essay film in Chinese cinema today? Is it providing more Chinese filmmakers with an individual voice?*

Like you said, a lot of interesting personal forms of documentary films have emerged in the past two decades in China. I also find some interesting patterns. Artists who use voice-over – the more standard essay film format – are mostly from the younger generation, especially those who have studied overseas. Artists from the older generation barely use voice-over in their films. The Chinese independent documentary film scene started in the 1990s, with a group of people who had access to cameras because they worked for public television. When they borrowed cameras for their personal works, they wanted to break away from the public television style, which often used a didactic or even authoritarian voice-over. Shinsuke Ogawa and Frederick Wiseman were the two most influential filmmakers for the filmmakers of the 1990s. Letting things unfold themselves in front of the camera and letting the camera explain the scene, for a while, was the unwritten norm for filmmakers who wanted to work against public television conventions. The young generation seems less concerned about the 'sin' of language.

*I believe you have been working on a project called* Hong Kong: A Story of Space, *which will eventually become or comprise an essay film. Can you say more about it? How is it progressing and how is it impacting on your way of thinking about the essay film as a form and as a practice?*

Yes, I have been working on one project about Hong Kong since 2012, in collaboration with my friend Pan Lu. 'A Story of Space' is the working title. We are trying to approach Hong Kong's current crisis (identity anxiety, stagnant social mobility, etc.) through an examination of its urban space.

The production and presentation of urban spaces always have some distinct logics to follow, and the processes of making these spaces are often shaped by different powers and ideologies. So, the way we look at urban space is very similar to the way I deal with images. I believe that by going through both the appearances and the structures behind the appearances, one can gain a deeper understanding of the powers behind the crisis, whether it's capital, nationalism, or something else. The new film in this project, *Many Undulating Things*, is coming out in 2019.

## Susana Barriga

Born in 1981 in Santiago de Cuba, Cuba

*You describe your nonfiction works as essay films rooted in reality. What is the essay film to you, and in what ways do you find it relevant to your practice?*

First of all, I must say it has been a while since I made a film, so my answers will be based as much on practical experience as on my work in recent years, which is linked to theory. If I think about the context in which those films were made, it was only after I finished them that I started to see my work as potential essays. I remember being surprised, when one of them received an award at the Chicago International Film Festival in 2009, that they called it an essay in the citation. At the time, I had already been immersed in a radical questioning of nonfiction cinema, essentially understood as documentary, which, even when accompanied by the adjective 'creative', still carries with it the pretension to knowledge.

What interests me in the essay is its anti-systemic nature, the possibility of reinventing the normative, whether in relation to the cinematographic narrative, politics or aesthetics. Bearing in mind that the ideological entails finished, established forms, it seems crucial to me that essay practice presupposes a radical contortion of form, to the point of its revocation. To summon the emptiness of images, as Godard says. In this sense, I am interested in its experimental vocation: I think about the composability of divergent elements, the spatialisation and transversality of time, and the deliberate search for the unfinished. It is also significant to me how these structural aspects depend on process. Because the essay shuns the programmatic, formal resolutions are at the mercy of the specific creative process. I think that, in general, it is a space for the production of subjectivity in which what the essayist knows about herself is of no use to her, and the reason why she makes an essay is to know herself in relation to the world. But what finally unfolds is a non-knowledge, a form of knowledge which is not the kind that can satisfy the typical demand from the spectator of documentary for information or verisimilitude. That peculiar

Figure 1.3  *The Illusion*, Susana Barriga, 2009. Courtesy of Susana Barriga.

knowledge is never given, nor should it be understood outside the discursive framework that the essayist constructs. In the best of cases, the result is a film as a space of freedom and autonomy, especially in the construction of truth.

*Your work is characterised by a distinctive mix of political documentary, experimental ethnography and personal reflection. Both* Cómo construir un barco *(2006), in which a fisherman discusses his failure to receive the permission to fix his boat or build a new one, and* Patria *(2007), in which a young labourer, who has been working for four years repairing the same road, dreams of leaving, portray very specific local realities while asking broader societal questions. Do you feel your cinema is equally informed by the Latin American tradition of social concern and by forms of personal documentary? Who are your model essayists, both in the west and in non-western countries?*

In general I think so, although it depends on how these definitions of the social and the personal are used. With regard to the former, what concerns me is that it serves to foster an expectation of the type of films, especially documentaries, coming from underdeveloped countries and, in the case of Latin America, with its political realities marked by being in the geopolitical orbit of the United States, to put it simply. Seen in this way, it is a limitation for the cinema of the region that is, moreover, absolutely diverse in its stylistic and production aspects. With regard to the personal, the risk is that it could be understood as a correlate of a point of view or a specific identity. But I think it has nothing to do with those premises. It is difficult to categorise my model filmmakers as essayists, due to the very nature of the essay and also because I am interested in the possibilities of cinema as language in a wider sense. I think that any categorisation would reduce the value of their works. Tomás Gutiérrez Alea and Nicolás Guillén Landrián are important to me in Cuba. Outside Cuba, I think of Jack Chambers, Andrei Tarkovsky, Chris Marker, Chantal Akerman, Johan Van der Keuken. Many of these filmmakers are not considered essayists and there are substantial differences between their films.

*The Illusion (2009), in which you surreptitiously document your meeting with your father in London, where he had been living in exile after leaving Cuba fourteen years before, is a work of courageous autobiography that also provides a personal insight into aspects of Cuban history. How do you understand the intersection of the personal and the societal through the essay form? In what way is this convergence important to you as a filmmaker?*

I believe the possibility of formal syntax encompasses social and personal syntaxes. Of course, a film is not life. The space of freedom that a film creates is not necessarily verifiable or possible in life. Paradoxically, this difference is fundamental when it comes to speaking in your own name. To say 'I' is to position oneself in an unknown – or at least unforeseeable – place. I do not speak in the first person to assert an identity. It is a process of depersonalisation, interrogation and invention, for which desire is fundamental. In other words, I open myself to the world to return as an other, as a stranger to myself. This necessary fluidity of the self is perhaps the greatest difficulty when it comes to making an essay. *The Illusion* tries to express such a process through form. That is why the film is built with images that in principle could be considered waste material, through which we can barely see. Images that deny their condition as image. In the violence and inevitability of that gesture the film finds its truth, but that is not then reduced to a point of view. Everything we see is the ruins of the attempt to build a reality so that it, at least, exists. Something as precarious as that. Then, there also is the informational layer, through which we understand what is at stake in this attempt, at both personal and social levels. But what matters is how the form of the film expresses it.

*I am aware that you have been teaching and also writing a doctoral thesis on the essay film. Have you also been working on new films?*

Yes, I have several projects that I have been working on. I am planning to complete them after I finish my doctoral thesis. One of the projects in progress is called *El recorrido del sol cuando cae* (*The Sun's Course When It Falls*). I shot the footage in Cuba. I am still uncertain about the presentation format, but I think it will be an installation.

*The essay film is the epitome of an idiosyncratic, non-aligned and subjective form of intellectual engagement with reality. Is the troubled history of a filmmaker like Nicolás Guillén Landrián representative of the status of the essay film in Cuba in the past? What is the role of the essay film in Cuban cinema and society today?*

It is difficult to generalise because there were other notable essay-style films, from other directors, that aligned better with the thinking of the ICAIC (Cuban Institute of Cinematographic Art and Industry) as an institution. *Memorias del subdesarrollo* (*Memories of Underdevelopment*, 1968) is an example. Having said that, I also believe that the essayistic radicalism of Nicolasito's cinema is unparalleled in that context. Where those who read history as progression saw, and ended up producing, stasis, he recorded the discontinuity, the coexistence of the old and the new, its friction, the mending of a not-so-uniform social fabric, and the possibility of the future as a diverse state, as a state of conflict, that slipped through the cracks of that present. In the course of filming, he perfected the art of provoking those instants where, as Walter Benjamin would say, the past 'flashes up'; each look that Nicolasito provoked, and that was returned to him in his images, is a potential temporary lapse in the unitary narrative of what was. In a context in which everything had to change, this filmmaker glimpsed the regresses and the leakages that constituted the image of change; he did not seek to simulate a hypothesised, unilateral, parametrised rhythm. His images recorded the transformation, incubated it, as only a true revolutionary could create them.

### References

Kafka, Franz [1917] (1995), 'Eleven Sons' ('Elf Söhne'), in Franz Kafka, *The Complete Stories*, New York: Schocken Books, pp. 473–4.
Rascaroli, Laura (2017), *How the Essay Film Thinks*, Oxford and New York: Oxford University Press.

# 2. ESSAY FILMS ABOUT FILM: THE 'FILMED CORRESPONDENCE' BETWEEN JOSÉ LUIS GUERIN AND JONAS MEKAS

## Fernando Canet

### INTRODUCTION

*Todas las cartas. Correspondencias fílmicas* (*The Complete Letters: Filmed Correspondence*) is a collective project conceived with the intention of having filmmakers with similar concerns engage in a productive dialogue through filmed letters. The filmmakers participating in the project come from different geographies, and were brought together by their particular vision of cinema. Five pairs of filmmakers participated in these filmed dialogues: Albert Serra–Lisandro Alonso, Isaki Lacuesta–Naomi Kawase, Jaime Rosales–Wang Bing, Fernando Eimbcke–So Yong Kim and José Luis Guerin–Jonas Mekas. This innovative project has its precedent in the film correspondence exchanged between Spanish filmmaker Víctor Erice and Iranian director Abbas Kiarostami.[1] All of these cinematic correspondence projects were possible thanks to support from museums;[2] due to their experimental nature, they would not have been produced through the regular channels of the film industry.[3] However, as Jordi Balló and Iván Pintor suggest, '[t]he originality of [this type of work, which they call "exhibition cinema"] consists in the fact that, although they are created as an interaction between the cinema and the museum, they never lose their nature as film' (2014: 36).[4]

I argue that these filmed correspondence projects constitute essay films. In recent world cinema there has been a developing trend of essay films, heirs to various traditions, including literary ones, and movements, including cinematic ones, that had their day in different periods of the last century, such as

Figure 2.1  *The Complete Letters: Filmed Correspondence.*

the avant-garde and documentary practices of the 1920s as well as the foundational cinematic essays of the 1950s. For example, as Timothy Corrigan notes, 'Marker's *Letter from Siberia* [1957] and André Bazin's prescient characterization of that film the same year as an "essay film" are key historical markers in the emergence of the essay film' (2011: 50). In these films a strong artistic impulse, spirit of experimentation and the audio-visual inscription of subjectivity can be noted. The rejection of objectivity as the only way to approach social reality opens up multiple possibilities for working with the documentary; a recognition, as Hans Richter suggests, 'that the picture postcard is not the ideal for the documentary film' ([1940] 1992: 195).

Not only is the objective, descriptive impulse no longer incompatible with a more subjective, reflective impulse. As Michael Renov suggests, 'it is their obsessive convergence that marks the essayistic work' (1992: 228). Paul Arthur underpins this intersection with his assertion that in essay films, 'the rhetorical focus is at once directed outward to concrete facts and inward to a realm of mercurial reflection' (2003: 60). Drawing on Richter's postcard image, one may also argue that the postcard turns into an essay when a reflective comment about one's personal experience is written on the back, in what Renov calls 'the mediation of the real through a cascade of language, memory, and imagination' (1992: 217). This personal approach to the world was already prefigured by Michel de Montaigne when he states his purpose in his *Essais* to declare 'the measure of my sight, not the measure of things' (1948: 298). Authorial reflection, in other words, is a key feature of the essay film. This reflective process brings to the surface thoughts and ideas about the subject under consideration.

As the postcard suggest, such reflection may not only be verbal or vocal but can be evoked in or through the interplay between words/voice-over narration and images. A postcard is different from a letter because of the presence of the image on the front and the relation it has with the words on the back. Although André Bazin, who was looking at Chris Marker's *Letter from Siberia* (1958), stresses that what makes Marker's work different from documentary is his use of voice-over, he also attributes great value to the dialectic between word and image proposed by the French filmmaker. He argues that 'a given image doesn't refer to the one that preceded it or the one that will follow [unlike the avant-garde works], but rather it refers laterally, in some way, to what is said' (2003: 44). In Marker's work, words are related to images, because the filmmaker focuses on how images work. The main subject of his movie *Sans Soleil* (1983) is not so much memory as how images *represent* memory. By doing this, Marker takes full advantage of the multitrack feature of cinema and therefore of the creative potential that the relationship between the two tracks, visual and verbal, allows. Indeed, some scholars propose that it is precisely the relationship between words and images that makes the most remarkable essays possible (Arthur 2003: 60; Corrigan 2011: 6).

Reflexivity is central to the essay film's definition, as Noël Burch suggests; it is the main feature of a 'cinema of pure reflection, where the subject becomes the basis of an intellectual construct' (1981: 162). Obviously, the subject of this reflection can be diverse; but I am interested here in film projects that reflect on the nature of cinema. It is hardly surprising that one of the possible topics of conversation between two filmmakers should be the film medium itself. Various critics and scholars, such as Alain Bergala (2011: 266) or Phillip Lopate, have argued this way, either with specific reference to the filmed correspondence projects or with reference to the essay film in general. Lopate notes that '[o]ne of the natural subjects for personal essay-films is movie making itself, since it is often what the filmmaker knows and cares about most' (1992: 257). Christa Blümlinger defines essay films as 'essays on the cinema' (2004: 57) and more recently, Corrigan refers to them as 'refractive essay films', one of the essay modes he proposes in the second part of his book titled *The Essay Film: From Montaigne, After Marker*. For Corrigan, these films 'concentrate the representational regime of the essayistic on the cinematic itself' (2011: 191).

One of the most enlightening examples of essay films exploring filmmaking in the correspondence project is the unique dialogue between Guerin and Mekas. From December 2009 to April 2011, the two directors exchanged nine video letters or, in Rob Stone's words, nine 'essay[s] on film instead of on paper' (2013: 174). Both filmmakers are cinephilic and fervent enthusiasts of their trade; they live by and for the cinema, and typically express their personal reflections on cinema in or through their filmmaking practice. Their filmed letters generate 'ideas' about film as a reflective and critical response as well as an alternative approach to traditional criticism. Before I embark on a closer analysis of the filmed correspondence between Guerin and Mekas, something needs to be said about the distinct ways essayistic strategies are employed in the larger *Todas las cartas. Correspondencias fílmicas* project.

### Filmed Correspondence between Filmmakers: Topics and Strategies

Correspondence projects have a long tradition in the art world. One of the first examples was the sustained dialogue that existed between the young Portuguese architect and humanist Francisco de Holanda and Michelangelo. Nicole Brenez dates this foundational correspondence project back to 1578. Through this dialogue, she argues, both artists 'addressed numerous questions that were to become the topoi of art history [. . .] from an eminently critical viewpoint' (2011: 280). Another contemporary example is the productive correspondence between Theodor W. Adorno and Thomas Mann from 1943 to 1955 (the latter's year of death). It constitutes one of the most passionate reflections on artistic creation.

Filmed correspondence is of a much younger age, as the creative dialogue between the avant-garde theatre director Terayama Shuji and the poet Tanikawa Shuntaro shows. Their correspondence in 1982, lasting until Shuji's death in 1983, can be considered as pioneering. The experimental project was called *Video Letter* and was the inspiration for a subsequent correspondence in 1996, also between Japanese artists, but now the filmmakers Yutaka Tsuchiya and Naomi Kawase. This project was sponsored by the Yokohama Museum of Art. Between these two Japanese dialogues, another form of filmed correspondence took place in 1991, in this case between the filmmakers Robert Kramer and Steve Dwoskin.

*Todas las cartas. Correspondencias fílmicas* must be viewed within this larger tradition of artistic and cinematic correspondences. It was first shown in different museums around the world and was then distributed on DVD. These alternative paths, away from the mainstream, allow for a greater level of experimentation and freedom in the creative process. The promotion of these cinematic projects is only possible through cultural institutions like these, which are less focused on money-making products than on artistic value. Moreover, the filmmakers involved in these projects are not internationally well-known filmmakers, but rather representatives of world cinema, whose countries of origin – Spain, Lithuania, Japan, Mexico, Argentina, China and South Korea – highlight their geographical diversity, and whose recognition comes from the attention of specialised critical circles and participation in reputable film festivals.

Typically, these are filmmakers who are geographically distant but close in terms of their conception of cinema. As Balló suggests, 'the letters show that the affinities aren't created in closeness but in distance, and are sealed in a friendship forged through cinema itself' (2011: 258). Thus these filmmakers are less emblematic of a particular national cinematic tradition, than of a nomadic dimension of cinema that refuses to be classified in geographical terms.[5] They all reflect a kind of 'polycentric multiculturalism', a concept proposed by Ella Shohat and Robert Stam in their book *Unthinking Eurocentrism* (1994: 8) and echoed by Lúcia Nagib in her advocacy for 'the inclusive method of a world made of interconnected cinemas' (2006: 34). In this sense, the filmed correspondence project may be considered as an example of the third definition of world cinema proposed by Vinzenz Hediger, namely 'an ensemble of films that may or may not be the product of a national culture but that transcend their parochial national origins and become part of something larger – a transnational communication through art' (2013: n.p.).[6]

Thus, the filmed correspondence project relates to elements that are central to contemporary essayistic film practice. According to Rascaroli, essay films constitute 'a transnational form, made by international filmmakers in dialogue with one another' (2009: 18). This transnational dialogue shows us how filmmakers from diverse geographies and cultures can understand one another, because they share a language, that is, a corresponding way of thinking about cinema, which is what unites them as members of world cinema. I therefore understand filmed correspondence as a journey exploring the diversity of the world using a shared conception of cinema as unique vehicle for transport, allowing us, as Dudley Andrew suggests, to '*know the territory differently*, whatever territory it is that the film comes from or concerns' (2006: 28; original emphasis).

The documentary and the avant-garde film are often seen as the main points of reference of essay films. Indeed, it is precisely the combination of these two approaches to filmmaking that prompted Hans Richter to propose a new type of cinematic practice in 'The Film Essay: A New Form of Documentary Film' (1940). As Richter suggests, the artistic 'free reign' (sic), innovation and potentiality offered by this form 'allows the filmmaker to transgress the rules and parameters of the traditional documentary practice' (in Alter 2003: 14). Theodor W. Adorno also notes the transgressive and experimental feature of essay films when he suggests that 'the essay's innermost formal law is heresy' (1991: 23). This feature of essay films has been identified by numerous other scholars (Alter 1996: 171; 2002: 8; 2007: 44, 50; Arthur 2003: 58, 62; Rascaroli 2008: 39, 43; Corrigan 2011: 8).

As the above postcard simile suggests, any correspondence implies the presence not only of a writer, but also of an addressee. The 'I' usually addresses a 'You'. Essay films, as Robert Stam suggests, 'favor the I-You of "discourse" to the He-She-It of "histoire"' (1992: 149). Indeed, as Rick Warner points out, this dialogical dimension was already implicit in Montaigne's seminal *Essais*, where it is 'central to the essayist's working manner and principles' (2013: 7). Émile Benveniste's formulation of discourse 'demarcates the [essay film] from the diverse range of presentational treatments common to fiction and non-fiction alike [. . .] in which the third person impersonal verbal inflection issues from "the one who is absent"' (Renov 1989: 10). Rascaroli's claim is 'that the (real) spectators of [essay films] are called upon in an unremitting effect of interpellation' (2009: 14).[7]

In correspondence, the dialogue between 'I' and 'You' ceases to be figurative and becomes a literal dialogue between two interlocutors.[8] Consequently, 'You' assumes the role of 'I' and vice versa in a suite of alternating roles. Normally, the exchange of letters occurs in the private sphere. However, in the filmed correspondence project the interlocutors, that is, the filmmakers, are very aware that their relationship is not an intimate exchange but rather a public dialogue whose ultimate recipients are the spectators. Hence, the spectators are invited to share the author's reflection not directly but through an intermediary, the actual receiver of the letters.

Obviously, the topics addressed in the letters depend on the agenda of each filmmaker. Their professional activity is an important factor in the establishment of the topic of the letter. Thus, the film that the filmmaker is working on or promoting at the time can become part of the correspondence. If the filmmaker travels, the journey itself becomes part of the exchange through the adoption of the travelogue form. On other occasions, the subject is specifically developed for the project without necessarily being drawn out of the filmmaker's personal and professional activity. For example, the correspondence between Rosales and Bing focuses less on their private lives than on ethnographic and sociological aspects of their respective remote societies. Lacuesta and Kawase reflect on the differences between mourning traditions in Japanese and Spanish culture. As a result, geographically distant realities become a reason for correspondence.

In other examples, the private sphere is what prevails over other considerations. This can be explained by the desire that the interlocutor has to introduce him- or herself to the other. With this approach, the filmmakers explore their private world and reveal it to the other, following both Montaigne's motto 'I am myself the matter of my book' (1700: 254) and Georg Lukács's assertion that 'the essayist must now become conscious of his own self, must find himself and build something of himself' (1974: 15). For example, Eimbcke offers Kim an emotive and personal letter about his childhood, explaining to her how a slow disease took the life of his father; to tell this story, he uses images from his family album. Lacuesta also looks back on his personal history by visiting the places of his childhood in the present. In this way, the gaze on the past, on personal memories, becomes a recurrent theme in the letters. However, the filmmaker's life can also be dealt through the exploration of the present. In this case, everyday life, that is, how the filmmaker lives today, becomes the subject matter for the dialogue. The correspondence between Eimbcke and Kim and that between Lacuesta and Kawase are examples of this approach.

An important part of these filmmakers' lives is the cinema; more than just a profession, it is their passion. It is thus not surprising that these correspondence projects should turn into a perfect excuse for engaging in reflective dialogue about the nature of their own medium of expression. In this way, the work of their fellow filmmakers becomes the subject of the essays, as each filmmaker talks not about him- or herself but about the other filmmaker, and what he or she knows about the other is the other's movies. For example, the inaugural dialogue of this correspondence series, Kiarostami's *Where Is the Friend's Home?* (1987), forms the core of Erice's third letter to him. In turn, Kiarostami answers Erice with a tribute to Erice's *The Quince Tree Sun* (1992). The motive of this homage is not only a specific film, as the subject of the letter could be the cinematic style of the other filmmaker or the themes explored in his or her movies. Lacuesta, in his first letter, following in the footsteps of his interlocutor, Kawase, whose career has been characterised by explorations of her own private world (as she did as early as her first film, *My Family, One Person* [1989]), portrays his partner and collaborator, Isa Campo, in intimate terms.

Returning to the 'I', in his last letter Lacuesta turns his gaze to his own filmic universe; specifically, to that which at that time was his latest film, *The Double Steps* (2011). In this case, images from his own movie, from its 'making-of', and his reflections on the creative process, are central to the last instalment of his correspondence with Kawase. Similarly, Alonso and Serra (the most succinct of the correspondence projects, as only two letters make up their dialogue) focus their interest on their particular conceptions of cinema. While the former, as Olivier Père suggests, addresses his spectators with the aim of telling them 'where his cinema is going' (2011: 296), the latter turns his gaze to the past by inviting his actors to recall their first cinematic adventures.[9]

## REFRACTIVE ESSAY FILMS: THE FILMED CORRESPONDENCE BETWEEN GUERIN AND MEKAS

Dziga Vertov's *Man with a Movie Camera* (1929) foregrounds not only the filming stage of cinematic production but also the editing and reception stages. Abandoning the illusionist procedure, Vertov has no intention of concealing the signs of the construction process; on the contrary, his aim is to reveal the cinematic apparatus as a didactic and ideological device. Filmic representation is thus the subject of reflection, of a critical evaluation carried out by the filmmaker himself through the practice of filmmaking. The generation of reflections on cinema is the main defining feature of essay films about film as a subcategory of this genre. As Corrigan remarks, '[Georg] Lukács' model especially emphasises how the essay generates "ideas" about art and literature in its critical responses to those practices' (2011: 197). He makes use of the phrase 'refractive cinema' to support his argument that the main feature differentiating the essay film from other modes is this critical, self-reflexive response to one's own practices of writing or, by extension, filming.

'It was in this way – through writing – that one day I began to think about cinema, and discovered another way of prolonging its vision', argues Víctor Erice in 'Escribir el cine, pensar el cine' ('Writing Cinema, Thinking Cinema') (1998: 3). This Spanish director is an emblematic example of the group of cinephile filmmakers who worked as critics before becoming filmmakers or have expressed their reflections on cinema in both means of expression over the course of their careers; a group which includes the filmmakers of the French New Wave and especially Jean-Luc Godard.

One of the best examples of this reflective dialogue on cinema is the filmed correspondence between José Luis Guerin and Jonas Mekas, which forms the focus of my chapter here. From December 2009 to April 2011, Mekas and Guerin exchanged nine video letters, of which five were filmed by Guerin and four by Mekas. The former started the correspondence (Guerin's first letter, November 2009, 4'54") by reflecting on something the latter had said during their first meeting in New York: 'I react to life.' It is precisely Mekas's reaction to his everyday life in Brooklyn that forms the focus of his answer to Guerin (Mekas's first letter, January 2010, 9'42"). Because the images were filmed in wintertime, the snow assumes an important role, as it does in Guerin's second letter (March 2010, 7'22"), which was filmed in the frozen landscape of Lake Walden. In Mekas's second letter (April 2010, 9'06"), the present gives way to the past as the temporal focus, as we see Mekas in his editing room revisiting some old film footage of his past life. Guerin, in his third letter (May 2010, 9'41"), also revisits images from the past, in his case with the purpose of paying tribute to a young film critic, Nika Bohinc, who died under tragic circumstances after they met at the Lisbon Film Festival. The memories of the past are also the subject of Mekas's third letter (July 2010, 13'11"), as he goes back to his roots by visiting locations in Poland and Slovakia that were sites of barbarities in Europe's history. Taking advantage of his participation in the Břeclav Film Festival in Poland, Guerin equally engages in dialogues about the Jewish genocide in his fourth letter (November 2010, 9'57"). Winter, the season that opens Mekas's dialogue, is also the season that ends it, in his last letter (January 2011, 19'49"); in this case, the filming coincides with the fortieth anniversary celebrations for the Anthology Film Archive, a legendary independent film institution founded and directed by Mekas. Finally, Guerin's last letter (April 2011, 14'51") is sent from Japan, and in this case the object of homage is the legendary Japanese director Yasujirō Ozu, who is buried in the Kita-Kamakura cemetery.

The fact that Mekas is a cinephilic filmmaker has been of special importance to Guerin. Over the course of his long career, Mekas has not only made very personal films but has also written or promoted publications on cinema, such as the magazine *Film Culture*, founded by him and his brother in 1954, as well as his articles of film criticism published in the *Village Voice* from 1958 to 1970. In his fifth (and last) letter, Guerin pays homage to Mekas's prolific life as a cinematic agitator and the influence he had on his own work. In his visual correspondence with Mekas this discussion is complemented by the inclusion of objects such as Mekas's *Movie Journal: The Rise of a New American Cinema, 1959–1971* (1972), which marked Guerin's cinephilic youth.

Although Guerin has not been a prolific writer, his thoughts about cinema are dispersed over numerous transcriptions of his talks and interviews, in which he reflects not only on his filmography but also on his understanding of his medium of expression. His relationship with the cinema began very early; from a young age, he took an interest in watching and studying the classics, such as the films of Jean Renoir, Charles Chaplin, John Ford and Ozu. His cinephilia developed over time and very soon was given expression in his first short film at the age of fifteen. From his first feature, *Los motivos de Berta* (1983), to his latest, *La academia de las musas* (2015), the reflexive nature of the cinema is a constant that defines his films. His most reflexive film is undoubtedly *Tren de sombras* (1997), his personal celebration of the centenary of the cinema.

In Guerin's first letter Mekas's cinematic formulation 'I react to life' is Guerin's point of departure for a reflection on a way of conceiving filmmaking. Reacting to the world with the camera is a core idea that has accompanied Mekas throughout his career, as well as Guerin in his *Guest* (2011), a film shot with his digital camera over the course of almost two years. *Guest* is the outcome of a long journey through international festivals or events to which Guerin was invited to talk mainly about his previous film, *In the City of Sylvia* (2007). Undoubtedly, *Guest* is his most spontaneous and least calculated film, the one that responds most faithfully to the idea of reacting to life. Guerin himself describes the film as 'made with a single line', suggesting that it resembles the drawings of French artist Henri Matisse, 'which are made without lifting the pencil from the paper, where it is something irreversible; the line in the present moment' (in Barrachina 2012: 65).

In his first letter, Guerin compares Mekas to 'the camera operators working for the Lumière Brothers who travelled like this, alone, with their cameras'. As Guerin points out, 'the Lumières were very important to Mekas; he had even made a film about *L'arrivée d'un train en gare de La Ciotat* ("The Arrival of a Train at La Ciotat Station")' (in Brenez 2011: 281), as well as dedicating his first completed diary film, *Walden: Diaries, Notes and Sketches* (1969), to them. The supposedly aimless path that Guerin takes through the streets of Paris does finally lead to a destination, the Grand Café where the Lumière Brothers held their first public screening of the film on 28 December 1895. On his arrival there, Guerin aims his camera and shows us the inscription that commemorates that mythical moment in film history. Guerin confesses to Mekas that he thinks of him as one of those camera operators, perhaps the last one, while we see the shadow of his figure with the camera cast onto the street. Obviously, Guerin, as he himself admits, also identifies with that 'romantic image' (Losilla and Monterde 2010: 15) of the travelling filmmaker who captures the world around him with his camera wherever the whims of fate take him.

The fondness for this idea is shared by Mekas. In 1996, in commemoration of the centenary of cinema, Mekas wrote what he titled the 'Anti-100 Years of Cinema Manifesto', in which he offered the following description of independent avant-garde filmmakers: 'they took their Bolexes and their little 8mm and Super 8 cameras and began filming the beauty of this world, and the complex adventures of the human spirit, and they're having great fun doing it' (2012: 19). These filmmakers embodied the metaphor of Vertov's 'film eye' (*kino-glaz*), responding to life with a camera and inscribing in film their personal and subjective vision. Guerin portrays this idea of first person cinema at the end of his fourth letter through filming two different reflections of himself: one in the mirror and the other in the pupil of his model. Moreover, Guerin repeatedly films his own shadow carrying his small digital camera, thereby making visible his authorial presence in his letters. In his third letter, during his visit to Slovakia, Mekas also imprints his shadow on the film. In both cases, the figures are very recognisable. When Mekas turns his camera on himself – as he, for instance, does in his first letter – he emphasises even more the enunciation of his personal discourse. While Guerin, however, addresses his interlocutor using a voice-over, Mekas does so more directly by talking to him straight into the camera. At the end of his first letter, he does this to say goodbye to Guerin, after having given him a glimpse into his life. From the next letter on,

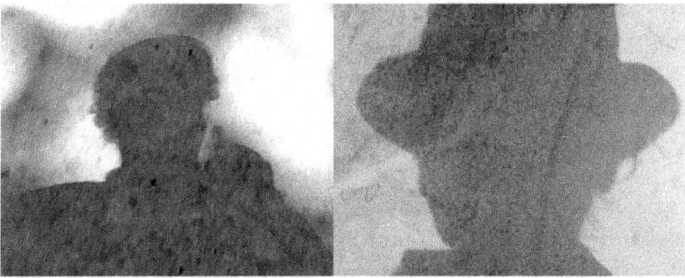

Figure 2.2  Guerin's and Mekas's shadows in *The Complete Letters: Filmed Correspondence*.

this method becomes increasingly prevalent. Mekas makes comments while filming, his voice thus leaving the territory of 'over' to become either 'off' or even 'on' when he decides to turn the camera on himself.

While in his first letter Mekas introduces Guerin to his everyday life, in the second he turns his gaze towards the past, revisiting old footage by means of using his old editing system. In *Lost, Lost, Lost* (1976), Mekas's voice-over already acknowledges his desire to recover the past. The journey back in time, on which he embarks in his second letter, shows Guerin a part of his filmed history, both public and private. He wistfully recalls filming this old footage, including shots of himself in New York and London with his close friends some thirty years earlier. In doing so he offers Guerin reflections in the present on past historical events, reminding him, as Renov phrases it, of 'the distances that separate the profilmic event and the voiced narration written years afterward' (1992: 223). However, Mekas does not just film his present and remember his past; he also thinks about his future. Despite his advanced age, he is still looking forward, commenting that he wants to edit these out-takes into what he says will be his last film, 'Footages'.[10]

In this way, the reality filmed by the filmmakers is subsequently taken up again in the editing room, the place reserved for a re-encounter with the material which, after some time has passed, engages the filmmaker's attention once more. In Guerin's third letter, in response to Mekas and following his letter structure, he also places two windows face to face, that is, the window through which reality is filmed and the window of the editing system through which previously filmed reality can be revisited and thought. In Guerin's case, the new form of digital editing replaces analogical technology, and the computer and Avid editing software substitutes the old Moviola. In his case, the footage is made up of images from a festival in Lisbon two years earlier. The protagonist of these images is Nika Bohinc, a Slovenian film critic whom Guerin met at this festival, who was murdered some time later. Thus, through the editing system Bohinc's lifeless body can, at least in a metaphorical sense, be brought back to life. With this practice, Guerin reflects on the idea formulated by André Bazin that the cinema embalms fragments of time, which thanks to the magic of filmmaking are recovered in each projection. Roland Barthes also evokes this idea when in his *Camera Lucida* he writes of 'that rather terrible thing which is there in every photograph: the return of the dead' (1981: 9).

Similarly, it is possible to find details in today's world that evoke the past. At the beginning of his third letter, Guerin shows Mekas through his window a date on the façade of the building opposite. In this case, these temporary traces in the present remind him of certain episodes in film history. As Guerin tells Mekas, 'dates on buildings automatically take me back to the cinema of the time . . . while the workers were constructing this building, Fritz Lang was shooting his first *Doctor Mabuse* and [F. W.] Murnau was making *Nosferatu*'.

The details of reality remind him of his cinematic heritage. Another reality – but in this case far away in the forest of Walden Pond, Massachusetts, where he looks for the myth of Henry David Thoreau – reminds him also of another historical landmark film, Robert Flaherty's *Nanook of the North* (1922). Guerin here looks at reality with an eye educated and trained in cinema. His cinephilic vision allows him, in his fifth letter, to see Ozu's films in some Japanese workers who are working on the opposite building. He comments to Mekas that these are '[o]ffice workers that would never have caught my interest, if it weren't for the fondness transmitted by the filmmaker Ozu in his films'.

Guerin takes advantage of his journeys to visit legendary places with the aim of recovering collective memories. As noted above, he visits the place where the Lumière Brothers screened their first film and the hut that Thoreau built with his own hands following his philosophy of living a simple life in nature. Mekas begins his third letter by addressing Guerin directly again, telling him that as a response to his journey to the New World, the forest of Walden Pond, he wants to offer him another travelogue, in this case of two places in the Old World, Krakow (Poland) and Banská Štiavnica (Slovakia). Mekas defines both journeys as a mistake, since both places are testimonies to the death and torture that define the worst parts of European history.

In his fourth letter, Guerin responds to Mekas by showing him images shot in Poland during his visit to the Břeclav Film Festival. While a screen in a square is shown and people can be seen to move in and out of the frame, Guerin is heard to tell Mekas that he also 'decided to visit the scenes of horror'. Already on the train, he confesses his purpose, 'to see whether actually being there, close by, would allow me to understand some more', and thus perhaps to empathise better with the victims of the brutality. He shows images of the train ride, but it is not his trip but rather the route to the death camps that Holocaust victims had to take many years earlier. Guerin represents this idea mainly by means of two absent images in which the figures are off-camera: wire fences and people marching as if in formation, both visualised through their reflection in puddles made by the rain. What seemed like a trip to Auschwitz was really a trip to the film festival in Venice – a very different place. However, Guerin takes the opportunity of his stay in Venice to show Mekas the gateway of what was Europe's first ghetto, 'the first place where Jews were segregated from the rest of the population [. . .] in the 15th century'.

In his fifth (and last) letter, Guerin proposes another twist in the direction of the correspondence. He decides to open this letter, on the one hand, with a reflection on Mekas as filmmaker, cinematic agitator and key figure in the rise of underground cinema in New York and, on the other hand, with a consideration of how the figure of Mekas influenced him and his generation in the decades of the 1970s and 80s. Initially, these thoughts were meant to form a dialogue with a long sequence showing Mekas walking to his office at the

Figure 2.3  Guerin's fourth letter in *The Complete Letters: Filmed Correspondence*.

Anthology Film Archives, but instead of focusing on his figure he decides to show images of Tokyo, as if those images had been taken by Mekas himself. This change was made because Guerin, emulating Mekas to a certain extent, decided to make a tribute to the Japanese people, who were suffering from the collective trauma of the Fukushima nuclear disaster when Guerin was planning his visual letter. The historical event and its aftermath prompted him to go back to the images he had filmed in Japan the previous year. Once again, Guerin takes advantage of a journey to visit another emblematic place; in this case, the town of Kita-Kamakura where the master filmmaker Ozu is buried.

In their eagerness to portray the life around them, both filmmakers capture not only the landscape or the people who inhabit it, but also the many small details that usually go unnoticed. Both invite us to contemplate what is irrelevant to the majority; for example, in a very long sequence (around three minutes) in his last letter Mekas shows us the apparently insignificant strutting and playing of a pigeon in the streets of New York, and in response Guerin shows us a five-minute scene of the hard-working ants on Ozu's grave. While the unstaged reality filmed by Mekas offers no greater pleasure than simple contemplation, in Guerin's case the reality he films offers us an unexpected lesson about life. Perseverance and collective work ultimately bear fruit. Sometimes, patient observation of reality can reward the filmmaker with an extraordinary revelation. It is precisely this attitude that leads both to engage with John Grierson's third principle: 'Spontaneous gesture has a special value on the screen' (1966: 147).

The patient observation in search of an unexpected internal order is also the subject of reflection at the beginning of Guerin's fourth letter. A long take of a screen in the background and the movement of the people in the foreground allow him to think about how reality creates its own order without the intervention of the filmmaker, whose role in these cases is simply to be aware of being able to reveal the secret order within the frame. As Guerin tells Mekas, this order is constructed by 'the figures that move in and out ... the rhythm ... the movements ... the intersection of different scales ... at times things seem to become diluted ... but then suddenly something happens ... something that brings back a sense of orchestration or composition, to the image'. However, the world around Guerin allows him not only to identify this unpredictable order, but also to make up stories. The inhabitants of public spaces are the protagonists of these stories, especially those who share the same quality of 'rootlessness'. Thus, Guerin looks and fantasises about what he sees around him, his notebook is always open with empty pages waiting for new stories that practices of close observation may provide. At the end of his fourth letter, Guerin points to this idea with his appearance on screen, gesturing to a Thoreau quote: 'the world is but a canvas to our imagination'.

The imagination thus can translate ideas into images using fragments of reality. Guerin's first letter concludes with a rhythmic construction made up of random fragments of people going in and out through the revolving door of a restaurant, until an anonymous hand halts its mindless movement. The background noises of the station are replaced with outdoor sounds: the wind is shaking the leaves in the trees, which here form the leaves of the revolving door. Images and sounds finally give meaning to Guerin's words addressed to Mekas at the beginning of his letter: 'Now I will attempt to capture some interesting reflections in the revolving door before me. It turns, like a series of small, random films. You know: the wind blows wherever it pleases.'[11]

## Conclusion

Correspondence projects like the one between Guerin and Mekas allow filmmakers to address one another across national and institutional borders, engaging in a rich dialogue between images and words, the present and the past, and amongst different generations of filmmakers; they also make the enunciation process self-conscious. While Guerin does this by predominantly using the voice-over, Mekas anchors himself in the pro-filmic space, addressing Guerin from either behind the camera or in front of it. In his third letter Mekas ends by addressing the camera directly and reflecting on the reasons that motivate him to film moments of reality. Through such self-conscious gestures a shared conception of cinema is proposed, which also offers possibilities for the formation of a meta-referential discourse that aims at the medium of cinema itself and its multiply refractive practices.

## Notes

1. For a further discussion of this seminal correspondence, see Linda C. Ehrlich's article 'Letter to the World: Erice-Kiarostami: *Correspondences* Curated by Alain Bergala and Jordi Balló' (2006).
2. The foundational project, the filmed correspondence between Víctor Erice and Abbas Kiarostami, was co-produced between Centre de Cultura Contemporània de Barcelona (CCCB) and La Casa Encendida (Madrid), and was also screened at Centre Georges Pompidou in Paris. This project was curated by Alain Bergala and Jordi Balló. *Todas las cartas. Correspondencias fílmicas* was also produced by Centre de Cultura Contemporània de Barcelona (CCCB) and La Casa Encendida (Madrid), but with the additional participation of Centro Cultural Universitario Tlatelolco (CCUT) of the National Autonomous University of Mexico (UNAM) and Acción Cultural Española (AC/E). The curator in this case was only Jordi Balló.
3. For a further discussion of this trend, see Alter, 'Translating the Essay into Film and Installation' (2007).
4. Raymond Bellour had already anticipated this idea in his book titled *La Querelle des dispositifs. Cinéma – Installations, Expositions* (2012).
5. In using the term 'nomadic' I am drawing on an idea posited by Gilles Deleuze and Félix Guattari in their chapter titled 'A Treatise on Nomadology', in *A Thousand Plateaus* (1987).
6. For a further discussion of Hediger's definitions, see his article titled 'What Do We Know When We Know Where Something Is? World Cinema and the Question of Spatial Ordering' (2013).
7. Orson Welles's *Filming Othello* (1978) can serve here as a palpable example. In this film, Welles speaks directly into the camera to the spectator, with whom he establishes an open discourse as if the addressee were in the same room. At the beginning of the film, Welles invites his viewers to strike up a conversation about *Othello* (1952). He addresses us directly with the words, 'I don't know your opinion. I want to tell you mine.' His self-inscription in the text and his interpellation to the spectators makes the enunciation process self-conscious. We are invited to reflect (with the filmmaker) on cinematic enunciation for meta-cinematic purposes.
8. Indeed, Montaigne sought an impersonal receiver as a substitute for his deceased correspondent. As Warner notes, 'the *Essais*, in their very conception, were inspired by the premature death of Montaigne's close friend and correspondent, Etienne de La Boëtie, and Montaigne frames his essaying as an effort to continue their intellectual exchanges' (2013: 7).
9. For a further discussion of three of the five encounters (Serra–Alonso, Lacuesta–Kawase and Guerin–Mekas), see Steven Marsh's article 'Turns and Returns, Envois/Renvois: The Postal Effect in Recent Spanish Filmmaking' (2013).
10. In 2012, Mekas's film *Out-Takes from the Life of a Happy Man* was released, and he continues to make films, his most recent being *Reminiszenzen aus Deutschland*, a short film released in 2013.
11. For further discussion of this and for an exploration of the main themes or motifs that have inspired Guerin's cinematic work, from *Innisfree* (1990) to his most recent work released in 2011, see my article 'Praise for the Muses of José Luis Guerin' (Canet 2014).

REFERENCES

Adorno, Theodor W. (1991), *Notes to Literature: Volume One*, ed. Rolf Tiedemann, trans. Shierry Weber Nicholsen, New York: Columbia University Press.
Alter, Nora (1996), 'The Political Im/perceptible in the Essay Film', *New German Critique*, 68 (Spring/Summer), 165–92.
Alter, Nora (2002), *Projecting History: German Nonfiction Cinema, 1967–2000*, Ann Arbor: University of Michigan Press.
Alter, Nora (2003), 'Memory Essays', in Ursula Biemann (ed.), *Stuff It: The Video Essay in the Digital Age*, Zurich: Edition Voldemeer, pp. 12–23.
Alter, Nora (2007), 'Translating the Essay into Film and Installation', *Journal of Visual Culture*, 6:1, 44–57.
Andrew, Dudley (2006), 'An Atlas of World Cinema', in Stephanie Dennison and Song Hwee Lim (eds), *Remapping World Cinema: Identity, Culture and Politics in Film*, London: Wallflower Press, pp. 19–29.
Arthur, Paul (2003), 'Essay Questions: From Alain Resnais to Michael Moore', *Film Comment*, 39:1, 58–62.
Balló, Jordi (2011), 'Filmed Letters', in Jordi Balló (ed.), *Todas las cartas. Correspondencias fílmicas*, Barcelona: Centre de Cultura Contemporània de Barcelona e Intermedio, pp. 256–59.
Balló, Jordi and Iván Pintor Iranzo (2014), 'Exhibition Cinema: A Crossroads between the Cinema and the Museum in Contemporary Spanish Filmmaking', *Hispanic Screen Arts*, 15:1, 35–48.
Barrachina, Santiago (2012), 'La pantalla como lienzo. Entrevista con José Luis Guerín', *L'Atalante. Revista de estudios cinematográficos*, 13, 60–70.
Barthes, Roland (1981), *Camera Lucida*, trans. Richard Howard, New York: Hill and Wang.
Bazin, André (2003), 'Bazin on Marker (1958)', trans. Dave Kehr, *Film Comment*, 39:4, 44–5.
Bellour, Raymond (2012), *La Querelle des dispositifs. Cinéma – installations, expositions*, Paris: P.O.L.
Bergala, Alain (2011), 'I'm Writing You These Images . . .', in Jordi Balló (ed.), *Todas las cartas. Correspondencias fílmicas*, Barcelona: Centre de Cultura Contemporània de Barcelona e Intermedio, pp. 259–67.
Blümlinger, Christa (2004), 'Lire entre les images', in Suzanne Liandrat-Guigues and Murielle Gagnebin (eds), *L'Essai et le cinema*, Paris: Champs Vallon, pp. 49–66.
Brenez, Nicole (2011), 'Mimesis 2. Correspondence between Jonas Mekas and José Luis Guerín', in Jordi Balló (ed.), *Todas las cartas. Correspondencias fílmicas*, Barcelona: Centre de Cultura Contemporània de Barcelona e Intermedio, pp. 280–7.
Burch, Noël (1981), *Theory of Film Practice*, Princeton: Princeton University Press.
Canet, Fernando (2014), 'Praise for the Muses of José Luis Guerin', *Hispanic Screen Arts*, 15:1, 49–60.
Corrigan, Timothy (2011), *The Essay Film: From Montaigne, After Marker*, Oxford and New York: Oxford University Press.
Deleuze, Gilles and Félix Guattari (1987), '1227: Treatise on Nomadology – The War Machine', in Gilles Deleuze and Félix Guattari, *A Thousand Plateaus: Capitalism and Schizophrenia*, trans. Brian Massumi, Minneapolis: University of Minnesota Press, pp. 351–423.
Ehrlich, Linda C. (2006), 'Letters to the World: Erice-Kiarostami: *Correspondences* Curated by Alain Bergala and Jordi Balló', *Senses of Cinema*, 41, <http://sensesofcinema.com/2006/feature-articles/erice-kiarostami-correspondences/#1> (last accessed 17 October 2015).

Erice, Víctor (1998), 'Escribir el cine, pensar el cine', *Banda Aparte*, 9:10, 3–4.
Grierson, John (1966), 'First Principles of Documentary', in Forsyth Hardy (ed.), *Grierson on Documentary*, London: Faber & Faber, pp. 145–56.
Hediger, Vinzenz (2013), 'What Do We Know When We Know Where Something Is? World Cinema and the Question of Spatial Ordering', *Screening the Past*, <http://www.screeningthepast.com/2013/10/what-do-we-know-when-we-know-where-something-is-world-cinema-and-the-question-of-spatial-ordering/> (last accessed 17 October 2018).
Lopate, Phillip (1992), 'In Search of the Centaur: The Essay-Film', in Phillip Lopate, *Totally, Tenderly, Tragically: Essays and Criticism from a Lifelong Love Affair with the Movies*, Amsterdam: Anchor, pp. 19–22.
Losilla, Carlos and José Enrique Monterde (2010), 'José Luis Guerín', *Cahiers du Cinéma. España*, 37 (September), 14–16.
Lukács, Georg (1974), 'On the Nature and Form of the Essay', in Georg Lukács, *Soul and Form*, trans. Anna Bostock, London: Merlin Press, pp. 1–18.
Marsh, Steven (2013), 'Turns and Returns, Envois/Renvois: The Postal Effect in Recent Spanish Filmmaking', *Discourse*, 35:1, 24–45.
Mekas, Jonas (2012), 'Antimanifiesto del centenario del cine', *Caimán Cuadernos de Cine*, 11 (December), 19.
Montaigne, Michel de (1700), *The Essays of Montaigne*, trans. Charles Cotton, 3rd edn, London: Printed for M. Gillyflower et al.
Montaigne, Michel de (1948), *The Complete Works of Montaigne*, trans. Donald M. Frame, Stanford: Stanford University Press.
Nagib, Lúcia (2006), 'Towards a Positive Definition of World Cinema', in Stephanie Dennison and Song Hwee Lim (eds), *Remapping World Cinema: Identity, Culture and Politics in Film*, London: Wallflower Press, pp. 30–7.
Père, Olivier (2011), 'LA/AS Wild Thought and Grandiose Minimalism', in Jordi Balló (ed.), *Todas las cartas. Correspondencias fílmicas*, Barcelona: Centre de Cultura Contemporània de Barcelona e Intermedio, pp. 291–9.
Rascaroli, Laura (2008), 'The Essay Film: Problems, Definitions, Textual Commitments', *Framework: The Journal of Cinema and Media*, 49:2, 24–47.
Rascaroli, Laura (2009), *The Personal Camera: Subjective Cinema and the Essay Film*, London: Wallflower Press.
Renov, Michael (1989), 'History and/as Autobiography: The Essayistic in Film & Video', *Framework: A Journal of Image and Culture*, 2:3, 6–13.
Renov, Michael (1992), 'Lost, Lost, Lost: Mekas as Essayist', in David E. James (ed.), *To Free the Cinema: Jonas Mekas & the New York Underground*, Princeton: Princeton University Press, pp. 215–39.
Richter, Hans [1940] (1992), 'Der Filmessay: Eine neue Form des Dokumentarfilms', in Christa Blümlinger and Constantin Wulff (eds), *Schreiben Bilder Sprechen: Texte zum essayistischen Film*, trans. Richard Langston, Vienna: Sonderzahl, pp. 195–8.
Shohat, Ella and Robert Stam (1994), *Unthinking Eurocentrism: Multiculturalism and the Media*, London: Routledge.
Stam, Robert (1992), *Reflexivity in Film and Literature: From Don Quixote to Jean-Luc Godard*, New York: Columbia University Press.
Stone, Rob (2013), 'En la ciudad de Sylvia/In the City of Sylvia (José Luis Guerín, 2007) and the *durée* of a *dérive*', in Maria M. Delgado and Robbin W. Fiddian (eds), *Spanish Cinema 1973–2010: Auteurism, Politics, Landscape and Memory*, Manchester: Manchester University Press, pp. 62–182.
Warner, Rick (2013), 'The Cinematic Essay as Adaptive Process', *Adaptation*, 6:1, 1–24.

# PART TWO

# MOBILITIES AND MOVEMENTS

# 3. ACCENTED ESSAY FILMS: THE POLITICS AND POETICS OF THE ESSAY FILM IN THE AGE OF MIGRATION

## Igor Krstić

> You sit in your homes . . . but I speak with an accent . . .
> and you don't even know where I come from.
> (Jonas Mekas, *Lost, Lost, Lost*)

> The world is but a perennial movement.
> All things in it are in constant motion.
> (Michel de Montaigne, *Essays*)

> The twenty-first century will be the century of the migrant.
> (Thomas Nail, *The Figure of the Migrant*)

This chapter brings together the notion of 'accented cinema theory'– which has been put forward by Hamid Naficy in his ground-breaking *An Accented Cinema: Exilic and Diasporic Filmmaking* (2001) – with the category of the essay, in order to conceptualise a burgeoning body of film, video and other moving image practices in what sociologists have termed 'the age of migration'.[1] Through this confluence of a supposedly generic category (the essay film) with a theory that has, undoubtedly, been of great importance to film scholarship since its emergence, I hope to provide new perspectives on an emerging transnational body of films (which I would only reluctantly describe as a kind of 'sub-genre' of the essay film), all of which have been produced by diasporic, exilic or interstitial documentary and/or essay filmmakers in the recent past. In applying Naficy's terminology, I argue that one can describe these examples as 'accented essay films' because they all deal with displacement, exile or migration in the essayistic format. These include better-known examples, such as *The Nine Muses* (John Akomfrah, 2010), but also lesser-known 'world cinema' examples, if you like, such as the (South and North) Korean film *Grandmother's Flower* (Jeong-hyun Mun, 2007), the Czech film *Home* (Margareta Hruza, 2008) or the Brazilian essay film *A Hungarian Passport* (Sandra Kogut, 2001) – even though these national labels are highly problematic when it comes to 'accented essay films', as we shall see.

The central question that I would like to address with regard to this filmmaking practice is related to notions of authorship – a concept that was, and to a certain extent still is, a hotly debated one in film studies: how is the experience of first-, second- or third-generation migration worked through in the essayistic format and what role does the filmmaker's subjectivity play in this process? The centrality of the author/filmmaker's subjectivity to essay film practices has been emphasised by numerous essay film scholars (cf. Rascaroli 2009; Renov 2004), as has the centrality of the filmmaker's personal or autobiographical experiences in what Naficy termed 'accented cinema' (2001: 277). However, it has also often been remarked that the essay (film) is characterised by its 'epistemological uncertainty' (Renov 2004: 70), as well as by its very questioning of the notion of an autobiographical or clearly identifiable authorship. This is why this chapter will not only present the way in which 'essay film' and 'accented cinema' interlace aesthetically or formally, but also the way in which the predicament of being a migrant corresponds with the essayistic mode of expression in terms of identity politics. The chapter starts with an analysis of what one might call the *Ur-text* of all 'accented essay films' – *Lost, Lost, Lost* (1976) by recently deceased filmmaker Jonas Mekas – in order to derive in the second section some symptomatic features that accented essay films share. The last section will then use these defining features in order to look at two more recent essay films – *Passing Drama* (Angela Melitopoulos, 1999) and *The Nine Muses* (John Akomfrah, 2010) – both of which not only merge the essayistic form with the accented style, but also the personal with the political.

## *Lost, Lost, Lost* as Historical *Ur-text*

Sociologically, one can argue that many 'accented essay films' are the result of social consequences and family dislocations following the Second World War, the Cold War and globalisation. And one can equally argue that it is because of this instance that the 'accented essay film' emerges in the early 1970s for the first time – a time which announces the era of globalisation.[2] Above that, the 1970s witness cities in crisis, caused particularly by the advent of post-Fordism, privatisation and neoliberal policies. US-American cities are affected by this political-economic 'sea-change' as well, while decades-long racial ghettoisation of black as well as of first-, second- or third-generation immigrant populations in inner-city areas deepen the crisis significantly. This is the troubling socio-political context in which Jonas Mekas's classic diary film *Lost, Lost, Lost* appears, a film which is set in New York, the 1970s crisis-city *par excellence*. However, the film was actually only edited in the 1970s, because it shows the filmmaker's footage of his daily life between 1949 and the early 1960s in a more or less chronological order. It is therefore not exactly a 'film diary' about Mekas and New York, but, as David James has argued, a 'diary film'. The distinction between diary film and film diary makes sense, because the footage that Mekas shot after his arrival as a Lithuanian DP ('displaced person') in post-war New York was edited almost three decades later, that is retrospectively and not immediately.[3] Nevertheless, even though *Lost, Lost, Lost* is a highly autobiographical (or diaristic) film, it was not only perceived as an 'autobiographical documentary', a 'film diary'/'diary film', but also as a 'film-poem', an 'experimental documentary' and, last but not at least, as an 'essay film'.

As for the latter, it was the prominent American documentary scholar Michael Renov (2004) who categorised Mekas's film for the first time as an essay. In his 'Lost, Lost, Lost: Mekas as Essayist' (first published in 1992), Renov argues that even though it has a strong affinity to the diaristic form, Mekas's film displays, just like Montaigne's *Essays*, an 'unyielding attentiveness both to the measure of sight and to the measure of things' (2004: 73). In other words, Mekas displays in *Lost, Lost, Lost* an attentiveness to both 'the self' and 'the world' and his films are therefore both (self-)reflective (or pensive) and documentarian, that is, attempting to document reality 'as it happens'. However, even though Renov's discussion of the essayistic features of *Lost, Lost, Lost* is detailed and to the point, he reduces his analysis somewhat to formal elements, focusing less on what one might experience on initial viewing as the film's most pertinent feature: the immigrant filmmaker's subjectivity and how the very intimate, but emotionally upsetting experience of feeling 'lost, lost, lost' in a foreign country permeates each and every sequence of the film's 180 minutes. *Lost, Lost, Lost* can, in this respect, very well be regarded as a predecessor, a historical *Ur-text* of the kind of contemporary 'accented essay films' that I will discuss later on. However, Mekas's film 'constitutes a singular case within cinematic immigrant autobiography', since 'most of the attempts to portray the immigrant experience autobiographically in film have been done by second and third generation immigrants' (Cuevas 2006: 54). So, how does the film portray the immigrant experience autobiographically from a first-generation perspective, and, through that, adhere to the notion of 'accented cinema' as well as to that of the essay film?

In the most parts of *Lost, Lost, Lost* Mekas documents his everyday life in New York, from 1949 to 1963, exhaustively pondering over his status as an

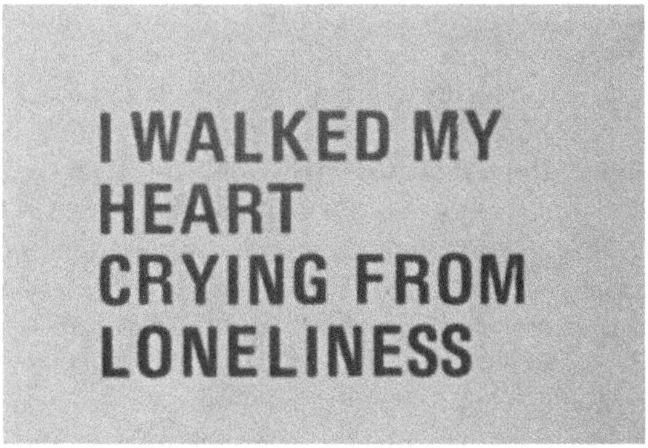

> I WALKED MY
> HEART
> CRYING FROM
> LONELINESS

Figure 3.1   Homesickness in *Lost, Lost, Lost*, Jonas Mekas, 1976.

immigrant from Lithuania to the United States. Right at the beginning we see the arrival of 'displaced persons' at New York harbour's 'Welcome Center' in the late 1940s – two of which are Jonas and his brother Adolfas, who both arrived in 1949 from Germany, where they had been incarcerated in a labour camp by the Nazis. Homesickness and thus home video-like footage of Lithuanian diaspora festivities, weddings and gatherings are the main content of the film's first parts, while later, when Mekas moves from Brooklyn to Manhattan, we predominantly see, often fast-edited, impressions of the change of the seasons, New York street life or artists at work, which give us the sense that the immigrant-artist has now become 'integrated' and 'adapted' to his new environment – to use these problematic phrases of daily migration policies. Hence, in the course of the film (and the years passing) Mekas turns his camera/gaze away from Lithuania towards his new home, but without submitting his life story to the clichéd US-American meta-narrative of the immigrant success story; instead, we witness Mekas's increasing unease with notions of national identity and his growing admiration for nature, the arts and particularly the art of cinema and so, in a way, a merging of his rural past (his native village Semeniškiai, to which he devoted *Reminiscences of a Journey to Lithuania*, 1972, and much of his poetry) with his urban present – which is why the reference to Henry David Thoreau in his earlier *Walden* (1969) is, of course, particularly revealing. Mekas frequently appears himself, as if the diary's author insists on inscribing his face and body onto the film's 16mm reels. Another form of self-inscription is, however, the author's voice – a voice that has an Eastern European accent. Most of the time that voice speaks in a lyrical tone, reciting a continuous string of self-made poems, sayings or anecdotes. It also often repeats certain words or phrases, such as 'lost . . . lost . . . lost', suggesting that the meaning of that particular word or phrase only manifests through repetition and the materiality of its sound. However, it sometimes also addresses us more directly, emphasising, for instance, that we will 'never know what a displaced person thinks'. Addressing those 'who do not know the pain of the exile', hence those who sit comfortably at that apparently secure and stable place called 'home', the filmmaker with an accent makes us constantly aware that he is in search of that place throughout the film.

Two of the key features of *Lost, Lost, Lost* are thus its continuous reference to the materiality of the filmmaker's or (enunciator's) presence and voice, its 'accentedness', as well as a direct way of addressing the audience in what constitutes a typically essayistic mode of address, that is, the highly personal, even intimate I-You mode. Indeed, essay films often employ a first person narrator, but because of their inherent self-reflexivity they often put the 'authority' of the author in doubt. For Rascaroli this results in an ambivalent 'presence-absence' of the essay film's enunciator (2009: 37), in which the author is neither fully inscribed, nor totally absent from the filmic images and sounds. In other words, in essay films the identity of the enunciator is often unstable, shifting or assuming different shapes. In *Lost, Lost, Lost* this strategy is already introduced in the opening shots, where we see what we would call today a 'selfie' shot of Mekas in his new flat in Brooklyn. Mekas thereby inscribes himself bodily from the very beginning as both enunciating author and performing actor of the film. Simultaneously, however, we see his brother Adolfas, who resembles Jonas quite a bit, in a mirror shot with Mekas's beloved Bolex camera, introducing the notion of doubling, but also, and more importantly, immediately confusing the viewer with regard to the identifiability of the film's author. During that opening sequence we also hear a quote from Homer's *Ulysses* via Mekas's accented voice-over, suggesting that this newly arrived immigrant in New York thinks that he is in fact embarking, just like Ulysses, on a heroic journey. The purpose here is to ironically destabilise the notion of an author who is in full control of his destiny/biography: as it turns out, the filmmaker neither is the hero of a home-coming journey, nor will he encounter obstacles that need to be overcome in order to return to Semeniškiai/Ithaka.[4] Mekas thus establishes right from the beginning multiple 'selves': as an amateur filmmaker with a handheld camera; as an autobiographical author of an audio-visual diary; as an epic poet, who turns out to rather be a romanticist, or even a modernist one; as an actor, performing the role of a 'hero' of a home-coming journey, not to be taken too seriously.

With regard to its cinematography and editing style, *Lost, Lost, Lost* equally displays some typically essayistic features, most obviously perhaps, its tendency to fragmentary heterogeneity and indeterminacy. Not only can the film be regarded as an inconsistent mixture of (filmic) poetry, diary and essay, but it also contains a wild mixture of disparate shot styles: black-and-white and colour, handheld and static, documentary- and home video-like. These shots are frequently interrupted by intertitles which sometimes contain diary-like information on places, dates or people, but sometimes also quotes, poems or short haikus; in one sequence – the famous 'Rabbit Shit Haikus' sequence – the intertitles simply consist of numbers. The audio track at times runs more or less synchronous to the images, but at other times it juxtaposes poetic, essayistic or expository voice-over commentary with the images. The same strategy is applied with regard to music, since Mekas employs a kaleidoscope of different musical styles, from Lithuanian accordion folklore to classical piano music, to go along with the images. Such multilayered sound–image combinations provoke the viewers to think with the author about what is recorded and screened, since they create contrapuntal, ironic or even contradictory meanings. Rather than to create a linear, chronological (or diaristic) and neutral account of immigrant life in New York, it is an audio-visual 'dialogue of ideas' (Corrigan 2011: 51) into which we are asked to enter. Mekas himself has reflected upon this, when he claims that, throughout time, his ambition shifted from being a 'camera historian of the exile' (hence, a classical documentary filmmaker) to someone who assembles incomplete and personal notes, creating a filmic notebook, so to speak – which brings to mind Alexandre Astruc's notion of cine-writing with a *caméra-stylo* ([1948] 1999).

Another important feature of filmic essayism is reflectivity, which could even be described as the form's default logic. Phillip Lopate, an American essayist, has described the essayistic mode of thinking most fittingly as a 'search to find out what one thinks about something'; according to him, essayistic thinking is a 'continuous asking of questions – not necessarily finding "solutions"' (1992: 19). This definition also resonates with the notion of the essay as an (incomplete, unfinished) 'probe' or 'attempt', as Montaigne originally defined his *Essais*. Of course, the alignment of Ulysses and Mekas at the beginning of *Lost, Lost, Lost* is then not only a way of ironically destabilising the notion of a heroic home-coming journey, but also an announcement that the film we are about to see is an essayistic 'attempt' to find out what 'home' (Ithaka, Semeniškiai, Lithuania, USA or New York?) really is or means. Typical for the essayistic rationale, we do not receive an unambiguous answer to that question, even though the film diarist suggests (rather than defines) that the search for a 'home' is a tedious and time-consuming journey that 'leads to nowhere', as Mekas recounts during the 'Rabbit Shit Haikus' sequence. This road that leads nowhere may have some benefits, such as finding new friends or a purpose in life (in this case, a life wholeheartedly dedicated to cinema), rather than family roots or a specific place to inhabit. Not coincidentally, not only poetry, but also asking questions rather than answering them, as well as tentative insinuation and purposeful incompleteness lie at the very heart of Jonas Mekas's essayistic strategies in *Lost, Lost, Lost*.

## The Poetics and Politics of Accented Essay Films

If we bring some of the points that have been made in the previous section with regard to *Lost, Lost, Lost* together with comments and observations made by (essay) film scholars on accented (exilic, migrant or diasporic) cinema, (autobiographical) authorship and the essay film, we may define some of the most characteristic features of 'accented essay films' as follows. First, Mekas's shifting authorial positions and manifold performative (or bodily) appearances within *Lost, Lost, Lost* not only point to some formal essayistic practice; if we consider Mekas's 'autobiographical' position of longing for and belonging to different socio-cultural spheres (Lithuania and New York, his rural past and his urban present), one can say that it is exactly the kind of spatial, temporal and cultural interstitiality which creates authorial ambiguities. This point has also been raised by Naficy in regard to accented cinema, when he explains that accented 'filmmakers are engaged in the performance of the self [. . .]; because of their interstitiality [. . .] exilic authors tend to create ambiguity regarding their own real, fictive or discursive identities' (2001: 35). This observation also corresponds with the notion of the 'presence-absence' (Rascaroli) of the essayistic author. Indeed, even though the essay's fragmentary heterogeneity is often only held together by little more than the author's voice, the kind of knowledge that is produced by this voice is provisional and unstable, contributing to a subjectivity that is in constant flux. In fact, one can say that essayistic writing becomes only truly essayistic when the author speaks from a position of instability, flux and movement, rather than from one that assumes stability, firmness or an Archimedean vantage point – a notion that was already expressed by the founder of the essay, Michel de Montaigne. In his essay 'On Repentance' he famously states that

> the world is in perennial movement. All things in it are in constant motion. [. . .] I cannot keep my subject still [. . .] I do not portray being, I portray passing. [. . .] If my mind could gain a firm footing, I would not make essays. (Montaigne [1580] 1958: 610–11)

The notion of the migrant as a 'political figure of movement' that is only adequately approachable from the *position* of movement has only recently been acknowledged by political philosophy (cf. Nail 2015: 3) – with notions such as 'hybridity' (rather than identity), 'becoming' (rather than being) and other similar concepts, post-colonial theory has acknowledged these inherently political migrant issues frequently and to greater effect. Hence, one can say that a second characteristic of 'accented essay films' like *Lost, Lost, Lost* is that the essayistic voice corresponds with a voice that speaks from a position of movement, instability or flux and is therefore infused with a 'politics of identity' that acknowledges the migrant's fluctuating and non-fixable (and perhaps to some, particularly to those at the right-winged end of the political spectrum, irritating) speaking position. I am rephrasing here a very similar observation made by the essay filmmaker and scholar Ursula Biemann, who has argued that the essayistic form is particularly good at capturing 'the more abstract, untangible processes of social and cultural transitions', and particularly the intangible 'movements of diaspora, dislocation and migration'; video essayists, Biemann claims, respond with their films to 'an increasingly ambivalent experience of place, nation and belonging' in a globalising world, which 'has prompted them to develop an artistic language that corresponds to the essayistic voice, a voice that speaks from a position of placelessness' (2003: 10).

We can derive a third characteristic from this observation, namely that such a 'position of placelessness' necessarily also leads to a questioning of notions like home, mother tongue or national identity, and hence to a form of what Walter D. Mignolo calls 'border thinking'[5] – which corresponds to the notion of the essay film as an intermedia (literary-cinematic), genre-crossing (docu-fictional), indeterminate practice *par excellence*. In fact, this is an issue that prominently runs through Mekas's film and finds its most explicit expression after thirty minutes, at the end of Reel 1, when Mekas declares, somewhat disillusioned, that all the diasporic festivities and gatherings he recorded are nothing more than sad attempts at holding onto something (an idea of a nation) that does not exist in exile anymore. While Mekas traces in *Lost, Lost, Lost* his loss in the belief of belonging to a certain place or nation across two decades (and this is what is ultimately 'lost' in *Lost, Lost, Lost*), Nora Alter suggests that it is not only anti-patriotic sentiments, but also a general disbelief in notions of 'identity' that concern most essay filmmakers:

> Most [essay filmmakers] question or reject the notion of a fixed identity as filmmaker, be it national, sexual, or cultural. Many, like Chilean-born but Paris-based Raul Ruiz, or Vietnamese-born, French-educated, and U.S.-based Trinh T. Minh-ha, have been working in exile. It may even be argued that it is this state of 'in-between-ness' which leads these filmmakers to adopt the essay film as a medium of expression in the first place. Falling themselves between categories, more or less finding a home in multicultural lands, they have been inspired, if not forced, to look for their inspiration to a similarly multilayered practice of filmmaking. (Alter 1997: 263)

We can thus say that for the 'accented essay filmmaker', art (or indeed the essay film) itself becomes his or her multicultural/multilayered homeland and this is why *Lost, Lost, Lost* not only traces the loss of an individual's national identity, but also the discovery of an artist's true vocation.

Finally, and derived from this, we can state that today, in the 'age of migration', accented essay films have become a decidedly transnational film practice. This is also because the essay film itself has 'extended since the 1970s'; it is 'now a transnational practice' since it 'proliferated through many new wave cinemas and various film cultures around the world', as Timothy Corrigan has observed (2011: 70). Naficy has, on the other hand, proposed the category of 'independent transnational cinema' to describe films by interstitial or exilic filmmakers, who partake in a form of 'cine-writing' and self-narrativisation linked through themes of memory, desire, loss, longing and nostalgia (1996: 121). Hence, one can say that both 'accented cinema' and 'essay film', and therefore also 'accented essay films', extended since the 1970s on a transnational scale, particularly those who, like *Lost, Lost, Lost*, have memory, desire, loss, longing and nostalgia as their primary subject. While *Lost, Lost, Lost* is a 1970s prime example, many other essay filmmakers made these themes, alongside migration and identity, an issue of their essayistic quests, among them Chantal Akerman (*News from Home*, 1976), Jill Godmilow (*Far From Poland*, 1984), Trinh T. Min-ha (*Surname Viet Given Name Nam*, 1989) or Boris Lehman (*Looking for My Birthplace*, 1990). Each of these examples operates within very different essayistic modes of expression, as diaries, notebooks, travelogues or (self-)portraits, but they all explore migration-related topics like these. Geographically, these filmmakers have made most of their movies either in the USA or in Europe; yet, unlike before, 'accented essay films' are today not only made by émigrés to the United States and Western Europe, but also by Indian, Japanese, Mexican, Brazilian, Armenian or Chilean filmmakers – even though, to repeat Alter, these national identity categories would not be suitable to describe these filmmakers anyway.

### Contemporary Examples

Given its transnational appeal as well as its affinity to transnationality as a subject (or 'way of life') in itself, it comes as no surprise that the 'accented essay film' becomes a more and more topical practice of global film culture in 'the age of migration'. Films such as *Passing Drama* (Angela Melitopoulos, 1999), *A Hungarian Passport* (Sandra Kogut, 2001), *That's My Face* (Thomas Allen Harris, 2001), *Algerian Dreams* (Jean Pierre Lledo, 2003), *Stone Time Touch* (Gariné Torossian, 2007), *Harat – A Journey Diary* (Sepideh Farsi, 2007), *Grandmother's Flower* (Jeong-hyun Mun, 2007), *Fotografías* (Andres Di Tella, 2007), *I for India* (Sandhya Suri, 2007), *Domov* (Margareta Hruza, 2008), *The Nine Muses* (John Akomfrah, 2010), *Nostalgia for the Light* (Patricio Guzman, 2010), *Beyond the Mountains* (Aya Koretzky, 2011) or *Purgatorio, A Journey into the Heart of the Border* (Rodrigo Reyes, 2013) present decidedly subjective, but nevertheless also essayistic quests for the meaning of home, family, memory, nation or national identity across a variety of continents and borders. While some of these films were made by exilic or diasporic filmmakers in the first generation (Guzman, Lledo), younger filmmakers often attempt to retrace the migratory routes of their parents or grandparents. For instance, in *Beyond the Mountains* Koretzky tries to interrogate her parents' reasons for moving from Tokyo to a remote mountain village near Coimbra in Portugal; in *A Hungarian Passport* Kogut, granddaughter of Jewish-Hungarian refugees to Brazil, embarks on a Kafkaesque journey through embassies and government agencies in France, Brazil and Hungary in order to apply for a Hungarian passport; in *Domov* Hruza tries to reunite her divorced parents, émigrés from communist Czechoslovakia, in Oslo, where she grew up, travelling to Los Angeles and Prague to convince her parents to do so; and in *I for India* Suri uses her father's Super 8 film archives to create a deeply personal essay film on her family's migrant experience in the UK, spanning four decades, from the 1960s to the 2000s.

Hence, unlike in the 1970s, the fates and hardships of 'far-flung families' (Berghahn 2013) is a particularly prominent issue of today's 'accented essay films'; and it is also one that is approached in *Passing Drama* – a 1999 video essay by Angela Melitopoulos. It has a more experimental approach to the topic, but is no less personal. This film has, just like *Beyond the Mountains* or *Domov*, buried family histories of migration, separation and displacement at its heart, but it is less conceived as a travelogue and more like an essayistic 'hypertext [. . .] of images and sounds visualizing memories and remembrance, thanks to the techniques of non-linear editing', as Melitopoulos has put it herself.[6] This stylistic strategy – one that works with snippets of sounds, found footage, testimonial interviews and digitally manipulated close-ups of landscapes, walls or faces, that puts an emphasis on fragments, discontinuities and non-linear narratives – matches the film's content, that is, its preoccupation with a family history of fragmented memories, discontinuities and ruptures. The film shows a number of interviews with elderly people from the Greek town of Drama, among them also Melitopoulos's grandparents, who recount their memories of the exodus of Greeks from Asia Minor in 1923 after the break-up of the Ottoman Empire, which brought them to Drama – a small city predominantly inhabited by refugees from Asia Minor. But Drama was for Melitopoulos's family also just a 'non-place' (to use Marc Augé's term), that is, a transit station. Her family was literally only 'passing through Drama', which is why the film's title *Passing Drama* actually describes a migratory movement in itself: the film recounts how they had to flee Drama during the Second World War because of the Bulgarian occupation, which finally brought the Melitopoulos family as refugees or so-called *Gastarbeiter* to Germany.

*Passing Drama*, in this way, portrays the history of a people with no nationality; as Melitopoulos puts it, 'This film expresses the point of view of a minority whose past seems to have been eaten out by industrial machines for the privileges of the majority.'[7] One can even say that *Passing Drama* addresses, just like many other 'accented essay films', a 'people yet to come' – as Gilles Deleuze and Félix Guattari have put it with regard to what they called a 'minor literature'– and in this way becomes a case of political cinema (of a silenced minority), rather than just one that is concerned with personal traumas and private memories. The notion of a, according to Deleuze and Guattari, decidedly political 'minor literature' is, it seems, particularly applicable to 'accented essay films'. Naficy (2001: 45) used a few of Deleuze and Guattari's characteristics of 'minor literature' to define his notion of an accented cinema: it is infused with politics, Naficy says, and it is a style that is best described as a gesture of refusal of dominant cinemas – which recalls Deleuze and Guattari's statement that the minor writer 'hates all languages of masters' (1986: 26).

In this sense, *Lost, Lost, Lost* can be considered as 'minor cinema' *par excellence*: it is an avant-gardist essay film that not only refuses the dominant cinema of its time and place (Hollywood and the industrial production mode), but also subverts the status quo uses of dominant languages, that is, the language of narrative cinema as well as that of the English language via the narrator's strong Eastern European accent. Furthermore, by becoming, in a double sense, an 'immigrant in one's own tongue',[8] Mekas has reinvented the language of cinema (in regard to the essayistic diary form) as well as deterritorialised that of a 'proper' English (via his accented poetry). *Lost, Lost, Lost* is also a political kind of cinema, because it remains aware of, and even celebrates, its minoritarian identity, or that 'road that leads nowhere'. After all, for Deleuze and Guattari, 'becoming-minoritarian' is primarily a political act or, indeed, a daily practice. This is why I call 'accented essay films' like *Lost, Lost, Lost* – which Mekas himself described as 'a small film, that does not force anything upon you' (in Naficy 2011: 143) – not a 'minor cinema', but a 'minor film *practice*', since it really showcases an artist's daily practice, a film diary of 'becoming-minoritarian' in a Deleuzian sense.

As many of today's accented essay filmmakers prove, this kind of daily, cine-writing or documentary practice might very well be the future of a new, political kind of migrant or 'minority cinema', because it empowers those with fewer resources, providing a public platform for a politics of subjectivity that is denied to them in the mainstream media. Hence, one can say that unlike in the 1960s and 70s, political (minority) cinema is today less accusatory, protesting or inclined to grand revolutionary gestures; it is more essayistic and, therefore, perhaps more decidedly 'minor' within a film industry that continues to be thoroughly capitalist and consumer-oriented. This is a tendency that can also be recognised in the work of one of Britain's most innovative artists:

Figure 3.2  Arctic landscapes in *The Nine Muses*, John Akomfrah, 2010.

John Akomfrah. From *Handsworth Songs* (1986) to *The Nine Muses* (2010), Akomfrah has produced some of the aesthetically most experimental and politically most radical films of recent British film history. However, while *Handsworth Songs* forms an accusatory protest against racist stereotyping of blacks in British media, anchored in a concrete historical event (the Handsworth riots of 1985), *Nine Muses* is best described as an audio-visual meditation on what Akomfrah perceives to be a timeless topic. Slow-edited archival footage (taken from the BBC archives) is constantly contrasted with a set of long takes, in which a lonely figure, dressed in a yellow suit, stares at Arctic landscapes, as well as with a variety of musical pieces, songs and quotes, which are read by professional actors. These image–sound combinations let us reflect on the experience of migration in more general terms. Akomfrah thus suggests that migration is more of an anthropological constant of humankind, rather than a 'social problem' of our post-colonial age; that it is less an exception and more of a rule in human history. To emphasise this point, Akomfrah uses the wisdom of poets and thinkers which spans not only the globe transnationally, but also almost two millennia of multiple 'ages of migration': actors read poems, passages or verses by Dylan Thomas, Rabindranath Tagore, Homer, Shakespeare or Nietzsche, each of which reflects on the experiences of dislocation, exile or the loss of one's home. This truly 'intertextual' audiotrack is mostly juxtaposed with found footage from TV archives, predominantly from the 1950s and 60s, which shows African, Jamaican or Indian immigrants arriving, working or dwelling in the cities of the UK. However, despite the imagery's concrete socio-historical context, Akomfrah's audio-visual meditations are structured in nine chapters, each of which refers to one of the nine muses of Greek mythology, thus emphasising once again not only the transnational but also the 'transhistorical' nature of migration as an anthropological constant for people of all ages in human history.

## Conclusion

With the more recent rise in autobiographical (cine-writing) film, video and new media practices – which find their expression either in the documentary film or through social media – one finally needs to ask whether the accented essay film really contributes to a more subtle political acknowledgement of the migrant's subjectivity; after all, it is a somewhat elitist, truly 'minoritarian' film genre that reaches, at best, only a spectatorship of international cineastes, film students or artisans. However, and assuming a filmmaker's perspective, one can say that today, in our postmodern digital era, in which neither narratives nor documents can be taken for granted and in which potentially everyone can document his or her life in an autobiographical diary fashion on blogs, vlogs, Facebook, Instagram, YouTube or elsewhere, essayistic reflectivity with its implied state of detachment and uncertainty seems to offer one possibility of escaping the traps of conventional (social) media representations as well as the pseudo-authenticity that is promised via instantaneous self-presentations on the web. Assuming a migrant's perspective, we can say that today, in our globalising world, in which (involuntary or voluntary) mobility as well as the feeling of *not*-belonging has become a rule rather than an exception, the essay film offers a veritable mode of expression because it can respond to the challenges of living a life 'in-between' in adequate ways. Finally, and assuming, this time, the perspective of the 'accented essay filmmaker', we can also say that it is exactly the essay's ability to interweave intellectual reflectivity with emotional trauma, documentary detachment with autobiographical involvement, that can adequately address the complexities and paradoxes of our new 'age of migration'.

## Notes

1. With the phrase 'age of migration' I refer to a volume that offers wide-ranging transnational and comparative perspectives on migration flows in the twentieth and twenty-first centuries by social scientists (see Castles et al. 2013).
2. As, for instance, the Marxist geographer David Harvey puts it, who has coined the term 'time-space compression' to describe the effects of globalisation: 'There has been a sea-change in cultural as well as in political-economic practices since around 1972. This sea-change is bound up with the emergence of new dominant ways of how we experience space and time' (1990: vii).
3. In other words, technically speaking, *Lost, Lost, Lost* is not a film diary, but a 'diary film', as James (1992) argues, because Mekas edited the material he shot in this time span in retrospect (in the 1970s) – which also distinguishes the diary film from the written diary. This, too, makes for the essayistic qualities of the film, as one might

argue, because the retrospective perspective lends itself to reflection and introspection.
4. A notion that Mekas made quite explicit with the title of his book of poems titled *There Is No Ithaka* (1996).
5. Rather than 'post-colonial', the concept of border thinking ought to serve as a 'de-colonial' thinking practice, as Walter D. Mignolo (2000) has argued – hence, a decolonisation of the mind or of (eurocentric, disciplinary) knowledge systems. I am referring here to Mignolo's concept because one can say that the essay (film), with its creation of 'epistemological uncertainties' and its tendency to be interdisciplinary, intermedial and genre crossing, is an ideal form for a kind of border thinking that creates, as Mignolo puts it, 'epistemic disobedience' (2).
6. Qtd in an abstract of the film on the website of *Heure Exquise! Centre international pour les arts vidéo*, available at <http://www.exquise.org/video.php?id=75&l=uk> (last accessed 6 September 2016).
7. Ibid.
8. This is, in essence, how Deleuze and Guattari describe Kafka's speaking position and, hence, that of a minor writer, but also, according to them, the way in which a minor writer ought to write (1986: 19).

## References

Alter, Nora M. (1997), 'Essay Film', in Tracy Chevalier (ed.), *Encyclopedia of the Essay*, London: Routledge, pp. 454–9.
Astruc, Alexandre [1948] (1999), 'The Birth of a New Avant-garde: La Caméra-Stylo', in Timothy Corrigan (ed.), *Film and Literature: An Introduction and Reader*, Saddle River, NJ: Prentice Hall, pp. 181–4.
Berghahn, Daniela (2013), *Far-Flung Families: The Diasporic Family in Contemporary European Cinema*, Edinburgh: Edinburgh University Press.
Biemann, Ursula (2003), 'The Video Essay in the Digital Age', in Ursula Biemann (ed.), *Stuff It: The Video Essay in the Digital Age*, Zurich: Edition Voldemeer, pp. 8–11.
Castles, Stephen, Hein de Haas and Mark J. Miller (eds) (2013), *The Age of Migration*, 5th edn, Basingstoke: Palgrave Macmillan.
Corrigan, Timothy (2011), *The Essay Film: From Montaigne, After Marker*, Oxford and New York: Oxford University Press.
Cuevas, Efren (2006), 'The Immigrant Experience in Jonas Mekas's Diary Films: A Chronotopic Analysis of *Lost, Lost, Lost*', *Biography*, 29:1, 55–73.
Deleuze, Gilles and Félix Guattari (1986), *Kafka: Toward a Minor Literature*, Minneapolis: University of Minnesota Press.
Harvey, David (1990), *The Conditions of Postmodernity*, Hoboken, NJ: Wiley-Blackwell.
James, David E. (1992), 'Film Diary/Diary Film: Practice and Product in *Walden*', in David E. James (ed.), *To Free the Cinema: Jonas Mekas and the New York Underground*, Princeton: Princeton University Press, pp. 145–79.
Lopate, Phillip (1992), 'In Search of the Centaur: The Essay-Film', *The Threepenny Review*, 48 (Winter), 19–22.
Mekas, Jonas (1996), *There Is No Ithaka*, trans. Vyt Bakaitis, New York: Black Thistle Press.
Mignolo, Walter D. (2000), *Local Histories/Global Designs: Coloniality, Subaltern Knowledges, and Border Thinking*, Princeton: Princeton University Press.
Montaigne, Michel de [1580] (1958), *Complete Essays of Montaigne*, Stanford:

Stanford University Press.
Naficy, Hamid (1996), 'Phobic Spaces and Liminal Panics: Independent Transnational Film Genre', in Rob Wilson and Wimal Dissanayake (eds), *Global-Local: Cultural Production and the Transnational Imaginary*, Durham, NC and London: Duke University Press, pp. 119–44.
Naficy, Hamid (2001), *An Accented Cinema: Exilic and Diasporic Filmmaking*, Princeton: Princeton University Press.
Nail, Thomas (2015), *The Figure of the Migrant*, Stanford: Stanford University Press.
Rascaroli, Laura (2009), *The Personal Camera: Subjective Cinema and the Essay Film*, London: Wallflower Press.
Renov, Michael (2004), *The Subject of Documentary*, Minneapolis and London: University of Minnesota Press.

# 4. *COTTONOPOLIS*: EXPERIMENTING WITH THE CINEMATOGRAPHIC, THE ETHNOGRAPHIC AND THE ESSAYISTIC

## Cathy Greenhalgh

In this chapter I consider the making of my feature film *Cottonopolis* (90', 2020). The film combines memories of 'Manchesters', that is, historical mega-textile cities Manchester (England), Ahmedabad (Gujarat, India) and Łódź (Poland), with observations of contemporary handloom and power loom cotton manufacture. I employ documentary techniques, reflexive essay and meditation, sensory and material culture ethnography, oral historiography and experimental visual immersion. I describe film production concerns related to questions of the cinematographic, ethnographic and essayistic. This analysis is underpinned by a practice point-of-view, conversations with Indian film colleagues and theories of essay, ethnographic and documentary film, eco-criticism and world cinema/diaspora aesthetics.

### CONTEXT AND APPROACH

I am influenced by artist-filmmaking collaborations with animators, choreographers and composers and by working as a professional cinematographer. My praxis fuses pedagogy, anthropology and filmmaking. *Cottonopolis* is an example of practice-as-research undertaken in (and out) of the academy, made over several years on a low budget. Making the film whilst working in higher education meant reflection became embedded more deeply as time stretched, expanded, contracted and evaporated. It is also as if my cotton ancestors kept showing up with their demands in pushing the eventual form of the film. I am a diasporic Lancastrian and my autobiographical route incorporates family

Figure 4.1 Appliquéd and animated title panel in *Cottonopolis*, Cathy Greenhalgh, 2020. Designed with and made by Lokesh Ghai in Ahmedabad and animated by Nina Sabnani in Mumbai.

background and genealogy in the cotton trade. My relatives, going back to the 1820s, worked in cotton mills, beginning as half-timers (half-day at school, half-day in the factory from the age of twelve).

I was invited to Ahmedabad, Łódź and Manchester for work. Ahmedabad was known as 'the Manchester of the East' which, with Mumbai (originally in the same Indian state), was India's main centre of cotton manufacture. The National Institute of Design based in Ahmedabad was one of India's earliest centres of photography teaching, co-founded by Haku Shah with the support of Henri Cartier-Bresson. Łódź was known as 'the Manchester of Poland' and served the former Soviet bloc as the main textile centre. Łódź is home to the Polish National Film School (PWSFT) and became Poland's filmmaking centre, relocating from Warsaw after the Second World War. Andrzej Wajda shot his film *The Promised Land* (1975) about the textile mill capitalists of Łódź in the 1800s. Manchester was an early centre of photography and filmmaking with some of the earliest film footage (1900s film shot by Mitchell and Kenyon) being discovered in 2011 in Blackburn, a former mill town north of the city. It is no accident that filmmaking and textiles are linked in this way as the chemicals needed for both were produced in these cities. Early celluloid was made from highly flammable gun cotton and the very earliest edited splices were stitched with cotton. This dawning realisation influenced the film in the direction of becoming a reflexive essay.

Each of these mega-textile city administrations still uses the 'Manchester' name as part of their tourist experience and cultural heritage. Manchester's decline took several decades, that of Łódź much less, and rapidly reindustrialising cities such as Ahmedabad discard and recycle, reinvent and rebrand, displace migrants and outsource skills at an alarming speed. Ahmedabad has a few large mills, though most trade relocated to Coimbatore; Manchester revived a few couture and high-end furnishing mills in the 2010s after years of closure. *Cottonopolis* (Manchester's nickname, originally given by a London newspaper in the 1800s and intended as derogatory) is still there as a 'state of mind' mingling loss and pride for textile city inhabitants. Recent gentrification of former mill areas may erase physical evidence, but older people recall sensory memories of noisy factories and the smell of cotton and they pass on the attitude of having an eye for fashion and good cut of cloth to the young. The agency of cotton as material and commodity is implicated in the flows of economy and politics, labour and health.

The film's structure combines narrative threads under major themes such as heritage, labour, material, migration, shoddy (waste), repair, resilience, thread, utility. The essay begins from my own story and family tree and ends with my dialogue with filmmakers. This hopefully roots the complexity and reach of the film's subject. First, we follow the process cotton goes through (though we begin with weaving in Lancashire's past, then move to the present day cotton fields in Gujarat); from sowing, picking, ginning, carding, spinning, weaving, bleaching, dyeing, sewing, selling, wearing and recycling. Second, a global historiography of the cotton trade is told via songs, poems, paintings, archive photography, film and quotations (Dickens, Engels, Gandhi, Gaskell, Kabir, Kerouac, Lowry, Marx, Spender, Wajda). Third, this is shot through with sensory recollections of participants (their voices or with them handling cotton, not as talking head interviews). There are sometimes small re-enactments or performative modes of storytelling as inspired by encounters with contributors.

I do not pretend to speak about varied Indian cultures, but there are similarities displayed in the feelings and experiences of people in cotton cities and certain repeating visual tropes (e.g. shuttles, looms, chimneys, clocks). Main contributors speak English, but also other languages (Gujarati, Hindi, Tamil, Polish). Though the cotton trade has a much older history across the Indian Ocean, I begin with its global commodity status cemented during the British Empire and colonialisation. This necessitates a dialogue which is transnational, diasporic and infused with what Mieke Bal has termed 'migratory aesthetics' (2008). Movement and migration characterise the paradigm for our contemporary world. For the essay film mode this mobility maps the subject, the process and its interdisciplinary travel and synthesis. It allows or even demands that poetics and politics combine to thread links together.

My approach to *Cottonopolis* has been influenced by working in India. In western academia it is difficult to combine the spiritual, activist, political and performative as unified. I am challenged by thinking about the material realities, shifting identities and changing landscapes that are important in *Cottonopolis*. Amrit Gangar's concept of 'Cinemā of Prayōga' is an alternative to the Euro-American idea of the avant-garde, describing experimentation in Indian cinema. Avoiding the duality of documentary or fiction, he considers cinema influenced by older forms of Indian music, myth, poetry and performance. Gangar's formulation derives from a pre-modern idea of innovation that understands time as cyclical and a 'cinematographic idiom that is deeply located in the polyphony of Indian philosophy and cultural imagination' (2006: 11). His provocation that Prayōga cinema is a practice that 'emphasises the excessive possibility of any form of contemplation – ritualistic, poetic, mystical, aesthetic, magical, mythical, physical or alchemical' (11) is inspiring.

Gangar suggests a 'ritualistic or alchemical force' is possible with immersive moving imagery. He states: 'if we contextualise experiment environmentally, or environment experimentally, we get a transcendental experience of the realm of cinematography. It is always in the process . . . [It] . . . would produce an ecology of aesthetics' (11). Praxis occurs within particular environments and temporalities and is affected by artistic, cultural, collaborative, ecological and economic contexts. An ecology of aesthetics inculcates a state of being, producing, writing and critiquing which can be specifically located and materialised, but is simultaneously diasporic, inclusive and interdisciplinary. A polymathic dialogue, both contemplative and political, can coexist. *Cottonopolis* contains both historiography of Empire and post-colonial subjectivities that draw on pre-industrial sensibilities in England, Poland and India. The film developed from my praxis (reflection on action) during production. Praxis 'arises from practice, not from integrating practice and theory. It is tested in practice and research imperatives arise from observations made through practical activity' (Greenhalgh 2018: 144).

*Cottonopolis* did not begin life as an essay film. It was first conceived as a short art film with choreography, set only in Lancashire. As research accumulated it grew into an ethnographic documentary feature film project and Indian colleagues encouraged me to expand the idea. Attending *Camerimage*, the International Festival of the Art of Cinematography held for many years in Łódź, regularly brought textiles and cinematography together in my mind. Finally, I found a form of the essay film to be the most appropriate solution, a way to allow the images and my dialogue with participants to build up a critique of accounts of the global cotton story and both 'implicate' and immerse myself (a female, white, western subject) in the experiment. What evolved incorporated cinematographic, ethnographic and essayistic modes. I continue by taking these three ways of thinking through the 'world cinema and the essay film' theme of this book, using the making of *Cottonopolis* as the 'lens'.

## Cinematographic

I define 'cinematographic thinking' (via years of pedagogic practice, filmmaking and interviewing cinematographers) as a way of thinking and being in which one sees light, movement and composition (framing) as a means of cohering and representing the world. These elements of the medium may be found and selected in documentary situations, or used to enhance locations and build fictional worlds on artificial sets. An essay film may fall somewhere in-between with fictional reconstruction or documenting taking place in production. For me, cinematography is a form not only of thinking, but also of scripting, performance and incorporation – how to 'make images feel'. Indeed 'writing-with-light-in-motion' produces a particular kind of knowledge and is the method of discovery and engagement. Here I outline the cinematographic use of chronotope and camera choreography, colour and texture as important components of *Cottonopolis*.

*Cottonopolis* has a chronotope (time-space frame) which both mirrors cotton manufacturing processes and opens out fissures of memory where the essayistic manifests. Michael Chanan argues that documentary has particular tropes and practices in relation to time as a fourth dimension of space. Though a genre is characterised by its chronotope (taking Bakhtin's notion), it is also open and dialogic. Chanan posits:

> A documentary shot is [...] the outcome of a process: the result of discovering, capturing, selecting and arranging appropriate elements to be found within actually existing social-historical space [...] [T]he documentarist discovers that representational space is highly malleable, for it includes people, places, events, the results of the provocations of the camera, and already existing images of every sort. [...] In the documentary mode, the visual and geographical leap is bridged by a logic of implication, where the organizing principle does not rely on plot and story but rhetoric, argument, or poetry. [...] Where the space of the fictional narrative produces continuity, documentary space is composed of discontinuities, both spatial and temporal, produced by dialectical (and dialogical) associations across time and space. (Chanan 2000: 60)

The chronotope is a helpful way of identifying how different subjectivities and perceptions are inscribed or can be produced in a film. In relation to diasporic cinema and world cinema, Hamid Naficy posits that filmed 'chronotopes are organising centres [...] not just visual, but synesthetic [...] temporality often structures feeling' (2001: 153). Timothy Corrigan considers time in the documentary (diaristic) essay form as 'a record of the dispersed and reflective subject across (this) temporally layered landscape' (2011: 140).

Cinematography can be used as a portal to 'supra-normal' kinds of experience; slowness and speed changes can amplify presence, immanence, awareness and resilience for participants, filmmakers and audience. Long takes can add intensity; potentially meditative, contemplative, emotionally intense or physically fascinating. Differential focus, low- or high-resolution imaging, combined with attention to the minutiae of performance, physiognomy and surface texture of objects, clothing, faces and landscape, are revelatory techniques available to the cinematographer when considered as temporal indicators.

My attitude to the materialities of both cotton and film production was influenced by conversations with filmmaker colleagues. Indian documentary cameraman and scholar K. P. Jayasankar understands cinematography as an embodied activity, where one is in tune with the process as contemplation, what he calls 'yielding' or being 'submissive to the image one finds', derived from a Buddhist stance. He tries 'to look at the image as a layered entity [. . .] And also the idea that you make Buddha icons with ice or butter, knowing that they would melt away [. . .] you build them all the same' (Jayasankar interview in Rutherford 2011: 303). This attention may help to bring an aliveness to the image. Filmmaking became a realisation or reinscription of time as practice and ritual which birthed this kind of contemplation whilst shooting *Cottonopolis*. This experience was prompted by the literal and psychic travel from filming deafening, monotonous, power loom environments to handloom, wherein I had to 'slow right down' to the pace of making, observing different rhythms and the arresting 'song of the handloom' (Shamji Vishram interview, Greenhalgh 2012b).

All cinematography involves a type of choreography, that is, blocking within mise-en-scène or moving in an improvised alignment with characters or people in documentaries. The craft, timing and movement involved in camerawork means this embodied relationship can also be intense labour for the operator. Here is a conversation from *Cottonopolis* with cinematographer S. B. Saksena about filming millworkers in Ahmedabad:

> Saksena: 'It's no longer a machine for them, it becomes like their life, you know. Some people retire when their machine has been discarded, because they are so much in love with that machine . . . They treat it more like a human being. Because of that long relationship of thirty, forty years on the same loom. It brings a love and hate relationship that persists.'
> Greenhalgh: 'Cameras can be like that.'
> Saksena: 'Yeah, ha! I completely agree cameras could be like that.'
> (Saksena interview, Greenhalgh 2012a)

K. P. Jayasankar and Anjali Monteiro's ethnographic films include *Saacha* (*The Loom*, 2001) about the emblematic figure of the migrant in mercantile

Mumbai's former cotton economy (Jayasankar and Monteiro 2016: 168–70). On the loom as a metaphor, Jayasankar suggests: 'The loom is a space of dynamism ... of twinning ... a dialectical space ... of nothingness, but all these forces that (come) together in that fabric' (Jayasankar interview, Greenhalgh 2010). Machines involved in cotton manufacture feature in *Cottonopolis*, wide shots of many people at work (looking like a textile) functioning as frames within the frame, a useful device to fuel recursive discourse, mise-en-abyme. The loom and shuttles, especially 'boat shuttles' become a metaphor of the labouring body. Shuttles carry weft threads across loom warps; mirror shutters revolve inside movie cameras exposing film stock to light (the most recent now are data-driven shuttle-less looms like digital camera sensors). This technical mediation crosses boundaries and borders, the etymology of both words emphasising travel back and forth and a continuous opening and closing.

The moving image essay and cloth textiles are both spaces of expression and a mosaic of time travel. Nomadic groups can no longer cross borders where previously they carried textiles for barter, yet the global cotton trade uses migrant labour and does little to combat human trafficking. *Cottonopolis* reveals materialities and memories of making ubiquitous cotton calico, denim and shoddy items (recycled waste textile) such as blankets, towels, sleeping bags for the military, schools and refugees. The visual strategy and 'look' of *Cottonopolis* was influenced by the textiles I experienced – from utilitarian to intricate hand-woven cotton fabric – and the manner of making.

A filmic 'tactile epistemology' (Marks 2000: 138) is a delicate sensibility to play with in shooting and editing. One cannot know the effect a film will have on the audience, but it is intended they should feel something of having been through all the processes cotton material goes through; at every stage wet, then dry, steamed, then soaked again, stretched and tensioned, twisted and spun out; exhausting, but also strengthening. The viewer goes through the mill, watching and feeling the cotton, attending the machine, making the pattern, assembling the completed garment, wearing it out and recycling it. The phrase 'going through the mill' refers to being teased, dragged, pushed and pulled through a rigorous process. 'Trouble at mill' refers to the politics and humour of workers, the strikes by workers and the sudden fires that would break out at factories full of highly flammable cotton in the past.

Henri Cartier-Bresson (1908–2004) worked intensively photographing the dyers along the Sabarmati riverbanks in Ahmedabad. He was a follower of various Indian mystics and of Gandhi, whose ashram is by the river. Local photographer Parmanand Dalwadi was trained by Cartier-Bresson and documentary photographer Parthiv Shah was his young assistant. Both tell their stories and visions of mill environments and cotton millworkers in *Cottonopolis*. Across Ahmedabad and in the villages of western Gujarat

Figure 4.2  Mise-en-abyme, the loom like a camera. A handloom weaver at work in Chennimalai, Tamil Nadu in *Cottonopolis*, Cathy Greenhalgh, 2020.

(Kaachch and Saurashtra) there are still many dying factories and small workshops specialising in bandhani (tie-dye). The dying process reminded me of being at the film laboratory when shooting on celluloid in the past, when one would give instructions for bleaching and grading film. Film uses a lot of water in processing, as does cotton. I became interested in the way water moves across the frame and the after-effects – stains, drying, unpicked stitched and tied blur patterns.

In *Cottonopolis*, the repetition of light and colour effects and choreographic intensity hopefully provide a sense of the world, of migration and travel, yet of different 'Manchesters' connected through a shared 'cotton consciousness' and collective memory. Cotton calico and denim are the principal materials followed, and a key aesthetic of the film is the gradual movement from so-called grey-cloth (pre-bleaching) to colour. The chromatic plan mirrors temporalities and affective relations with processes of ginning, weaving, dyeing or recycling cotton. The colour shift is recalled through memories and archive, the difference in attitudes to colour and light in Manchester's and Łódź's past (of smog and factories) and contemporary India.

*Cottonopolis* therefore includes these cinematographic aspects and techniques: long slow takes that amplify the choreography and energy expenditure of labour; close-ups of cotton sliding, rushing or jabbing through frame; use of bolls, seeds, threads as transitions with mesmeric textural and musically resonant quality; use of stills versus moving sequences (e.g. stills of ruins or archive, where cotton is no longer made – left places 'for dead', and moving images in factories that are active and 'full of industry'); no slow motion or speeded up motion to allow perception of the range of authentic sound and image speeds in power loom and handloom to be felt, heard and seen; occasional repetition of time tropes (loom shuttles, factory mill clocks, bell and hooter sounds); handheld, but steady camerawork with few pans or follow-shots; small movements and 'reveals', trying to give corporeal sensation within workshop and factory space; close-ups of hands touching cotton, eyes and ears, inspecting cotton (workers can be seen while participants' voices and sensory memories are heard on the soundtrack); loom-like frame within frames compositions (film as a search, loom-like point-of-view, mise-en-abyme); vertical drop views and left to right movement across central frame (warp and weft); moving from monochrome, grey to rich colour though the film (moving painting textile, imbued light, light through cloth); shimmering effects and textural differences (repetition of vibrating material); all filmed in digital HD.

### Ethnographic

In this section I draw attention to questions of material agency and aesthetics, sensory ethnography and ekphrasic expression within anthropology. The ethnographic research for *Cottonopolis* began with collecting archive material, doing interviews, drawing and shooting video sketches, taking photographs as well as finding songs and poems. Filming involved a bricolage activity of walking and shooting still, then movie, around old Manchester then later Indian and Polish cotton factories, discovering connections. I also received 'video letters' from colleagues and friends in Connecticut, Georgia and Mississippi as well as from Uzbekistan cotton fields and mills. Conversations with local consultants, filmmakers, academics and students informed development. The research was transnational, multi-sited, 'home and away' and used narrative as a fieldwork technique with participants. Fieldwork and film research involved repeated visits to people and settings in different seasons and to build sensory expression. I met experts and historians, but sought everyday voices. Footage was acquired through the material, embodied process, improvised performance and reflexive, contemplative periods of editing, rather than rigorous structuring methods. Filming and fieldwork throw up many surprises and each trip altered the film.

The ethnographic filmmaking and visual anthropology disciplines have often distrusted aesthetic positioning. Observation was seen as a key activity within anthropology as a science. Though 'sensing' experiences of researchers and participant narratives of the sensory often featured in fieldwork notes, these stories did not make it into the more official accounts. Anthropology, like film studies, has seen ontological, sensory and ecological turns, amongst others, in the last twenty-five years. Critical practice in sensory ethnography has recast vision as embodied (Cox et al. 2016). The sense of how cotton looks and smells, sounds, tastes and feels to the touch in different states accumulates and intensifies in *Cottonopolis*.

Aesthetics can anchor identity and meaning, mobility and creativity through tacit or explicit means. There can be an 'aesthetics of organization' (Strati 1999: 9), in other words, specific ways in which an individual within a community of practice or organisation conducts their work. So I have preferences, accrued knowledge and affective moods I prefer and try to inculcate on a film project. Work has an organisational texture, suggests Silvia Gherardi (2006). Getting on with work requires skills of bricolage (such as darning, patching, quilting and various repair practices), using 'what is to hand to invent something new and make imaginative re-use of what is old and left over' (Gherardi 2006: 183).

In India, practices of making do (sometimes linked now with entrepreneurialism) are known as *jugaad*, a Hindi word for innovative fix and ingenious use of resources. I saw numerous examples of old spinning machines and looms (often old ones shipped from Lancashire to India years ago) held together with ingenious use of bicycle wheels and car parts. There is a history of using waste cotton (shoddy) in Lancashire, where the 'posh' end of the valley made fine muslins (Bolton), and the poorer end tea towels and blankets (Oldham). My own great-grandmother ran a 'fent shop' (ends of rolls which people used to buy to make up patchwork shirts) by the side of a mill. I began to think of the filmmaking process as this kind of patchwork and making do, both industrial and handmade.

Gandhi visited Lancashire in 1931 to petition the cotton workers and call for 'Swadesh', for India to make her own handmade cotton fabric and not be beholden to the English industry. Everywhere in Ahmedabad there are symbols of the *charkha* (simple spinning wheel) which Gandhi spun cotton on every day. Government officials and many ordinary Indians still wear *khadi*, handspun and handwoven cotton, following the Gandhian tradition. Knowledge of thickness and 'count' of cotton is widespread, as it is in Lancashire, where my mother recalls lines of cotton rope hung along the streets in the spinning district near her home. My uncle remembers with pride the famous advertising phrase after the Second World War: 'Britain's Bread Hangs by Lancashire's Thread'. In *Cottonopolis*, kite string appears in a sequence of stories of spinning threads. *Uttarayan*, the 14 January kite festival in Ahmedabad, celebrates *Makar Sankranti* (the entry of the sun into Capricorn after the winter solstice). The renowned strength of 'number one' cotton kite string, dipped in pink and orange sugar glass to cut opponents' strings, is essential for the ensuing fighting frenzy of kites above the rooftops. A popular image on kites and string bobbin reels in 2014 was of Prime Minister Narendra Modi, himself a child of Ahmedabad.

Anthropologist Tim Ingold identifies the creativity between object and maker, 'making-ness' as the place of intent and action, which he calls the 'textility of making' (2011: 210). He argues that there has been a lack of attention to what people do with materials in favour of general definitions of materiality. Ingold uses the example of kite flying, emphasising the movement between hand and kite as a moving line, and the wind as agency, as much as analysis of person or object (215). Whilst I was filming women making quilts from waste cotton in Ahmedabad, a kite suddenly dive-bombed into frame from above, and the women stood up to shout and chastise the 'culprit' children. This serendipitous energetic moment connects the activity to previous scenes. The camera can capture this kind of timing and 'enhance this wondering about the nature of things', according to anthropologist Ivo Strecker (2013: 54). He notices the 'co-presence of phenomena that appeared' (52) in scenes he had shot, but did not discover until editing, finding these provoked 'astonishment, evocation, and the spell of culture' (52) as they were 'nonanticipated' (53). This is the kind of event one cannot script before shooting but which formulates during editing.

Whilst making *Cottonopolis*, conducting interviews, visiting factories and workshops, archives and museums, finding cotton materials and filming, I wrote field notes. This became a way of making sense – between cinematography and writing. There has been recent experimentation using fiction and poetry, incorporating ekphrasic expression, seeking polyphony in ethnographic writing (Pandian and McLean 2017). Michael Taussig promotes his idea of 'nervous-system writing'. He says, 'sometimes when you write field notes time stands still and an image takes its place. On occasions that image is tactile' (2015: 8). Ethnographic filmmaker David MacDougall argues that 'Films [. . .] recover a dimension of human experience often lost in texts [. . . and] are permeated with the imprint of human environments' (2006: 58). He says that making films 'can induce an intense engagement with the world [. . .] It is not uncommon to find yourself inhabited by your subjects . . . The possession is not so much a matter of spirit as of material being' (137).

Andrew Irving's sensory ethnographic studies of twilight show that 'diminishing amounts of available light, and visible impairment shape people's possibilities for practical action and ekphrasic expression' (2013: 77). He says, 'people's actions in the world produce a form of "living montage" that creates continuous juxtapositions of sight, sound, smell, touch and taste' (77).

In diasporic and world cinema subject matter, we often find stories in which other senses and realities are imagined. Filmmakers integrate aesthetics with participants, environment, story, sense of place, weather phenomena, specific texture of objects and the vibrancy of material culture. Listening to and observing participants requires time, intimacy and sensitivity to how our co-presence and performativity affects the environments filmed in. This somatosensory engagement may be what we identify with in a film, and perhaps words can be more usefully used as a counterpoint to this affective track in the essay form – rather than making images perform illustration, give information, or provide overarching narrative. The audience need to be allowed to personalise the experience of watching a film and 'complete the equation'. They can be 'crushed by the "frame of representation"', claims veteran Hollywood editor and sound designer Walter Murch (2018: n.p.). He uses fabric as inspiration: 'How to represent ineffable things? Avoid the particular scene to start with, think of the transition and how you want that to feel. I think of this as a fabric. There's tweed; wool, rough and warm and then a transition to silk; smooth, cold and glistening' (n.p.).

Some ethnographic points associated with *Cottonopolis* are: sensory ethnography, corporeal mode of knowledge (going through the mill); material culture of cotton (associated tools, documents, drawings, maps, archive photos – materiality as part of environmental ecology and agency); field notes and interviews as 'scripting' as well as filming; repeated trips to the field over several years and seasons (appreciation of the 'slowness' of fieldwork and reflexive research); incorporation of serendipity and accident as experience (and allowing the audience to engage with the surprise); variety of visual and sound textures as 'portals', as energies and material qualities; performative relationship with participant narratives and filmmaker's reflexive comment (significant voices, but not 'experts', passion not polemic); no talking head interviews (some interviews showing hands and cotton objects).

## Essayistic

My aim with *Cottonopolis* is to combine documentary, cinematography, ethnography and the essay by working with them in dialogic relation, that is, to try to make 'writing' with light and movement, writing about people and culture, and personal thesis writing speak, comment and perhaps productively unravel each by applying the lens of the other method. This is in order to show up gaps and projections between the cotton stories – official and sensory histories that differ across perhaps contested transnational perspectives. Here, I want to suggest some ways of thinking about authorship, dialogue, commentary and the gaze in *Cottonopolis*. The placing of the author problematises and underpins part of the essay film enterprise:

> the essayistic is most interesting not so much in how it privileges personal expression and subjectivity but rather in how it troubles and complicates that very notion of *expressivity* and its relationship to *experience* [. . .] essayistic expression [. . .] demands both loss of self and the rethinking and remaking of the self. (Corrigan 2011: 17; original emphasis)

The essay and the essay film are 'not so much the projection but the undoing of the self. This involves interrogation, mediation, insight' (Corrigan 2011: 17). Filmmaker and scholar Anjali Monteiro explains: 'it has a lot to do with questioning the boundaries of self and other, realizing the fluidity [. . .] whether it is oneself as a living thing or a non-living thing' (Monteiro interview in Rutherford 2011: 301). This dissolving and reconstructing of self occurred through responding to the environment, cotton materials, my relationships with participants and by my performance as the cameraperson.

There are at least three famous essay films in which the cameraperson is a pivotal character: Dziga Vertov's *Man with a Movie Camera* (1929), Chris Marker's *Sans Soleil* (1982) and Agnès Varda's *The Gleaners and I* (2000). Vertov begins with the title 'an excerpt from the diary of a cameraman'. Final montage scenes combine close-ups of eyes, split screens (the 'Kino-Eye') and the camera bowing to the audience, dancers, guns and a woman worker superimposed over a cotton spinning machine – followed by camera operator Mikhail Kaufman and editor Elizaveta Svilova. This worker is an 'icon of the new Soviet woman. The circular movement of the machinery creates a halo around her head. The axle point is situated at the centre of her forehead' (Roberts 2000: 87). This is 'visual apotheosis as a political act: life, the film studio and the movie camera at its socialist post' (88).

My time, travel and materials are implicated in the cotton story. I am acutely aware of cotton's massive draw on resources of labour, water, land and time. These musings exacerbate my sense of both machine- and handmade textiles and filmmaking practice. I display myself in *Cottonopolis* as the director/camerawoman grappling with what she sees, revealing herself and the film's mechanics. Nadia Bozak locates the consumption of energy in the making of films. She sees Vertov as 'extracting' or 'mining' for images in support of his Soviet industrial vision: 'montage associations such as creative geography relate the automobile to the factory, the factory to the street, and the street to the camera [. . .] traced back to the editing table and the film factory' (2012: 98). This '"film factory logic" exhibits the process and the labour expended and absorbed by all stages of the cinematic process' (143).

Sandor Krasna, Chris Marker's globetrotting cameraman character in *Sans Soleil*, exchanges letters with the unseen female narrator. Corrigan describes the film as a prototype of the 'travel essay' or 'pilgrimage' which 'discovers another self in the process of thinking through new or old environments and thinking of self as a different environment. They commonly represent subjective experience as epistolary, journalistic and conversational' (2011: 105). The film deals with memory and misperception using images of Japan, Iceland or Guinea-Bissau. I was a young camerawoman when I first saw this film and the persona of the cameraman made me feel weary. I could not identify with him as a realistic construction. I was looking for my own version of the 'female gaze'.

Varda invented the term 'cinécriture' (cinematic writing) because she 'fought [...] for something that comes from emotion, from visual emotion, a sound emotion, feeling, and finding a shape for that, and a shape that has to do with cinema and nothing else' (Varda in Bénézet 2014: 111). Varda generally does not identify with a specific female point of view in her interviews, but there is an embodied sense of the female in her work, particularly present in *The Gleaners and I*. The film moves between essay and painting-tableaux to handheld rummaging as Varda follows contemporary gleaners in fields of potatoes and amongst urban market rubbish, discovering multiple societal metaphors with her mini-DV camera. In front of Jules Breton's painting *The Gleaners* (1854) she declares she is 'happy to drop the wheat and pick my camera' and 'to film my one hand with the other hand'. This is Varda's camera-pen 'full personal cinécriture', now possible due to new handheld camera technology, making it 'much less utopian than when Astruc coined the term "camera-stylo"' (Rascaroli 2017: 4).

A feminist eco-critical reading can be elicited from Bozak's proposition that Varda's 're-instatement of gleaning is a necessary social, economic and cultural intervention' which 'positions the self-sufficient cinematic document as a composite of ideas and images gathered from the practitioner's immediate universe [...] then reorganized, restructured and reformulated into discrete, subjective visions' (2012: 164). Corrigan positions the *The Gleaners and I* slightly differently: 'constructed as a meditation on gleaning (2011: 70). Gleaning, 'like the essayistic identity, is a parasitically productive activity, a subversion or rejection of the authority and primacy of subjectivity and selfhood' (71). Visiting a field where pickers sort through huge mounds of discarded potatoes, Varda finds only 'special' potatoes shaped like hearts, which she holds up to the camera with her one elderly, creased hand as she films with the other. This is her imprint on the situation. She recasts the people she meets within her essayistic take on French life; that is, not ethnographic or contemplative through the imagery, so much as romanticised at times by her delight in capturing the scene. For example, the gleaners are cut between the scene where Varda films her hand pulling at her grey hair in the mirror.

Whilst I am inspired by Varda's essay film practice, I found a different means of expression through the transnational context of Cottonopolis. I was sometimes with others, but often shooting myself, a lone female. I am a cinematographer, with that training and adeptness, which is not the same as directors who are self-shooters. This 'cinematographer's gaze' and technical ability can both enhance and interfere with shooting. Having shot films for other directors, it is sometimes challenging also to direct oneself and inhabit that voice fully. An example of this dilemma happened when, literally I 'enter the field', in ethnographic terms, an Indian cotton field, with two (Indian) male companions. As I approach the women pickers, they come towards me holding bolls of cotton, pull my hand towards them and prick my fingers. In Gujarati dialect they explain the cotton has sharp thorns and it is hard work. I am filming my one hand with the other hand, but I keep the shot running in a long take until the women stand back, take a sip of water using their veils as a filter, and offer me some before they return to picking. This all happens within two minutes.

Later I discover the women say, 'I don't mind her filming us, she reminds me of my aunty, she's got a camera, she's always taking photographs.' My frame settles to a wide shot, and later I find this disturbing in its 'picturesque' quality. I find similar compositions in the paintings of black cotton pickers by American artist Winslow Homer and earlier etchings of slaves. I find a silent 1931 Pathé press film showing 5,000 Lancashire children 'dressed as a cotton field' – running up and down with 'bolls' on their heads. I realise my ancestors, like myself, would never have seen a real cotton field, nor understood what made Manchester so rich. My family tree shows they moved across the county looking for work during the American Civil War (1861–5) and the resulting Lancashire Cotton Famine blockading cotton at southern American ports. (Britain abolished slavery in the British Empire in 1833, the USA in 1865.) I worry about how I am picturing my subject. The cotton field scene gives me an opportunity to implicate myself, but also, through the inclusion of the women, to counter my own potentially colonial gaze with their contemporary view of me. The essayistic loop is used here to carry this complexity and 'trouble' readings of the image. After the field sequence, I cut to a montage of the Homer

Figure 4.3 Implicating the camerawoman in the essay. Cathy Greenhalgh filming in the ginning mill, Wadwhan, Gujarat. Photographed by Dhimant Vyas.

painting, the silent film archive, and to contemporary Calvin Klein cotton adverts overlaid with participant descriptions of cotton fields in Mississippi and India.

The ability to make connections in an essay film is encouraged by the use of devices such as competing texts, polyphonic narratives, rhizomatic rather than linear structures. Such use creates a spun and woven structure with different emphases and experiences from those caused by a linear narrative script. Essay films may have a 'kaleidoscopic nature (which) exceeds the realm of the visual to include the acoustic. [. . .] Their objective or subject matter tends to be labyrinthine, and largely open to the spectator's interpretation' (Alter 2018: 6). The female gaze in *Cottonopolis* is affected by the textiles and water in so many shots – an essentialist tone these days perhaps, but it is how I have experienced living my life, rather than how I theorise my work. Luce Irigaray argues with Friedrich Nietzsche about point-of-view and the nature of water: 'one by one, each of her surfaces takes its turn to shimmer. And the mirage falls into the gleaming abyss, endlessly. The sea shines with a myriad eyes. And none is given any privilege. Even here and now she undoes all perspective. Countless and shifting and merging her depths. And her allure is an icy shroud for the point of view' (1991: 47). This is more how I feel the female/cinematographer gaze operates in my own work – a silent interior and several points of view; intense focus on the process of yielding, rather than a penetrative single view.

In 2010, I visited Queen Street Mill, Burnley, Lancashire; a museum, the last still working steam cotton mill in Europe. This was the first time I had seen working machines and encountered the smell, dust and the sheer noise. I cried as a vague, and as yet unarticulated, ancestral memory welled up. It was completely unexpected and I was told this reaction was common amongst local visitors. It is this confusion and affective sense I hope to have captured for the audience viewing *Cottonopolis*. It was important to 'invoke' out of the material of cotton and also to implicate myself – to avoid any 'colonial voice' tone and because I want to include my immersive engagement with the material phenomenal world and relationships with documentary participants. *Cottonopolis* draws on well-documented historical sources, yet affective memories and the migratory aesthetics of hidden narratives, the historiography of cotton, are rare. A sort of 'spectrepoetics' accrued in making the film was challenging – ghosts filled old factory ruins, as if speaking through me. Writing about John Akomfrah's essay films, Nora Alter notes the 'fabrication of histories from spectral traces, from the "ghosts of songs", becomes one way of countering the relative absence of records or archives that locate diasporic subjects' (Alter 2018: 26).

In Karl Marx's *Capital* (1867), Friedrich Engels's footnotes give detailed insights into the labour of the Lancashire cotton workers he studied, particularly young women and children, in the mid 1800s: 'factory work exhausts the nervous system to the uttermost; at the same time, it does away with the many-sided play of the muscles, and confiscates every atom of freedom, both in bodily and intellectual activity' (Engels in Marx [1867] 1990: 584). In 1815, cotton operatives walked eight miles a day behind spinning mule machines. In 1832, speedier machines entailed walking twenty miles a day (537). The British Empire's wealth was built on the labour of slaves and workers – in Lancashire, '400,000 little girls made the Industrial Revolution' (historian G. T. Whitworth interview, Greenhalgh 2009). This labour continues in present day China, India and Uzbekistan. Gilles Deleuze sees history as arriving through rupture rather than continuity and uses the metaphor of the loom, the sudden break of threads caused by 'an accumulation of forces and timings' ([1988] 1993: 30). My own relatives haunt my reading and filming.

Essayistic aspects of *Cottonopolis* include: attention to the gaze (perhaps identifiably female); ellipses which reveal ethics of cultural and power difference; cinematography as a form of writing; chaptering via visual transition (not black screens/words on screen); words on screen as texture, including labels, embroidered signatures, mill names on brick chimneys, pub signs like 'Clogger's arms', street signs like 'Bobbin street' or 'Plantation street' in Lancashire towns, my maps of destroyed mills, lists of cotton samples, lettering on towels, child's drawings and essay; words as counter rhythms and voices as sonic compositional material texture, most notably accents, types and speeds of storytelling, songs, poems; my own voice-over and conversation mingled with participants; video letters – epistolary links from cotton locations; a sense of a 'spectrepoetics' with the past invading the present unexpectedly and emotively; the camerawoman as a character, the journeyer and gatherer of threads.

## Conclusion

In classical Sanskrit theatre the *sutradhar*, which translates as 'the one who holds the threads', is a producer, narrator or puppeteer. They control the flow of performance, maintain clear sense and comment on technical operations by connecting story links for the audience. Jayasankar and Monteiro maintain this is a powerful example of

> reflexive and critical work in the non-dualist artistic, performative, diegetic and philosophical traditions that flourished in the Indian subcontinent. These predate, by many centuries, [western] intellectual debates [. . .] The figure of the *Sutradhar*, [. . .] commenting constantly on the dramatic text put his foot in the door of the story [. . .] The audience does not see anything incongruous in this temporary narrative disruption. (Jayasankar and Monteiro 2016: 72)

She/he is not so much authorial, as acting as a facilitator. They try to make connections between different sub-stories, audiences and narratives. I hope to have explained here something of how I put my own foot in the door of the story and how working in India influenced my film project.

A dialogic approach to thinking through the making of *Cottonopolis* has been inflected by writing here. I am one thread in its complex weave, mingling with a distributed set of participant subjectivities and the agency of non-human materials. Within the crossover of the essayistic and the ethnographic and with the cinematographic positioning I have developed, I find that both intellectual and sensory ways of working with participants create interesting material elisions and provocations. My essay filmmaking praxis incorporates an improvisational aesthetic within a specific structure which privileges affective experience and contemplation, reflexivity and a poetics of revelation, providing uncertain answers rather than polemic. As a small child in the 1960s I scrawled words into the thick, black coal soot deposited on mill buildings along canals (cleaned away in the 1980s). My own essay film directing voice in *Cottonopolis* is enabled through threads back to the global cotton industry past, and the labour of those who came before that must be acknowledged and remembered. As the 'garment' is re-sewn/sown into the present, realisation comes in waves and loops. Films are threads, but also time-capsules like seeds which hopefully grow with the viewer.

## References

Alter, Nora M. (2018), *The Essay Film: After Fact and Fiction*, New York: Columbia University Press.
Bal, Mieke (2008), 'Migratory Aesthetics: Double Movement', *Exit*, 32, 150–60, <https://transaestheticsfoundationdotorg.files.wordpress.com/2016/01/bal-mieke-migratory-aesthetics-double-movement-exit-32-december-2008-january-2009-150-61.pdf> (last accessed 16 July 2018).
Bénézet, Delphine (2014), *The Cinema of Agnès Varda: Resistance and Eclecticism*, Chichester and New York: Wallflower Press.
Bozak, Nadia (2012), *The Cinematic Footprint: Lights, Camera, Natural Resources*, New Brunswick, NJ and London: Rutgers University Press.
Chanan, Michael (2000), 'The Documentary Chronotope', *Jump Cut*, 43 (July), 56–61.
Corrigan, Timothy (2011), *The Essay Film: From Montaigne, After Marker*, Oxford and New York: Oxford University Press.
Cox, Rupert, Andrew Irving and Christopher Wright (eds) (2016), *Beyond Text? Critical Practices and Sensory Anthropology*, Manchester: Manchester University Press.
Deleuze, Gilles [1988] (1993), *The Fold: Leibniz and the Baroque*, Minneapolis: University of Minnesota Press.
Gangar, Amrit (2006), 'The Moving Image: Looped, to be Mukt!1 – the Cinemā Prayōga Conscience', in Brad Butler and Karen Mirza (eds), *Cinema of PraYoga: Indian Experimental Film and Video 1913–2006*, London: no.w.here, pp. 9–26.

Gherardi, Sylvia (2006), *Organizational Knowledge: The Texture of Workplace Learning*, Malden, MA and Oxford: Blackwell.
Greenhalgh, Cathy (2009), Interview with G. T. Whitworth, Littleborough, Lancashire, May.
Greenhalgh, Cathy (2010), Interview with K. P. Jayasankar, Mumbai, August.
Greenhalgh, Cathy (2012a), Interview with S. B. Saksena, Ahmedabad, January.
Greenhalgh, Cathy (2012b), Interview with Shamji Vishram Valji, Preston, Lancashire, September.
Greenhalgh, Cathy (2018), 'Cinematography as Research, Research into Practice', in Craig Batty and Susan Kerrigan (eds), *Screen Production Research: Creative Practice as a Mode of Enquiry*, Basingstoke: Palgrave Macmillan, pp. 143–59.
Ingold, Tim (2011), *Being Alive: Essays on Movement, Knowledge, Description*, London and New York: Routledge.
Irigaray, Luce (1991), *Marine Lover of Friedrich Nietzsche*, New York: Columbia University Press.
Irving, Andrew (2013), 'Into the Gloaming: A Montage of the Senses', in Christian Suhr and Rane Willerslev (eds), *Transcultural Montage*, Oxford and New York: Berghahn, pp. 76–95.
Jayasankar, K. P. and Anjali Monteiro (2016), *A Fly in the Curry: Independent Documentary Film in India*, Los Angeles, London and New Delhi: Sage Publications.
MacDougall, David (2006), *The Corporeal Image: Film, Ethnography, and the Senses*, Princeton and Oxford: Princeton University Press.
Marks, Laura (2000), *The Skin of the Film: Intercultural Cinema, Embodiment and the Senses*, Durham, NC and London: Duke University Press.
Marx, Karl [1867] (1990), *Capital: A Critique of Political Economy*, vol. 1, London: Penguin Books.
Murch, Walter (2018), 'Imaginaries of the Desert – Frames of Reference', Film Symposium, Institute of Contemporary Arts, London (from notes, near verbatim), 29 April.
Naficy, Hamid (2001), *An Accented Cinema: Exilic and Diasporic Filmmaking*, Princeton and Oxford: Princeton University Press.
Pandian, Anand and Stuart McLean (eds) (2017), *Crumpled Paper Boat: Experiments in Ethnographic Writing*, Durham, NC and London: Duke University Press.
Rascaroli, Laura (2017), *How the Essay Film Thinks*, Oxford and New York: Oxford University Press.
Roberts, Graham (2000), *The Man with the Movie Camera: The Film Companion*, London and New York: I. B. Tauris.
Rutherford, Anne (2011), *What Makes a Film Tick? Cinematic Affect, Materiality and Mimetic Innervation*, Bern: Peter Lang.
Strati, Antonio (1999), *Organization and Aesthetics*, London, Thousand Oaks and New Delhi: Sage Publications.
Strecker, Ivo (2013), 'Co-presence, Astonishment, and Evocation in Cinematography', in Ivo Strecker and Markus Verne (eds), *Astonishment and Evocation: The Spell of Culture in Art and Anthropology*, New York and Oxford: Berghahn, pp. 52–62.
Taussig, Michael (2015), *The Corn Wolf*, Chicago and London: University of Chicago Press.

# 5. THE WORLD ESSAY FILM AND THE POLITICS OF TRACEABILITY

## Giorgio Avezzù and Giuseppe Fidotta

Located at the intersection between 'world cinema' and the tradition of the 'essay film', the label 'world essay film' designates a number of works in which the 'main idea' is, arguably, the whole world itself. This chapter investigates the world essay film from a theoretical perspective, focusing specifically on how the world's interconnectedness can be made visible, material and spatial – that is to say, geographical – through an essayistic form.[1]

At the same time, the works comprised under this label can be seen to thematise deep anxieties related to the invisibility of a late capitalist world, whose flows and networks seem to escape all forms of plain representation. The invisibility of contemporary capitalism undermines a typically modern attitude towards the world, an attitude historically reflected by some of cinema's traditional functions – namely, its ability to portray a 'worldist' perspective. Cinema was able to capture the spirit of its time because it contributed to the space-time compression of modernity, making the world a *knowable totality* – knowable by virtue of its imageability.[2] This very imageability should not be taken for granted today. In fact, as we argue, what is at stake in the world essay film is the very adequacy of cinema for the present times.

### DOCUMENTARY FILM AND THE ONE WORLD: TERMS FOR A DEBATE

'The true mystery of the world is the visible, not the invisible', reads the epigraph by Oscar Wilde (2005: 25) with which Walter Ruttmann's *Melody of the World*, the 1929 documentary commissioned by the shipping line HAPAG to promote their world tours, opens. Clearly grounded in the genre of travelogue, Ruttmann's film did not, however, portray anything mysterious about either the world or the visible. Rather, it aimed to 'capture the world in the archive of filmic images and reveal its secrets [. . .] residing [. . .] in the correspondences and regularities amid the seemingly endless varieties of visible life captured in moving images' (Cowan 2014: 83).

The possibility asserted by documentary filmmakers to grasp the world through the all-powerful means of cinema has such a familiar flavour that it could be considered as the foundation of what might be called the 'one-world film'. As prominent film theorists like Béla Balázs and Erwin Panofsky maintained in the same years when Ruttmann was roaming around the Earth to film it, cinema has a special relation with the world because of its visual character, its kinship with physical and material reality. Documentary film, of course, reinforces that claim with the authority of a cogent connection between reality, truth and representation.

The typically modern belief in an imaginable world fostered by documentary films like *Melody of the World* thus underpins an equal belief in cinema as a medium able to convey and articulate the deepest sense of the world. The term 'world' is understood here, following Franco Farinelli, as 'the complex of the (social, economic, political, and cultural) relationships in which human life unfolds' (2003: 6; our translation). According to modern thought (e.g. in social sciences, anthropology and human geography), such meaning can be inferred from an accurate depiction of the Earth's visual features. Cinema endorsed this conviction by legitimising its claim of appropriate representation through three interwoven beliefs, which should be brought into focus.

First, the world has to be conceived as a purely *visible surface* whose features cinema can capture and put together in a kind of inventory. This approach is exemplified by Albert Kahn's *Archives de la Planète* (1912–30), a utopian 'inventory of the surface of the globe', that is, an atlas, grounded in the certainty that photography and cinema are 'key tool[s] for extracting geographical knowledge from the disorder of reality' (phrases used by Kahn's associate Emmanuel Jacquin de Margerie in 1912 in a letter to Jean Brunhes inviting him to lead the project, in Amad 2010: 49, 71; see also Castro 2006; 2011: 176–91). A similar claim was advanced in the mid 1910s, not coincidentally just as Kahn's project was beginning, by Hermann Häfker's *Kino und Erdkunde* (1914), perhaps the first book to explore cinema's planetary mission. According to Häfker, both cinema and geography are meant to offer a sweeping depiction of the whole world and make the Earth home to human beings. Further, both disseminate knowledge of the homeland and of the colonies, support trade and business, and help shape a better transnational understanding of different countries and peoples as framed by a superior global vision.

Second, the world has to be conceived as a *relational space* dominated by correspondences and regularities, a place where rationality triumphs over irrationality, even in spite of appearances to the contrary. The *mondo* films of the 1960s and 70s (*mondo* being the Italian for 'world'), an exploitation genre of so-called shockumentaries exploring the rituals, myths and customs of both 'civilised' and 'primitive' societies, are telling in this respect. Built on graphic and often disturbing sensationalism, these extravagant forerunners of the essay film are organised around central topics (such as love, death, celebrity culture, women's issues and pollution) providing a structural coherence, which in turn mirrors the idea of an interconnected world (see Dalla Gassa 2014; Staples 1995; Goodall 2006, 2013). While the atlas rebuilds the entirety of the world through the gathering of devoutly collected fragments, the *mondo* film endlessly states the firm principle of coherence, maintaining that 'the world is the same wherever you go', and then enacts a symbolic appropriation of the all-knowable and transparent world akin to that of the atlas.

Third, the world has to be conceived as a *strategic field of action* regulated by global policies, to which cinema can provide a substantial contribution inasmuch as it can influence, mould and persuade both general public opinion and political elites. In this regard, the involvement of the Documentary Film Movement in post-war reconstruction through programmes commissioned by world organisations (such as UNESCO, FAO and WHO) provides a major example.

The movement addressed worldwide problems with the aim of impacting 'an economic and moral regeneration of the world', as Paul Rotha put it (1952: 56).[3] Such developmentalist one-world rhetoric expressed, first and foremost, a firm ideological belief. What Rob Aitken calls 'everyday internationalism', in fact, 'attempted to refigure film as a practice that could link distant everyday populations across global spaces of geographical and cultural difference' in order to 'help constitute a new world in the making' (2013: 660). The use of cinema for making the world visible – and then transformable – thus implied humanistic or even socialist dreams as well as a (neo-)imperialist faith in one-sided, top-down, exportable political strategies.

### The Global Imagery of the World Essay Film

The encounter between cinema and a distinctly modern idea of the world sets up the one-world film. At the core of this diverse tradition, wide-ranging enough to include aesthetic projects and strategies at odds with each other, we find a unifying conception of the medium's means informed by a positivist mindset. Behind this tradition stood, in fact, the idea of a filmable world, in which visible totality is predicated on relationality between the parts, as well as on the possibility of intervening to modify both the parts and the whole world system.

Few films could condense all this in a more unequivocal way than Paul Rotha and Basil Wright's *World Without End*, a 1953 documentary about UN development programmes in Mexico and Siam that soon turns into a plea addressed to all human beings, stating that 'beneath superficial differences of custom and landscape lies common experience, matters of life and death, the battle against disease and the desire for education' and therefore 'our primary responsibility is to love our neighbour' (MacDonald 2013: 469, 471).

The epistemic revolution introduced by the joint forces of postmodernism and globalisation should have made these strategies unviable and encouraged their being abandoned. In defining globalisation as 'the widening, deepening and speeding up of global interconnectedness', scholars have shown how postmodern culture, and cinema in particular, cannot actually grasp that always shifting, unstable, fragile totality as they previously seemed able to (Held et al. 1999: 14).[4] Given the nature of the postmodern world – neither ostensibly visible, nor visibly relational, nor strategically domesticated – the idea of a visible, filmable totality would seem outdated, or at least ideologically unviable. And yet, even 'progressive' forms of contemporary documentary fail to escape the conservative stance apparent in films such as Rotha and Wright's, inasmuch as they reaffirm the medium's 'burden of representation' in relation to the one-world perspective.[5]

The persistence of positivist and one-world perspectives is especially striking when considered in the face of recent debates addressing the essay film as 'inherently transgressive, digressive, playful, contradictory and political' (Nora Alter, in Rascaroli 2008: 27; see also Alter 1996). Such characterisations appear at odds with the straightforward relationship between the image and the real that documentary often implied without acknowledging 'the very impossibility of this aspiration' (Bruzzi 2006: 5). The emphasis put on reflexivity and subjectivity as main features of the essay film, however, constitutes nothing but a shortcoming, born from the desire to avoid the failure of documentary film to take on the liquidity paradigm around which many philosophical and sociological reflections on contemporary society have been constructed (see Rascaroli 2008). By embracing a dialectic approach in exploring 'the encounter between an open and protean self and social experience' (Corrigan 2011: 33), the essay film would likely clash with the presumptions of objectivity, totality, rationality and coherence associated with one-world films.[6] Hence the rebuttal of filmable totality.

As a matter of fact, and in spite of the disputes surrounding the precise definition of the essay film, most theorists who fashioned the term would not only oppose the positivist assumptions of the one-world perspective, but even reject their underlying framework of representation. Due to the multifaceted and heterogeneous corpus of films subsumed under this all-embracing label, however, it is difficult to say whether, in which forms, and to what extent this rejection is actually taking place. Nonetheless, certain telling approaches emerge once the scope of such exploration is reduced to a very specific, symptomatic case that somehow encourages a sharper consideration of the political, ideological and ethical values often taken for granted by scholars dealing with the essay film. Starting with Timothy Corrigan's assertion that the essay film depends on the 'idea of the cinema expressing ideas' (2011: 65), the following pages will analyse what will be called the *world essay film*, that is, a form of essay film *the main idea of which is the world*.

The world is a culturally and historically determined idea, and not a given or natural identity, so it requires images and discourses lending it reality and presence. Given the changeable nature of their cultural referent, these images and discourses can fall into obsolescence: the task of a symptomatic analysis is then to explain their interrelation with today's cultural reality, and point out the contradictions and anxieties inherent to both the essay film and the representation of a world built around forms of circulation, similarities, connections and forms of visibility. In order to do so, this chapter will look at three essay films that try to uncover, or rather to map, the contemporary economic world system and its networks, flows and processes from the standpoint of the global supply chain.

## Networks and Chains, Fruits and Seas

A focus on the supply chain, a favourite subject of one-world cinema, allows to bridge the gap between the local and the global. One-world films use the supply chain as a theme as well as a narrative structure, zooming out of the global scale into particular situations and vice versa. As early as 1943, however, Paul Rotha's documentary *World of Plenty* underscored the main contradiction regarding films on the food supply chain. In Rotha's film, the processes of food production, distribution and consumption are illustrated through a straightforward correspondence between image and reality and through mono-dimensional techniques that emphasise the one-world rhetoric (isotype animated maps, above all). At the same time, *World of Plenty* advocates internationalist interventionism to fight poverty or promote wealth redistribution. In other words, the film resorts to a reactionary representational strategy while purporting to support progressive, if not radical, political stances.

Do essay films accommodate politics and representation in a different mode? In the early 1980s, Israel filmmaker Amos Gitai was struck by the discovery that a pineapple could be cultivated in the Philippines, packaged in Honolulu, labelled in Japan and distributed in San Francisco. Willing to investigate further the forces and relations of production around the world that lead to the commercialisation of a can of pineapple, he realised the essay film *Ananas* in

Figure 5.1  *World of Plenty*, Paul Rotha, 1943.

1983. As Serge Toubiana comments, it is a film 'against globalization' (2003: 125) with a clearly strong political position against the relocation of industrial production and the search for a cheap labour force. Through the adoption of a first person perspective and frequent disruptions in editing and storytelling, Gitai also showed an oppositional stance towards a conventional documentary filmmaking style.

*Ananas*, however, is also a film that traces out and illustrates the relationships between social, economic and cultural phenomena occurring apparently independently of one another. As Gitai writes, 'A pineapple tells the story of the relationship between Filipino workers, San Francisco executives and the pre-Christian civilisation of Mindanao. A pineapple shows you why Christianity was introduced to homogenise the perception of reality' (Gitai 2001: 368). It is no coincidence that the first scene of the film shows a diegetic map of the world, used by a Dole Corporation agronomist, who is also holding the fruit in his hands, to illustrate the geography of their business. Despite the ideological distancing, this particular scene is emblematic of something pertaining to the whole film: it is at the same time a lesson in geography and an object lesson – the object is the pineapple fruit, which for the director is also metaphorical of the global economic system.[7]

Similarly interesting is Luc Moullet's *Genèse d'un repas*, made in 1978, which starts with the filmmaker eating his meal, wondering where it comes from and declaring his desire to unveil the meal's genealogy. This leads the filmmaker to track three basic food items – bananas, eggs and tuna – through France, Senegal and Ecuador, where he meets managers, grocers, trade unionists, dockworkers, unemployed people, executives and fishermen. Recognised by many critics as a model for documentaries denouncing the hidden face of today's world system economy, mainly because of the author's 'persistent reli-

Figure 5.2  *Ananas*, Amos Gitai, 1983.

ance on colonialism as an ideological grid relevant to the understanding of globalisation' (Evrard 2012), the film poses some problems that are also present in Gitai's *Ananas*, with the substantial distinction that it self-consciously addresses them (although it does not provide any answers).

Like *Ananas*, in fact, *Genèse d'un repas* relies on the essayistic form, favouring a dialectic narrative and diversified enunciation strategies over the authoritarian explanatory mode of traditional documentary film. Like *Ananas*, *Genèse d'un repas* works, to put it in Marxist terms, to de-fetishise the commodity by exposing labour and exploitation. So, if goods become commodities through what Marx calls the social hieroglyph, both films translate the latter into visible relations of production. More than *Ananas*, *Genèse d'un repas* is well aware of itself as part of this process, as it questions its own mode of production by showing how it enforces what it attempts to criticise. As Moullet comments at the end of the film:

> Even our film is part of the exploitation. With my tight budget, I paid 50 francs for interviews in the Third World, 120 francs in France. The profit I take from the film will be moral, but also perhaps material [. . .] When choosing my images, I found myself emulating the overseers at the cannery, as if knowledge were merely another subtle form of exploitation.

The film fades to black and so ends on this bitter note.

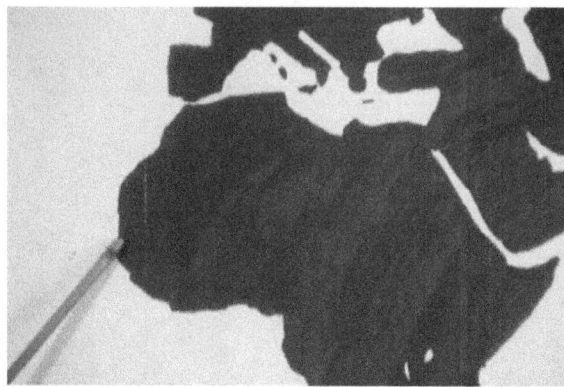

Figure 5.3  *Genèse d'un repas*, Luc Moullet, 1978.

It is worth noting that before this last sequence, Moullet too upholds the logic of total visibility through two rather clever solutions: a pan shot over a row of food items named through voice-over along with their country of origin, and a static shot of a woman stripping as the clothes' countries of origin are named. The effect is captivating insofar as it proposes a heterotopia, for which the world can be contained in a few metres, an idea that is interrupted in the next scene, which finally abandons any attempt at approaching the totalising image of the globe.

The third and last example is Allan Sekula and Noël Burch's *The Forgotten Space*, a 2010 world essay film that tries to achieve the very same goals as the

Figure 5.4  *The Forgotten Space*, Allan Sekula and Noel Burch, 2010.

former two but with a more explicit commitment to the essay film as a genre. Recently, Burch claimed to have invented the term in the 1970s as a reaction to the objective conception of 'documentary' of the English movement led by John Grierson. What in his view defines the essay film is 'a rambling structure, very largely discontinuous and often digressive' (2010: n.p.) – a structure that actually characterises *The Forgotten Space* while, paradoxically, succeeding in conveying the sense of a *totality* that would correspond to the breadth, the truly global scale of globalisation.

The film follows container cargo on ships, trains and trucks, from Europe to North America to Asia, trying to portray the whole global supply chain and the reality of the world economic system behind it. In spite of its formal and narrative complexity, the film addresses a very simple question: how is a world made up of producing and consuming countries bound together by trade?

Trying to answer this question by making the whole contemporary world economy visible, material and geographically extended, Sekula and Burch's film symptomatically insists that the maritime economy, even though it may appear obsolete, is more emblematic of globalisation than financial speculation, which, conversely, is fundamentally invisible.[8] The parallel between the visible, mappable, filmable maritime economy and the invisible, unmappable and unfilmable financial economy gives meaning to a film so strongly insisting that inasmuch as globalisation happens through space, it is representable as a whole. Therefore, the real space (of globalisation) is forgotten, but not actually hidden, and it is the task of cinema to show it and explain it. Such a Promethean endeavour might discourage the analysts, but not the filmmakers, who have given themselves the task of making sense of the world.

### Mapping and Representing: The Anxiety of Traceability

The directors' task in all these world essay films is what Fredric Jameson would refer to as 'cognitive mapping', the process by which individual subjects locate themselves within the larger boundaries of social totality in order to grasp its machinations. However, what prevents these films – as well as any other attempt in this direction – from being successful is the crucial problem of representability, for the complexity of late capitalism does not enable any adequate description, but on the contrary presents itself as the impossible, absent, unrepresentable totality. Capital and the 'hidden social order' have the form of an unimaginable, decentred, infinite, global network, which 'can never be perceived with the naked eye' (Jameson 1995: 31). Therefore, since cognitive mapping must be interpreted as a problem of representation and not as a task to actually be accomplished, it is impossible to illustrate the world system in an immediate way. On the contrary, it can only be figured indirectly (through an analogon, an interpretant, an equivalent or an allegory) as its depiction in realistic terms would produce nothing but a 'caricature', to stay with Jameson's terminology (see also Jameson 1992).

When applied to cinema, the problem turns out to be twofold: on the one hand, there seems to be a problem of visibility of the world system; on the other hand, there is a sort of anxiety of traceability of this system itself. In fact, even if it might be useful to keep the two aspects of the question distinct, they are intimately related: the anxiety of traceability is indeed also an anxiety concerning the visibility of interconnection. The visibility of the world system is of course a precondition for the traceability of the tracks of globalisation – not only essay films but also Hollywood movies have recently demonstrated this.[9]

The crux of the matter is that the global patterns of multinational capitalism are invisible in many respects. One-world films, nonetheless, keep displaying the same old belief that the functioning of the world system can be effectively captured even when it comes to globalisation and late capitalism. In a documentary such as *Darwin's Nightmare* (Hubert Sauper, 2004), for example, spectators witness gigantic Russian cargo planes landing in Tanzania carrying weapons that fuel wars in Africa and taking off again loaded with fish from Lake Victoria. Indeed, what the film so effectively summarises and successfully condenses in cinematic terms is not some hidden structure of today's impalpable economic system, but a rather customary neo-colonial trade that could have occurred almost identically two centuries ago.

Into a similar trap fell even the last great one-world filmmaker Michael Glawogger, whose 'Globalization Trilogy' sets out to interrogate what work and labour mean in a globalised world. Films such as *Megacities* (1998), *Workingman's Death* (2005) and *Whores' Glory* (2011), while trying to show globalisation, resort to fairly conventional, modernist strategies in representing forms of supply chain, industry and labour that look outdated and are certainly not those immediately associated with advanced capitalism, but rather with (early) modernity: Ukrainian miners, Indonesian sulphur-carriers, Nigerian butchers, Pakistani welders, Chinese steelworkers.

Glawogger can effectively show the 'globalised' world only when he can visualise labour, and he can do so only when labour is physical and material, and therefore less emblematic of late capitalism. His films aim at showing, often in an aestheticised way, 'places where the world's dirty work is done', but this dirtiness of labour is precisely a form of its own visibility. Indeed it is surely ironic that 'the world's oldest profession' should be considered allegorical of the new landscape of globalisation, as *Whores' Glory* attempts to illustrate in tracking the life and work conditions of prostitutes in Thailand, Bangladesh and Mexico.

In this regard, the answer that Glawogger gave to Scott MacDonald when asked about his choice of film locations is quite revealing:

I want to find places where I can *show* the world. If I cannot *show* I'm lost. For *Whores' Glory* I wanted to do something about escort services and Internet dating in Europe or the United States, but had no idea how to do it. Do I show some woman sitting in an office, taking phone calls? The idea bores the shit out of me. (Michael Glawogger, in MacDonald 2012: 45)

While the director seeks physical spaces where he can stage an operation of organisation and control of the visual field, he finds other spaces, such as the less appealing ones he would have had to use in order to depict online escort services, 'boring'. In fact, they are boring because the real functioning of those services does not happen through those spaces, but through virtual and immaterial 'spaces' belonging to the order of the invisible and which are therefore not filmable. The relevance of these kinds of spaces is increasing nowadays, and not only with regard to online prostitution, but also to information, society and economy on a global scale. And it is doing so with devastating effects on the cinematic medium, as Béla Balázs, the great theorist of the visual character of cinema, denounced as early as the 1920s:

The new focus on large-scale financial adventures has acted to the detriment of films as works of art. For the conflict between the safe-cracker and the detective was *visible* and gave rise to an inexhaustible wealth of fantastic situations into which a host of psychological subtleties and poetic insights could be smuggled where they were needed. In contrast, the essence of large-scale capitalism is that it is *abstract*, that the dominant forces in it and the conflict between them are *invisible*. A great financier may plunge into the most hazardous and fantastic adventures, but, however extravagant they may be, his exploits all take place in the mind: they are ideas, decisions, discussions with a trusted associate and, at most, a speech to the board. Even the decisive scene in which he appends his signature to a letter or a contract is not actually picturesque or dramatic enough to serve as the crucial scene of a film. In real life it is this invisibility that is so uncanny. In a film, however, it is not uncanny at all because it is not actually present. What cannot be seen cannot be photographed. (Balázs 2010: 82)

## Indicability: A Basic Limit of Cinematic Representation

There is a remarkable congruence between Jameson's thoughts on late capitalism and what cultural geographers such as Derek Gregory (1994), Gunnar Olsson (2007) and Franco Farinelli (2009) have been insistently preaching for the last two decades. Post-industrialism, globalisation and digitisation have introduced a new invisibility into the circulation of all the most valuable things, forcing the world to withdraw into a space beyond representation – a space that, indeed, is even beyond the traditional logic of space.

As a consequence, in our opinion, the real problem that cinema has to face concerns *not* the indexicality of the image, which may also have escaped unscathed from the revolution of digital imaging. Rather, the real threat to cinema concerns the *indicability* of the world. The problem originates from the world – from the invisibility of the contemporary world system, as Jameson says – not from the image. Fundamentally, it is a problem concerning the challenges that both the invisibility and the complexity of globalisation pose to cinematic representation and to cinema's traditional mission of making the world a knowable totality. Which is something that, as has already been noted, also affects mainstream Hollywood cinema – even, for example, in films trying to cinematically make sense of the financial crisis (see Kinkle and Toscano 2015) – but is especially visible in essay films thematising the whole world's visibility and connectivity.

'The true mystery of the world is the visible, not the invisible.' This time, Oscar Wilde's quotation comes from the opening sequence of Patrick Keiller's *Robinson in Space* (1997). Now it rings with a different meaning, because the problem of the relationship between world visibility and invisibility is crucial to the work of the English director, which – not by chance – has attracted the interest of several geographers.

In *London* (1994), the first film of Keiller's trilogy, Robinson, the (absent) protagonist, is said to have 'believed that if he looked hard enough he could cause the surface of the city to reveal to him the molecular basis of historical events, and in this way he hoped to see the future' – but at the end of the film (which from the opening titles announced itself as a 'journey to the end of the world') Robinson acknowledges the actual invisibility of the social, economic and cultural dimensions of London: 'the true identity of London, he said, is in its absence, as a city that no longer exists [. . .]: London was the first metropolis to disappear'.

Unlike Walter Ruttmann, with whom this investigation into the blind spots of global vision began, Patrick Keiller actually takes into account the mystery of the visible. The pilgrimage through which the two companions – Robinson and the anonymous narrator – explore the spaces of England works as a pretext for their essayistic travel, reflecting on the transformations of British landscape caused by modernity, industry and economics. But for Keiller there is no faith in the medium's capability of accurately mapping England or, for that matter, the world. On the contrary, he remaps, as Timothy Corrigan suggests, 'this contemporary landscape not as a teleological journey but as an excursion whose directions and geographies sequentially and simultaneously displace and dislocate each other' (Corrigan 2011: 116).

In this acknowledged failure lies the only meaning that the world can possibly carry today, and the only representational tactic that cinema can endorse. Accordingly, this chapter has stressed the problematic aspects of any attempt to cinematically depict the whole world system today, and has done so using terms that emphasise a self-reflexive approach to representation, such as 'imageability', '(in)visibility', 'traceability', 'indicability': the visual character of the contemporary world should not be taken for granted.

Indeed, the impossibility of illustrating the whole system and the incompleteness and precariousness of any actual cognitive mapping can also work as a sort of guarantee of the genuine political and confrontational quality of cognitive mapping itself. This is something that is sometimes overlooked when the concept of cognitive mapping is discussed in relation to the cinematic medium, such as when John Hess and Patricia Zimmermann advocate the political necessity of a new kind of transnational documentary film able to 'consciously and pragmatically, rather than only allegorically and unconsciously' map the spaces and webs of the 'new world order' (2006: 102).

Just as Luc Moullet considered knowledge to be another form of exploitation, this chapter has sought to propose the idea of a visible interconnected world as another form of what Mary Louise Pratt labelled the 'monarch-of-all-I-survey' tropes (1992: 201). Of course, this is not to say that the world essay film necessarily channels the tradition of imperial writing that Pratt analysed. Nevertheless, through the many contradictions of these representations, a profound discomfort can be located in this *aesthetics of evidence*, which is to say that a nostalgic attitude and a consoling formulation typical of the one-world cinema still inhabits a certain kind of cinema, one that still regards itself as the privileged standpoint from which reality can be grasped, understood and ultimately changed. An ideology of the visibility of the functioning of the world lurks in the world essay film, even in its most progressive manifestations. Consequently, a reactionary fantasy is also observable to a remarkable extent, a fantasy about the adequacy of cinema for the present times that flattens the viewer's position as privileged spectator of the world and aims at removing, while it symptomatically exposes, some of the basic limits of cinematic representation.

### Notes

1. This chapter was jointly conceived, discussed and drafted by the two authors. Giorgio Avezzù wrote the third to fifth sections; Giuseppe Fidotta wrote the first to third sections.
2. It is worth recalling here the definition of 'imageability' proposed by Kevin Lynch: 'that quality in a physical object that gives it a high probability of evoking a strong image in any given observer' (1960: 9).
3. It is worth recalling here the curious definition of Rotha given by Herbert G. Luft: 'the man whose mind conceives the world as a whole' (1955: 89).

4. The following is additionally relevant: 'One can speak of globalization [...] only when the growing interconnectedness of different regions and locales become systematic and reciprocal to some degree, and only when the scope of interconnectedness is effectively global' (Thompson 1995: 149).
5. For example, it is what nature and ecological documentaries do through their unproblematic depiction of a world reduced to an organic cell-like structure. Also films such as the *Qatsi* trilogy (Godfrey Reggio, 1983–2000), *Baraka* (Ron Fricke, 1992) or *Samsara* (Ron Fricke, 2011) display a global vision that, according to Martin Roberts, 'can be seen as a reaction to the threat the world poses to Euro-American cultural authority, which, in re-inscribing the world within the reassuring field of a Euro-American gaze, seeks to re-impose a neo-colonial order on a world slipping increasingly beyond its control' (1998: 78). On the 'burden of representation' see Shohat and Stam (1994: 182).
6. Globalist aspirations and weaker narrative forms can coexist, however, and the latter can also serve to justify the former in the context of crisis of traditional ethnographic authority. A film such as *Life in a Day* (Kevin Macdonald et al. 2011) well exemplifies the ancillary use of autobiographical–auto-ethnographic 'essayistic' micro-narration at the service of an all-encompassing, worldist vision.
7. This intention to present the world as object lesson connects Gitai's film with some early cinema practices, see Gunning (1994).
8. See also Sekula (1995), the photographic book from which the film has been adapted.
9. Network narratives of recent mainstream cinema too, such as *Babel* (Alejandro González Iñárritu, 2006) or *Contagion* (Steven Soderbergh, 2011), are often characterised by circulating objects – for example, the rifle in *Babel* – which help to connect geographically distant people and situations. On this topic, see Bordwell (2006: 97). On the current fascination with 'commodity biographies' in the academic literature on globalisation (and the cultural materialisation of the economic), see Foster (2006).

References

Aitken, Rob (2013), 'A *World Without End*: Post-war Reconstruction and Everyday Internationalism in Documentary Film', *The International History Review*, 35:4, 657–80.
Alter, Nora (1996), 'The Political Im/perceptible in the Essay Film: Farocki's *Images of the World and the Inscription of War*', *New German Critique*, 68, 165–92.
Amad, Paula (2010), *Counter-archive: Film, the Everyday and Albert Kahn's* Archives de la Planète, New York: Columbia University Press.
Balázs, Béla (2010), *Early Film Theory: 'Visible Man' and 'The Spirit of Film'*, New York: Berghahn.
Bordwell, David (2006), *The Way Hollywood Tells It: Story and Style in Modern Movies*, Berkeley: University of California Press.
Bruzzi, Stella (2006), *New Documentary*, 2nd edn, London: Routledge.
Burch, Noël (2010), 'Essay Film', *Notes on the Forgotten Space*, <http://www.theforgottenspace.net/static/notes.html> (last accessed 31 July 2015).
Castro, Teresa (2006), '*Les Archives de la Planète*: A Cinematographic Atlas', *Jump Cut*, 48, <http://www.ejumpcut.org/archive/jc48.2006/KahnAtlas/text.html> (last accessed 31 July 2015).
Castro, Teresa (2011), *La Pensée cartographique des images. Cinéma et culture visuelle*, Lyons: Aléas.

Corrigan, Timothy (2011), *The Essay Film: From Montaigne, After Marker*, Oxford and New York: Oxford University Press.
Cowan, Michael (2014), *Walter Ruttmann and the Cinema of Multiplicity: Avant-garde, Advertising, Modernity*, Amsterdam: Amsterdam University Press.
Dalla Gassa, Marco (2014), '"Tutto il mondo è paese". I mondo movies tra esotismi e socializzazione del piacere', *Cinergie*, 5, <http://www.cinergie.it/?p=4288> (last accessed 31 July 2015).
Evrard, Audrey (2012), 'Framing the World Economics in a Tuna Can: Luc Moullet Tracks the *Origins of a Meal/Genèse d'un repas*', *Jump Cut*, 54, <http://www.ejumpcut. org/archive/jc54.2012/evrardMoullet/text.html> (last accessed 31 July 2015).
Farinelli, Franco (2003), *Geografia: Un'introduzione ai modelli del mondo*, Turin: Einaudi.
Farinelli, Franco (2009), *La crisi della ragione cartografica*, Turin: Einaudi.
Foster, Robert J. (2006), 'Tracking Globalization: Commodities and Value in Motion', in Christopher Tilley, Webb Keane, Susanne Küchler, Michael Rowlands and Patricia Spyer (eds), *Handbook of Material Culture*, Thousand Oaks: Sage, pp. 285–302.
Gitai, Amos (2001), 'Histoires d'un cinéaste (parcours 1980–1990)', *Communications*, 71:1, 353–71.
Goodall, Mark (2006), 'Shockumentary Evidence: The Perverse Politics of the Mondo Film', in Stephanie Dennison and Song Hwee Lim (eds), *Remapping World Cinema: Identity, Culture and Politics in Film*, London: Wallflower Press, pp. 118–28.
Goodall, Mark (2013), 'Dolce e selvaggio. The Italian Mondo Documentary Film', in Louis Bayman and Sergio Rigoletto (eds), *Popular Italian Cinema*, Basingstoke: Palgrave Macmillan, pp. 226–40.
Gregory, Derek (1994), *Geographical Imaginations*, Cambridge, MA: Blackwell.
Gunning, Tom (1994), 'The World as Object Lesson: Cinema Audiences, Visual Culture and the St. Louis World's Fair, 1904', *Film History*, 6:4, 422–44.
Häfker, Hermann (1914), *Kino und Erdkunde*, Mönchengladbach: Volksvereins-Verlag.
Held, David, Anthony McGrew, David Goldblatt and Jonathan Perraton (1999), *Global Transformations: Politics, Economics and Culture*, Stanford: Stanford University Press.
Hess, John and Patricia R. Zimmermann (2006), 'Transnational Documentaries: A Manifesto', in Elizabeth Ezra and Terry Rowden (eds), *Transnational Cinema: The Film Reader*, New York: Routledge, pp. 97–108.
Jameson, Fredric (1992), *Postmodernism, or, the Cultural Logic of Late Capitalism*, Durham, NC: Duke University Press.
Jameson, Fredric (1995), *The Geopolitical Aesthetics: Cinema and Space in the World System*, Bloomington: Indiana University Press.
Kinkle, Jeff and Alberto Toscano (2015), *Cartographies of the Absolute*, Winchester and Washington, DC: Zero Books.
Luft, Herbert G. (1955), 'Rotha and the World', *The Quarterly of Film, Radio and Television*, 10:1, 89–99.
Lynch, Kevin (1960), *The Image of the City*, Cambridge, MA: MIT Press.
MacDonald, Richard (2013), 'Evasive Enlightenment: *World Without End* and the Internationalism of Postwar Documentary', *Journal of British Cinema and Television*, 10:3, 452–74.
MacDonald, Scott (2012), 'Knots in the Head: Interview with Michael Glawogger', *Film Quarterly*, 66:1, 40–9.
Olsson, Gunnar (2007), *Abysmal: A Critique of Cartographic Reason*, Chicago: University of Chicago Press.

Pratt, Mary Louise (1992), *Imperial Eyes: Travel Writing and Transculturation*, London: Routledge.
Rascaroli, Laura (2008), 'The Essay Film: Problems, Definition, Textual Commitments', *Framework*, 49:2, 24–47.
Roberts, Martin (1998), '*Baraka*: World Cinema and the Global Culture Industry', *Cinema Journal*, 37:3, 68–82.
Rotha, Paul (1952), *Documentary Film*, 3rd edn, London: Faber & Faber.
Sekula, Allan (1995), *Fish Story*, Düsseldorf: Richter Verlag.
Shohat, Ella and Robert Stam (1994), *Unthinking Eurocentrism: Multiculturalism and the Media*, London: Routledge.
Staples, Amy J. (1995), 'An Interview with Dr. Mondo', *American Anthropologist*, 97:1, 110–25.
Thompson, John B. (1995), *Media and Modernity*, Cambridge: Polity Press.
Toubiana, Serge (2003), *Exils et territoires: le cinéma d'Amos Gitai*, Paris: Arte éditions.
Wilde, Oscar (2005), *The Complete Works of Oscar Wilde*, ed. Russell Jackson, vol. III, *The 1890 and 1891 Texts*, Oxford: Oxford University Press.

# PART THREE

# LABORATORY OF MEMORIES

# 6. MEMORY AS A MOTOR OF IMAGES: THE ESSAYISTIC MODE IN APICHATPONG WEERASETHAKUL'S VARIATIONS OF *UNCLE BOONMEE*

## Christa Blümlinger

In the 1960s, Russian-American film historian Jay Leyda wrote in a retrospective of the 1920s: 'Today, the "film-essay" form is almost totally, and incomprehensibly, ignored. The only modern film-maker who employs a witty variation of it is Chris Marker' (1964: 30–1). From this observation the strong currency the essay film has had since the 1980s could never have been foreseen. But his foregrounding of Marker's work might already be illuminating in this respect. In his *Essai sur le jeune cinéma français* (1960), André S. Labarthe also commented on the specific filmic language developed by Marker who – as he argued – creates a poetic, interior world through imaginary landscapes.[1] Labarthe emphasised a new composite filmic form between documentary and fiction, which he dubbed a 'science-fictional cinema' (*cinéma science-fictif*, 1960: 39). The hybridity of this form is, however, just one aspect of essayistic filmmaking. I argue that its primary characteristic is the production of an interstitial space of memory and commemoration drawn from a particular play around and between image and word.[2]

Even then, but at the latest a decade after Leyda's statement, Marker was no longer the only one working in the essayistic mode. 'Wise visual commentaries',[3] produced by essayists such as Hans Richter working in multimedia contexts in the 1950s, soon inhabited the art space and, in increasing numbers, also the digital realm. Today, the essay film is seen as one of the 'most creative, ubiquitous, and important form[s] in modern media history' (Alter and Corrigan 2017: 2). Representative of this larger trend, filmmaker-artist of Thai origin Apichatpong Weerasethakul, whose imaginative, transmedial essayistic work is at the centre of my discussion here, produces both with his cinematographic preparatory work and in the museum a laboratory situation that corresponds to the original meaning of the essay as 'exagium', that is, both 'thinking' form and experiment.

In Weerasethakul's work even fiction takes on a test character and thus a political dimension, referring us to Friedrich Schiller and a particular aesthetic tradition. Recurring on this tradition, Jacques Rancière, more recently, developed a notion of fiction in which aesthetics and politics are entangled. Fiction here constitutes a model to produce political subjects that give the anonymous a voice, as well as a form that is indiscriminate with regards to genres or reference systems but aims at a general definition of a modern aesthetic mode. Fiction, according to Rancière, is

> [n]ot the creation of an imaginary world that is opposite to the real world. Rather, it is the work that makes *dissensus* possible, altering modes of presentation, of the sensuous and of enunciation by changing frames, proportions or rhythms, establishing new relationships between appearance and reality, the individual and the common, the visible and its meaning. (Rancière 2008: 72)

Such an 'aesthetic regime' determined by dissent is akin to the principle of the essay: it infiltrates the distinction between documentary and fictional forms as well as the demarcation between the arts. What determines essayistic memory art will therefore be explored not only through the medium of film, but also in ways that acknowledge memory art's heterogeneous constellation and forms of expression, its diversity and hybridity of 'life of forms' (Focillon [1934] 2013).

Not only in film, but also in art circles Weerasethakul has long been regarded as a highly esteemed innovator of moving pictorial worlds. He is known for crossing the boundaries between cinema and installation art, documentary film and fiction, and the work of memory, myth and fantasy. Weerasethakul's variations on the character 'Boonmee', including a documentary essay, a series of objects and video installations as well as a feature film, are hybrid and reflective aesthetic works that together form a larger imaginary space based on the interplay of image and word. From this space a theatre of memory evolves that originates from one singular historical motif but is developed in various ways through different formal and aesthetic means. The three works are linked together by a central motif, namely that of recurrence. Heterogeneous temporalities, however, challenge and disrupt the configuration of a more continuous cultural and political memory, as well as the viewer's individual perception.

Eulogy of Slowness: *Uncle Boonmee Who Can Recall His Past Lives*

From *Blissfully Yours* (2002) and *Tropical Malady* (2004) to *Uncle Boonmee Who Can Recall His Past Lives*, which won the Palme d'Or in Cannes in 2010, time is spent listening to and watching what is happening in the humming environment that Weerasethakul creates in his cinematic work, and which is full of astonishing gradations, sheltered from the modern life of the big city. At the centre of this world is the forest as a privileged space of imagery. Inhabited at once by animals, human beings and ghosts, it appears in several films as the uniform site for slowness that only the body can measure. The jungle, which Weerasethakul has been familiar with since childhood, is to him a scene of emotions, a 'mindscape' (Quandt 2009b: 126). The cinematic world he creates across different works forms a eulogy of slowness, as I want to suggest here. This is done not so much in the conceptual sense of the word (as this Thai filmmaker is often put too quickly in the same box as Andy Warhol), but rather in the sense of a certain aesthetic experience connected to the body and to perception. It is an experience that has become a rarity in fiction films today.

The opening of *Uncle Boonmee* immediately plunges viewers into this unusual, relegated world. The film's pre-credit sequence unfolds in half-light. At the edge of the jungle, a huge buffalo frees itself from its tether and gallops through the long grass to dive into the deep shadow of the trees and bushes. Its massive silhouette floats behind the leaves and branches and is soon followed by a young, bare-chested shepherd. In this twilight the buffalo appears to be a mythical, red-eyed creature: the monkey-ghost. 'Facing the jungle, the hills and vales, my past lives as an animal and other beings rise up before me', we are told by the first title card, in order to prepare us for these apparitions that are associated with Uncle Boonmee and are slightly invoking the cinema of Murnau. At the beginning there does not appear to be any passage between one world and the next, as the semi-mythical creature of the buffalo suggests that we are in the realm of fantasy. Once the opening credits are over, however, the film takes quite a sudden turn into the real. Viewers are permitted to enter into the world that Uncle Boonmee is preparing to depart from: a world governed by other measures and speeds. An abrupt cut leads us to the dazzling light of day and to the deafening sound of motors. Sitting in the back of a car, looking out of the window, Aunt Jen is driving through a tropical countryside in the company of her nephew Tong. The car's dirty windows frame their gazes, which are focused on the landscapes scrolling by outside. The low sun intermittently throws light on the face of this ageing woman, who has come to visit her brother-in-law Boonmee in his retreat. We can make out only what is far away in the world outside: anything close goes by too fast. But soon a scene shot in documentary style brings us back to slowness and calm. Viewers settle into a static shot, showing Uncle Boonmee lying on his bed, being meticulously cared for by the Laotian nurse who is tending to his kidney failure.

Weerasethakul makes us follow these medical gestures in one single shot, for three minutes, which allows us to measure their significance. In an interview, the filmmaker explains how he considered making a film shot in real time, which would have lasted forty-eight hours. For him, this desire is not so much connected to a conceptual idea in Douglas Gordon's sense, that is, to make the duration of a film match the duration of its story, as to a certain intuitive notion regarding the rhythm of human memory. For Weerasethakul, cinema is the privileged medium for creating 'a certain duration that is sufficient [. . .] to conjure up a feeling, a memory' (Weerasethakul in Tessé 2010: 12). His film, which tells the story of the last days of Uncle Boonmee's life, only lasts for two hours after all; but it is constantly filled with apparitions and transformations that emerge out of a specific type of attention and tranquillity, closely connected to the elastic concept of time as being linked both to perception and to memory.

'There are two kinds [of seeing]: an eye for details, which discovers new things, and a fixed look that follows only a ready-made plan and speeds it up for the moment' (Nadolny 2003: 129). Examining these ways of seeing, Sten Nadolny's novel *The Discovery of Slowness* uses very cinematographic terms to evoke the attitude of an exceptional nineteenth-century navigator who resists the acceleration of his life through exaggerated slowness. He is endowed with an acute sense of observation and attention as well as a memory that saves him from ever being surprised. The predisposition of Weerasethakul's shots and the character of Uncle Boonmee seem to be born out of a similar attitude, even if we tend to attribute it more easily to Buddhist culture than to a western novel.[4] Uncle Boonmee's taste for emptiness and chance has an impact on the composition and duration of certain static shots and sometimes produces the same kind of 'fixed look' as that described by Nadolny. Highlighting small details, the filmmaker allows us to comprehend a way of life that is not 'rhythmed' by clocks, and in which distances are essentially covered by foot: for example, when Aunt Jen drags her feet across Uncle Boonmee's house in the evening, her nephew Tong asks her not to crush any insects. Everything can have an effect on Uncle Boonmee's former or future life.

Becoming a monkey, a princess or an insect, as reincarnation is presented in *Uncle Boonmee*, is above all an issue for the viewer's affection. We are dealing here with a generalised empathy that goes beyond identification with the characters and touches on everything that the film renders perceptible, especially through sound. While the forest is filled with the humming of insects and the songs of birds that cannot be seen, they can be imagined at every step. The jungle creates a huge backdrop, a site for travelling back in time, beyond this Buddhist character with an exceptional memory (vaguely inspired by a book and a minor news item). Through Uncle Boonmee the filmmaker remembers in an eclectic manner different styles and stories, seen since his childhood in Thailand.[5] He also includes a great number of stories gathered throughout his work in this border region of the country's north-west, where the film is located. These stories are used more explicitly in Weerasethakul's 2009 exhibition, *Primitive* (see below), somehow foreshadowing the film he was preparing. Three 'reels' – this is how the filmmaker refers to the segmentation of this film shot in 35mm (see Delorme and Téssé 2010: 10) – recur on traditional styles of fiction, old television or costume dramas, while the other three sequences are more connected to a style of editing drawn from the documentary field. The more 'fantastical' sections tell the story of the visit of ghosts and spirits to Uncle Boonmee's table, the story of an ugly and solitary princess who is miraculously brought to ecstasy, and Uncle Boonmee passing through the darkness to reach the light. The more 'realistic' sections alternate with the old-fashioned fables to present us first with the arrival of Aunt Jen at the farm, then her visit to the tamarind trees, and finally a night at the hotel during her brother-in-law's funeral.

## Theatre of Memory: The *Primitive* Project

In Weerasethakul's work, figures and objects, motifs, subjects and shots are constantly being recomposed. They pass by and transform themselves not just from one sequence to the next, but also from one film to the next, from an installation to a film, from a book, a sketch or a model to this or that moving image. Thus, the hairy man-animal with luminous red eyes – who in *Uncle Boonmee* represents a ghost lurking in the forest at nightfall, sits down at Uncle Boonmee's table one evening and turns out to be his deceased son – already made an appearance in *Primitive* (2009), in an oneiric double projection that was part of the exhibition of the same name.[6] The complex care provided at length by the immigrant nurse to Uncle Boonmee at the start of the film, which is shot in a quasi-documentary style, is reminiscent of some scenes from *Mysterious Object at Noon* (2000) and, most notably, of the opening of *Blissfully Yours*, in which a young Thai woman brings her lover, an illegal Burmese immigrant, to a doctor for the treatment of his skin disease, while concealing his clandestine existence.

A very particular circulation of figures and subjects throughout the *Primitive* project thus creates a kind of platform that brings into play not just the exhibition bearing this title and the feature film *Uncle Boonmee*, but also the short essayistic film *A Letter to Uncle Boonmee* (2009).[7] In the museum, the multimedia exhibition, which oscillates between video, sculpture, drawing and installation, is focused on a film project, and shows life in and around a small village in the north of Thailand. Weerasethakul's representations of the

Figure 6.1   *A Letter to Uncle Boonmee*, Apichatpong Weerasethakul, 2009. © Chaisiri Jiwarangsan.

present and the past in the Nabua village interweave a series of animist popular mythologies, including the story of a monk who remembers the different stages of his reincarnations.

Foreshadowing the film to come, the letter-film that the filmmaker sends to this monk called Boonmee starts with a voice-over accompanying meditative gazes from the windows of a house on the edge of the jungle. Together with the intense rustlings of nature, this voice-over produces a volume that opens up an imaginary space of ghosts and spirits. The beginning of the 'letter' is presented as the origin of the whole project: 'I have been here for a while. I want to see a movie about your life. So I proposed a project about your reincarnations. In my script [. . .].' The form of possibility (*Möglichkeitsform*), which the cinematic letter as script here articulates, reiterates the essence of the cinematic essay, namely to provide an exploratory space in which imaginative and mnemonic processes coalesce.

The *Primitive* exhibition further explores precisely the determined 'wanting to see' that is expressed in the short film, which is included in but independent of the platform. The idea that *Letter to Uncle Boonmee* puts forward and encapsulates in form of a simplified visual sketch is used elsewhere, in a different space, as a preparatory extension. Here ghosts and lights as figures of transformation and reincarnation are connected to a type of reiteration or 're-enactment', in which acts are replayed that have a real origin. While they wait for the rice harvest in Nabua, male adolescents rest against buried objects created by the recent history of the region in which the village is located. Up until the 1980s, the state army savagely repressed the rural population in the north-east of Thailand, claiming that they were involved in communist activities.

This commemorative return becomes quite explicit in some videos that include games of shooting, explosions and projections, as well as scenes in which the story of the farmers' resistance is sung. The videos *An Evening Shoot*, *Nabua* and *Nabua Song* highlight the performative and experimental aspects of the commemoration.[8] These projections foreground both the gap and the possible relationships that might exist between a past suppressed by the elders and a precarious present experienced by the younger generation, living close to the Laotian border. In addition, the context of the theatrical work and the social research carried out by Weerasethakul in preparation for his larger project is documented by a number of accessories, photographs, drawings and a book entitled *Primitive*, presented in two versions within the framework of the exhibition (Weerasethakul 2009). Other projections create a very specific mix between history and fantasy, memory and imagination that is close to the world of *Uncle Boonmee*.

Upon entering the exhibition, through the encounter with *Phantoms of Nabua*, the viewer is thrust to the edge of fiction. The piece is performance art, film and installation at once: a sort of allegory of cinema, represented by a nocturnal game played by youths kicking a fiery ball towards a white screen, which receives projections of light until it is engulfed by the flames. Weerasethakul presents light here as matter and as medium: first, in the form of a 'film-within-a-film' by means of lightning; later, through the inclusion of a fireball; and, finally, by tracing the reflection of the street's and the screen's artificial lighting back to their sources.

The last section of the exhibition is closest to the initial project: the film-to-come. The double projection *Primitive*, which hangs at a slant, is the show's highlight and the final point on the viewer's journey. Its set-up is cinematic: the viewer is plunged into a dark space and encouraged to sit on a bench in front of the screens to watch the half-hour-long 'film', which is visually and aurally more intense as well as longer than the other videos. The aesthetic potential of the film-to-come is foreshadowed by the confrontation of two central motifs, dispersed across the two screens. On one side, the teenagers' actions are transformed into a nocturnal play of light, fire and masks. On the other side, viewers are drawn into the luminous interior of a spaceship, a futuristic and exhilarating object that we have seen the villagers build in a previous video. These scenes capture moments in which the teenagers meet to drink, play again or even sleep, and their gestures and postures are fictionalised by a narrative voice-over that attributes animist qualities and image-creating powers to the lights at the edge of the woods. The boys' red cavern becomes at once a stage on which to play and a space for projection. It appears as a time-travelling

Figure 6.2 *Primitive*, Apichatpong Weerasethakul, 2009. Courtesy of Kick the Machine Films.

machine, like Chris Marker's *La Jetée* (1962). In a highly sensory world, nourished with oneiric and fragmentary images, elements from a real past (interrogations, military outfits) and from an imagined future (ghosts, cinema) merge to form a theatre of memory suggesting at once historic events and folk mythologies.

In the feature film the historical context is only referred to on two occasions, in passing. The first instance is through an allusion to Uncle Boonmee. When 'the man who recalls his past lives', who is resting in the middle of his tamarind fields, refers to his karma during a conversation with Aunt Jen, he is not so much talking about the animals and ghosts that surround him as about his kidney disease, which he presents as the consequence of the violent state repression that he says he was involved in. Thus, less a historical time is evoked, which would be bound to knowledge and the past, than a mythical time, as Ernst Cassirer describes it: a time of natural processes and of human life processes. In contrast to the prophetic religions, which develop an active sense of the future, it is in Buddhism, as Cassirer explains, the activities, the *sankhâra*, our doing itself, which appears *as* the root and *at* the root of the suffering: 'Our actions, to the same extent as our sufferings, inhibit the course of the true, the inner life, because they draw this life into a "temporal form" [*Zeitform*] and entangle it' (Cassirer 2002: 146).

Then, during the fantasy cave sequence, Uncle Boonmee, escorted both by his living relatives (Aunt Jen and Tong) and by the spirit of his deceased wife

(Huay), in the midst of the shadows and lights, has visions and dreams. Sliding towards death, he sees fixed and disconnected images rise up (the *La Jetée* effect again), showing young people in camouflage gear resting in the forest, playing in the fields and playing at posing for the camera with a monkey-ghost. This is therefore neither the 'real' past of the soldiers who massacred farmers nor the magical reappearance of the red-eyed monkey-ghost, who is also present in the cave. These images come, according to Uncle Boonmee, from a previous future:

> Last night, I dreamt of the future. I arrived there in a sort of time machine. The future city was ruled by an authority able to make anybody disappear. When they found 'past people', they shone a light at them. That light projected images of them onto the screen. From the past, until their arrival in the future. Once those images appeared, these 'past people' disappeared. I was afraid of being captured by the authorities because I had many friends in this future. I ran away.

Like Uncle Boonmee wandering inside the cave, the boy-dreamers from the spaceship in *Primitive* talk about their physiological experiences of vision: 'I always fear that one day, when I open my eyes, I will see nothing,' says one of them. And the voice-overs in *Primitive*, just like the story of Uncle Boonmee's dream, allude to a machine that 'lets you see forever' and this crystalline moment of a contracted time: 'As soon as the image of your future arrival appeared, you disappeared.' Obviously, Weerasethakul makes this set-up look like real cinema: 'Somewhere in time, someone will discover my time machine. It will be covered with plants, roots and moss. They will think it is a prop from a movie shot a century ago.' The essential question thus concerns the connection between the function of cinema and the logic of memory. For Weerasethakul, magical apparitions, created and 'rhythmed' by vision machines, by the forest and by voices, always remain connected to the powers of cinema. This is why, in his films, issues of recording and of the real are subordinate to the principles of projection and invention. These are the forms of transformation and of the return of experience ('the past life') that constitute the essence of the project around Uncle Boonmee.

It would be a mistake to attribute 'fantastical' and 'realist' tendencies to one part of the film or another. There is a hint of the real in the fantasised and visually fabricated sections, just as there is something surreal to the passages in the film that are more documentary-inspired. Thus, the apparition of the 'ghosts' is variable: when Huay, Uncle Boonmee's wife, who died nineteen years ago, appears for the first time during the sequence in which the spirits of the dead return, she still looks like a ghost, transparent and almost incorporeal. When she reappears in Uncle Boonmee's room, during the oneiric sequence devoted to the jungle, she takes on a more realistic appearance. Huay administers his peritoneal dialysis, caresses him and discusses at length with her husband the subjects of death and fear. Then a medium shot shows the pair on Uncle Boonmee's bed, under the rolled-up mosquito net, holding hands, and framed from the front. When they go to the room where Aunt Jen is sitting with young Tong in front of the television, the camera passes from the television corner towards the table where Uncle Boonmee is spreading out his personal belongings to signal his imminent departure to Aunt Jen. Aunt Jen seems to be ignoring him, does not want to hear anything about Uncle Boonmee's end. From outside the frame of the shot, she speaks to Tong who remains alone in this corner in front of the television, until he ends up joining the others. From this quasi-quotidian scene an abrupt cut leads the four characters into the mythical forest, filmed using a day-for-night technique. This is the kind of transition from one world to the other that is constantly being used in the film, at different scales.

Towards the end, during Uncle Boonmee's funeral, a series of remarkable shots brings together three characters in a hotel room. We see Aunt Jen managing the details of the ceremony with the help of her friend, young Roong. Later at night, when the women try to distract themselves in front of the television, Jen's nephew Tong, wearing an orange robe, joins them. A Thai rite has transformed him into a monk for a day (see Tessé 2010: 12); he has just escaped from his cell in the temple in search of fresh air and company. Once Tong has taken off his religious clothing and had a shower, he suggests going to the restaurant – to which his aunt agrees. In this neutral setting lit with white light Weerasethakul frames the characters in quite an austere and repetitive manner, from the side or frontally, often in the foreground or looking off-screen, towards the television set, the sound of which fills the whole scene. Then the shots are suddenly split and separated into two opposing movements. It is worth carrying out a shot-by-shot analysis at this point.

On the one hand, Tong's aunt turns towards Tong to agree to his suggestion of going out for dinner (shot 1). We leave behind us the arrangement of bodies belonging to a previous shot, in which we saw the three characters sitting next to each other and from the back, turned towards the television screen. Tong now finds himself in the middle of the frame, standing, in a medium long shot, in front of the white wall; to the right, at the bottom of the frame, we see Aunt Jen's head, turned towards Tong. She has thus undertaken a whole journey through the frame to come to this point. Then, she holds out a hand towards him, gets up and pulls Tong towards the door, which is off-screen. Tong, still standing, continues to look towards the inside of the room. Shot 2 shows the three characters strangely sitting once more in front of the television screen, from the back. Its counter-shot (shot 3) brings in a virtual and fantastical dimension through an explicit figurative split. On the left, framed from the front now, we see Aunt Jen, Roong and Tong still sitting side by side on the

Figure 6.3 *Uncle Boonmee Who Can Recall His Past Lives*, Apichatpong Weerasethakul, 2010.

bed, turned to the left. And on the right, we see Aunt Jen's double leaving the room, pulling Tong's double to the right. The right-hand part of the frame thus follows on from shot 1, in which the two characters were preparing to leave. Thus, what might have seemed at first a continuity error (between shot 1 and shot 2) has ultimately helped to spread confusion at the level of both the narrative and the characters. Indeed, it has become difficult to know which character is located on the side of the double and the ghost, of memory or anticipation, and which in the real of the present.

### Creative Affinities: Warhol, Marker, Resnais

Critics have compared Weerasethakul's cinematic work to that of David K. Lynch or Abbas Kiarostami, for his capacity to connect the oneiric to the quotidian and documentary to fantasy. His films have also been compared to the experimental approaches of Nathaniel Dorsky and Bruce Baillie, on the basis of their sensitivity to colours, to micro-movements, to light, to sensations. The importance of Andy Warhol has often been noted, especially as far as irony and pastiche are concerned, especially in connection with Weerasethakul's years of training at the Chicago Art Institute.[9] When the *International Herald Tribune* asked him, in 2007, for the list of his five favourite films, Weerasethakul mentioned films that celebrate slowness or darkness, and which through their extreme length bring cinema and its apparatus to life: *Empire* by Warhol or *Sátántangó* by Béla Tarr, as well as other films that more frontally address the experience of nature or of life (the films of John Boorman, of Tsai Ming-liang and of Naomi Kawase; see Field 2009: 252).

In a more oblique way, a certain kinship is developed with Alain Resnais throughout the *Uncle Boonmee* and *Primitive* project. This kinship is not solely recognisable in terms of the narrative, even if Joachim Lepastier is right to compare *Uncle Boonmee* with *Je t'aime, je t'aime* 'in terms of its search for a memorial cocoon – be it a cave, a matrix or a machine' (2010: 8). Already in *Primitive* (the installation), especially in the final section, Chris Marker's *La Jetée* and the Resnais film derived from it are referred to fairly explicitly. In *Syndromes and a Century* (2006), James Quandt also locates the '*La Jetée* moments', in particular through the montage of the 'high-tech' city of Cholburi, which affects and accelerates the end of the absurd relationship between Nohng and Joy (2009a: 93). But a clandestine and complex relationship develops between Weerasethakul and Resnais/Marker above all through their renewed conception of memory, the mode of creation of heterogeneous temporalities identified by Gilles Deleuze as 'sheets of the past' (1989: 81), as well as by an essay-like or even more strictly experimental dimension revealing a predilection for the sciences. In an interview, the filmmaker explains that, originally, he had planned a story in tune with the concept of a 'random memory', rather than the relatively linear chronology that he ultimately used of two days in the life of Uncle Boonmee. The script, as Weerasethakul argues, told the story in a different order, and he had planned to introduce more abstract elements to create this impression of a random memory. Thus, the initial project required microscopic imagery to represent biological life, which recalls a certain type of insert used by Resnais in his films. In the same spirit, Weerasethakul shot scenes using a microscope to show single-cell beings (Delorme and Tessé 2010: 11, 12). His film includes a few transitions into abstraction left over from this idea, such as the extraordinary drawn-out moment when the princess's ecstasy in the pool at the bottom of the waterfall is retold. Viewers are provided with images of her luminous face and the movements of the mythical catfish, before the scene shifts to aquatic views and sounds that suggest organic and chemical processes on quite a different scale. This moment of suspension develops according to a specific slowness that allows the filmmaker to increase the viewer's attention and to open up towards strata of memory, be they internal or external to the film.

The above-mentioned 'other', that is, the anachronous but by no means ahistorical dimension of the images corresponds to a form of mythical time or, to put it in one of Cassirer's terms, a 'bio-cosmological' time (2002: 176). This moment of the abrogation of representation can be understood as part of the fiction itself, in Rancière's sense of the aesthetic mode of art as *dissensus*. Accordingly, new relationships can be established in the film between appearances and reality, the individual and the common, the visible and its meaning. Historicity and contemporaneity are never absolute, always relative; these are the lessons we learn from the Uncle Boonmee variations. In precisely this relativity – in the suggestion not to distinguish between the real and the imaginary, in the changing drafts of a multilayered memory theatre – lies the essayistic moment of the work of Weerasethakul.

Due to the many recent transgressions of formats in film production and distribution, the essay film is broadly defined as a hybrid genre that combines the categories of feature film, art and documentary film (Alter 2018). As much as these attempts at defining the essay correspond to the original impetus of the 1920s to 60s to renew outmoded forms of the documentary, so also do they require a precise localisation of what the essayistic is today. Because of their hybrid form and their subtly political component, Weerasethakul's variations on Uncle Boonmee can also be placed in the tradition of an essayistic 'third cinema'. The term originated in the 1960s from the post-colonial reception of Bertolt Brecht and Sergei Eisenstein in South America. Applied to contemporary essay films, however, the phrase denotes neither 'intellectual montage' (Eisenstein), nor political guerrilla cinema. Its function in the context of essay films today is rather to be/come a 'guardian of popular memory', as discussed by Nora Alter with Teshome H. Gabriel (1989), to produce an 'invaluable counternarrative to official history' (Alter 2018: 251). Such narratives require a mode of operation that also includes alternative forms of production, as well as a dissident 'look back to the future' (Gabriel 1989: 55).

Against this rhetorical background Weerasethakul's work can finally be characterised as a 'memory theatre'. As a phrase that originated in antiquity, today this term simply denotes the means that are 'used to remember' (Eco 1987: 132). Strategies of essayistic methods are in many ways analogous to those of the art of memory (*ars memoriae*), as described by medievalists: a way of communicating knowledge and a place from which the archive is generated and original thinking starts.[10] Precisely because it is necessary to grasp these mnemonic techniques in their historical specificity and with regard to the transformation of their devices, the term can be applied to certain methods of contemporary art and film. *Ars memoriae* is, as Mary Carruthers emphasises, primarily to be taken as a 'craft of composition' (1998: 3). Seen from this angle, Weerasethakul's films as well as his video installations tend to transform memories into composed 'scenes': in doing so, they investigate the ways film affects our perception and our memory.

### Acknowledgements

I would like to thank Simon Field for his material assistance while I was writing this chapter. Two-thirds of this chapter were initially written in French, the other third in German. My thanks go to Catherine McNaughton and Brenda Hollweg for their translations from French to English and from German to English, respectively.

## Notes

1. Labarthe writes about *Letter from Siberia* (1957): 'Through Siberia, Marker leads us [. . .] into the heart of a mythology, whose "reality" is indeed as valuable as that of Siberia' (1960: 39).
2. For the dynamic relationship that exists between image and word in essayistic filmmaking, see also Blümlinger (2016).
3. Leyda here makes reference to Hans Richter's *Inflation* (1928), a film based on archival material. In his history of the compilation film, Leyda defines the film essay, following Siegfried Kracauer, as a 'wise visual commentary' on socially interesting themes (1964: 30).
4. The English critic Tony Rayns talks of 'voidness' to translate the Buddhist concept of *sunnata* that supposedly inhabits the films of Apichatpong Weerasethakul. While his films rarely include Buddhist content, they are, according to this view, nevertheless impregnated with Buddhist thought. According to Rayns, one of Weerasethakul's favourite books is *Heartwood of the Bodhi Tree: The Buddha's Teaching on Voidness*, by Buddhadasa Bhikkhu (published in Thai in 1962, and in English in 1994). The author was one of the first Thai founders of forest monasteries (Rayns 2005: 134).
5. 'I wanted to start again from the films that inspired me as a child', explains Weerasethakul in an interview about the film (see Delorme and Téssé 2010: 10 for this passage). In a text about Weerasethakul's filmic work, James Quandt lists these local influences: Thai soap operas, local horror films, ghost stories, love songs, talk shows, tales for children, Buddhist fables and, more generally, a kitschy local culture (2009a: 16).
6. *Apichatpong Weerasethakul: Primitive*, Musée d'Art Moderne de la ville de Paris, 1 October 2009–3 January 2010, in coproduction with the Haus der Kunst (Munich) and FACT (Liverpool).
7. This film won a prize at the Oberhausen short film festival.
8. The second room of the exhibition presented Weerasethakul's performative work on location. In addition to two ink drawings, six video projections could be seen on plexiglass screens, on the side wall or on screens. The videos provided viewers with images of teens dancing to Thai pop music along the street (*I'm Still Breathing*), listening to a song dedicated to the country's history and the peasants' resistance (*Nabua Song*) as well as building a fairytale spaceship together with elders in the village (*Making of the Spaceship*). Later, this spaceship seems to float at dusk (*A Dedicated Machine*). Central to this exhibition space are two short films in which the historical repression of the peasants is playfully reconstructed. The first, *An Evening Shoot*, re-enacts in a Brechtian manner the persecution of male village members by the military through target practice with human targets and fake rifles. The second, *Nabua*, with its nocturnal explosions, is reminiscent of both the entrance projection *Phantoms of Nabua* and the fact that the former terror and persecutions were accompanied by flashes of lightning originating from the use of real arms.
9. In addition, Quandt compares him to other great Asian filmmakers such as Hou Hsiao-hsien or Jia Zhang-ke, due to his attachment to his native country. See Quandt (2009a: 93, 99; 2009b: 130), who furthermore highlights the inspiration drawn from painting and photography (Hans Memling, 1430–94, William Eggleston, 1939–).
10. In 2018, Apichatpong Weerasethakul received the FIAF (International Federation of Film Archives) Award to honour the director's long advocacy of film preservation.

REFERENCES

Alter, Nora M. (2018), *The Essay Film after Fact and Fiction*, New York: Columbia University Press.
Alter, Nora and Timothy Corrigan (2017), 'Introduction', in Nora Alter and Timothy Corrigan (eds), *Essays on the Essay Film*, New York: Columbia University Press, pp. 1–18.
Blümlinger, Christa (2016), 'Reading between the Images' (1992), in Erika Balsom and Hila Peleg (eds), *Documentary across Disciplines*, Cambridge, MA and London: MIT Press and Berlin: Haus der Kulturen der Welt, pp. 172–89.
Carruthers, Mary (1998), *The Craft of Thought: Mediation, Rhetoric, and the Making of Images, 400–1200*, Cambridge: Cambridge University Press.
Cassirer, Ernst (2002), *Philosophie der symbolischen Formen. Zweiter Teil: Das mythische Denken (1923–29), Gesammelte Werke*, vol. 12, Hamburg: Meiner.
Deleuze, Gilles (1989), *Cinéma 2: The Time-Image*, trans. Hugh Tomlinson and Robert Galeta, London: Athlone Press.
Delorme, Stéphane and Jean-Philippe Tessé (2010), 'Différentes réalités. Entretien avec Apichatpong Weerasethakul', *Cahiers du Cinéma*, 657 (June), 10–12.
Eco, Umberto (1987), 'Un art d'oublier est-il concevable?', in Huguette Briand-Le Bot (ed.), *Traverses Nr 40: Théâtres de la Mémoire*, Paris: Centre G. Pompidou, pp. 124–35.
Field, Simon (2009), 'Biography: A Guy Named Joe', in James Quandt (ed.), *Apichatpong Weerasethakul*, Vienna: Österreichisches Filmmuseum/SYNEMA, p. 252.
Focillon, Henri [1934] (2013), *Vie des formes. Suivi de Éloge de la main*, Paris: Presses universitaires de France.
Gabriel, Teshome H. (1989), 'Third Cinema as a Guardian of Popular Memory: Towards a Third Aesthetics', in Jim Pines and Paul Willemen (eds), *Questions of Third Cinema*, London: British Film Institute, pp. 53–64.
Labarthe, André S. (1960), *Essai sur le jeune cinéma français*, Paris: Éditions du terrain vague.
Lepastier, Joachim (2010), 'D'autres vies si proches', *Cahiers du Cinéma*, 659 (September), 7–9.
Leyda, Jay (1964), *Films Beget Films: Compilation Films from Propaganda to Drama*, New York: George Allen & Unwin.
Nadolny, Sten (2003), *The Discovery of Slowness*, trans. Ralph Freedman in association with Joseph Cullen, Edinburgh, London, New York and Melbourne: Canongate.
Quandt, James (2009a), 'Resistant to Bliss: Apichatpong Weerasethakul', in James Quandt (ed.), *Apichatpong Weerasethakul*, Vienna: Österreichisches Filmmuseum/SYNEMA, pp. 13–103.
Quandt, James (2009b), 'Exquisite Corpus. An Interview with Apichatpong Weerasethakul', in James Quandt (ed.), *Apichatpong Weerasethakul*, Vienna: Österreichisches Filmmuseum/SYNEMA, pp. 125–31.
Rancière, Jacques (2008), *Le Spectateur emancipé*, Paris: La Fabrique.
Rayns, Tony (2005), 'Touching the Voidness. Films by Apichatpong Weerasethakul', in James Quandt (ed.), *Apichatpong Weerasethakul*, Vienna: Österreichisches Filmmuseum/SYNEMA, pp. 132–42.
Tessé, Jean-Philippe (2010), 'L'Écran des sommeils', interview with Apichatpong Weerasethakul, *Cahiers du Cinéma*, 659 (September), 12.
Weerasethakul, Apichatpong (2009), *Primitive*, *CUJO*, 2:1 (special edition), limited edition (1,000 numbered copies).

# 7. 'TIME TURNING INTO SPACE': *INNOCENCE OF MEMORIES'* PRISMATIC ISTANBUL

## Tim O'Farrell

> I wanted to write a novel whose form resembled the objects in a museum, so that when you wandered around the museum, you would see the exhibits and remember the novel. Maybe some people think this is some kind of Borges joke.
> (Orhan Pamuk's narration in *Innocence of Memories*)

Like all accomplished essay films, Grant Gee's *Innocence of Memories* (2015) functions in multiple registers, principally as a kind of palimpsest, referring to and writing over Nobel Laureate Orhan Pamuk's novel *The Museum of Innocence* (2009). Indeed, the film begins inside Pamuk's apartment, with sweeping views over the Bosporus, as we see Pamuk writing the narration that is being spoken at the same time. Nothing too surprising there, given it has become commonplace to identify the literary heritage of the essay film. However, the relationship between *Innocence of Memories* and its literary forebear is further complicated by a unique link: significant parts of the film are shot in a museum also known as the Museum of Innocence. Located in Istanbul and established by Pamuk as a companion to his novel, this museum houses eighty-three display cases, each aligned with a chapter from the book and containing diverse everyday items such as clothing, jewellery, ceramics, photographs, newspapers, maps, clocks, watches and games.

The complex relationship between novel and museum becomes a veritable thicket when overlaid by Gee's film. The museum and the novel exist in a complementary relationship, each a perfect alibi for the existence of the other. The museum arranges its exhibits as shards of reality that buttress the novel, and together they work as an intricate project to conjure the environment and culture of Istanbul in the second half of the twentieth century. In recurring sequences throughout *Innocence of Memories*, the camera returns to the museum to linger over exhibits, which chart the novel's account of an affair between Kemal, an upper-class man, and his much younger, distant, lower-class relative Füsun. Their initial brief, passionate affair begins in May 1975, ending months later after a party for Kemal's engagement to another woman, Sibel. When Kemal later breaks off this engagement, he seeks out Füsun – too late, it transpires, as she has married another man, Feridun. Recovering from the shock of this revelation, Kemal assumes the mantle of the fond older cousin, visiting the couple in their home almost daily over the next decade. During this time he steals or clandestinely collects thousands of items from his former lover.

Both film and novel straddle a deep love of the past, a desire to preserve and understand it, and a fascination with the inexorability of time, transformation and notions of progress. Conceiving the idea of the museum and the novel together in the 1990s, Pamuk collected items for years, both before and during the writing of his book (the museum opened in 2012, three years after publication of the novel). When he started collecting items for the museum, he was chasing down the tangible objects, the infrastructure, that would reflect the novel's narrative. Pamuk's professed aim was, as he writes in his museum catalogue *The Innocence of Objects*, 'to collect and exhibit the "real" objects of a fictional story in a museum and to write a novel based on these objects' (2012: 15). Later he says, 'The more objects I collected for the museum, the more the story in my mind progressed' (21).

In her book *How the Essay Film Thinks* (2017), Laura Rascaroli posits the essay film as a category characterised by a disjunctive practice and interstitiality, key elements central to the forging of the in-between, atypical, thinking structure of the form. This definition acknowledges the flexibility of the essay film, while simultaneously identifying the profound questions it perennially interrogates: questions of genre, speaking position, subjectivity, narration, documentary, fiction and the dimensions of time and space (or, often more particularly, place). As Rascaroli puts it:

> the essay film is a fragile field because it must accept and welcome the ultimate instability of meaning and embrace openness as its unreserved ethos. The problematization of authorship is demanded by the essayist's aim of extending authorship to the audience [. . .] [T]he essayist asks many questions and only offers few or partial answers. (Rascaroli 2017: 16)

*Innocence of Memories* builds on the relationship between novel and museum, their blurring of reality and fiction and their roots in the physical evidence of the community of Istanbul which they document, to occupy the very territory Rascaroli refers to: a disruptive, in-between space where authorship is not straightforward but rather, 'extend[s] authorship to the audience'. I want to explore how *Innocence of Memories* conforms to the restless, questing model of the essay film by focusing on the film's employment of narrative techniques that blend fiction and reality, and its relationship to the indexical impulse. Examining these aspects of the film will illustrate its focus on point of view and memory in addressing Istanbul's history, politics and culture.

## Narrative as Medley

Point of view and narration lie at the heart of *Innocence of Memories*, playing a pivotal role in the film's strategies of engagement with the novel and museum. The collaboration between director-writer Grant Gee and Orhan Pamuk, credited as co-writer, consolidates and builds on Pamuk's creative role in the Museum of Innocence and the novel of the same name (the film's full title is listed in the opening credits as *Innocence of Memories: Orhan Pamuk's Museum & Istanbul*). Gee displays the text from Pamuk's novel on-screen frequently throughout the film, with relevant pages accompanying the voice-over narration, a strategy also employed in his previous film *Patience (After Sebald)* (2012), which dissected another work of literature (W. G. Sebald's *The Rings of Saturn*). The use of this technique renders the films' quotation from their literary sources explicit. These pages are often superimposed over other images of the landscape or interviewees, mapping the mindset of the literary author and the terrain covered by the literary text.

There is a distinct referential quality to the opening minutes of *Innocence of Memories*, as we can see Pamuk writing at his desk at night, commanding a panoramic view of the Bosporus Strait, which famously separates the European and Asian sides of the city. This opening acknowledges his role in the genesis of the film, as well as foreshadowing its true star: the city of Istanbul. It also echoes the novel's metafictional leaning, with the character 'Orhan Pamuk' knowingly, reflexively introduced late in the book by the words: 'Hello, this is Orhan Pamuk!' (Pamuk 2009: 516). The line between reality and fiction is further blurred when the novel culminates in Kemal, a fictional character and narrator, handing over the narrator's duties to Pamuk and tasking him with undertaking the museum project to commemorate Füsun.

For Laura Rascaroli, '[n]arration with all its components – including the adoption of specific narrative forms, plot structures, narrative functions, voice-over and captions, point of view, temporal organization and rhythm of the story, and music as narrative' (2017: 162) participates in the essay film's strategies of disjunction and interstitiality. *Innocence of Memories* exemplifies Rascaroli's notion that the essay film fundamentally destabilises and problematises notions of authorship, drawing on a number of recognisable traditions in essay films. First and foremost, as I have noted, it is organised around the creative work of Orhan Pamuk. However, it also uses invented characters to explore the notion of place and culture by surveying spaces and landscapes and probing cultural questions, like Chris Marker's *Sans Soleil* (*Sunless*, 1983) and Patrick Keiller's Robinson films (*London*, 1994; *Robinson in Space*, 1997; and *Robinson in Ruins*, 2010). On a different level altogether, it provides space for the testimony of a range of real-life citizens of Istanbul, in a similar manner to Agnès Varda's *Les Glaneurs et la Glaneuse* (*The Gleaners and I*, 2000).

Timothy Corrigan's description of *Sunless* as representing 'the triumph of an amalgamation and orchestration of modular layers' (2011: 9) could equally apply to *Innocence of Memories*. Switching between modes (adaptation of a novel, city film, documentary, guided tour), this philosophical meditation on time, memory and transformation is woven from a range of materials including photographs, old movie and newsreel footage, contemporary footage shot by Gee, content from Pamuk's novel and his museum, images from newspapers and magazines. More generally, the role of narrator is shared among a revolving cast, emphasising their collectivity even in their diversity. As I will demonstrate, this is a key technique separating *Innocence of Memories* from Pamuk's *The Museum of Innocence*, which is focused on Kemal's perspective. If Pamuk's novels and his nonfiction writings, such as *Istanbul: Memories and the City* and *The Innocence of Objects*, reinforce 'his inclination to see the city as a repository of collective memory', as Andrew Pulver argues in his *Guardian* review of Pamuk's film (2015), Gee's film actively represents the city as a repository of memory by shifting perspective between a range of narrators, both real-life and fictional creations, operating on an equal plane.

Through such real and fictional characters *Innocence of Memories* explores how memory, subjectivity and imagination construct life and imbue it with meaning. As Gee recalls it:

> I suggested we have a female narrator leading us on a night time journey through the museum and the city, looking for a lost girl and the lost city and blurring the lines between them. Orhan wrote the narration and had input into the shape of the edit. (in Hall 2015: n.p.)

Gee connects the Istanbul of the past to the present day, principally through his female character Ayla (voiced by Pandora Colin). Hers is a major narrative voice throughout the film, in contrast to Pamuk's novel, where she is only mentioned briefly. Ayla's narration begins from the present perspective, describing her Proustian flashback upon attending the Museum of Innocence:

> As soon as I saw Füsun's dress in the Museum of Innocence, I remembered it. We had bought it together cheaply, in a backstreet in Beyoğlu. My name is Ayla; Füsun was my friend. I was her neighbour for eleven years. From 1974 to 1985 we were her father, Tarik Bey's, ground floor tenants.

Conducted by Ayla's narration, the film moves from the darkness of the museum to the moody, dark, largely empty streetscapes of Istanbul at night.

The expansion of Ayla's character in *Innocence of Memories* and the invention of her backstory as a political exile returning to Istanbul in 2013, years after her friendship with Füsun, motivates changes in landscape, giving expression to the film's principal theme: transformation. Indeed, Ayla's continuing readjustment to the transformation of Istanbul is reflected in her voice-over narration: as renowned photographer Ara Güler's work appears, she notes that upon returning to the city she often confused his photographs with her own memory of the city. After the initial image of the dress in the museum, the visual landscape transforms dramatically as Ayla tells of losing touch with Füsun, moving first to Besiktas, then fleeing to Bremen in Germany as rumours spread that her unionist husband could get arrested after he 'got mixed up in politics'. The camera seems to float, as it accompanies and is directed by Ayla's narration in *Innocence of Memories*, alternating between the old neighbourhood of Çukurcuma, where the museum is located, and anonymous modern spaces.

This displacement effect, so prominent throughout the film, becomes manifest in this exchange between images of old Istanbul and the contemporary megalopolis. The quiet, static interior of the museum is replaced by gliding shots of modern Istanbul that would not be out of place in a J. G. Ballard novel: streetlights, multi-lane arterial roads, spotlit advertising hoardings, anonymous modern commercial buildings, freeway pedestrian overpasses, steel fencing, construction sites. Ayla's *flâneur*-like presence propels these images in *Innocence of Memories*, slipping between the past and the present, reflecting a rapidly changing metropolis in flux, a modern city, landscapes which have been refigured, time that does not stand still. Her personal memories and transformation are tied to the mutating signs and symbols of the city as expressed through her narration:

> when I returned to the city again in 2013, I found that the city had changed completely. Getting to know your city all over again is like making new memories. But all I did was search my old ones. And that's how I ended up in the neighbourhood where Füsun and I used to live.

In a film where meaning is layered and narrators multiply, the signs of the past are lovingly excavated, catalogued and placed alongside the present by these narrators. Gee's adaptation of the minor character of Ayla from the novel into an expanded role as a primary narrator, and returned exile to Istanbul, makes space in the film for her testimony as to the confronting nature of change, sending her in search of old memories. As the film progresses, this perspective is overlaid by a diverse range of narrators whose perspectives shift our experience of Istanbul, contributing to a mosaic portrait of the city.

Apart from Ayla, the following characters contribute voice-over narration to *Innocence of Memories*: Kemal, the main character in Pamuk's novel (voiced by Mehmet Ergen); Orhan Pamuk, seen both at work in his home and intermittently through segments of a television interview (staged for the film) that the audience sees from street level looking into shops and offices as the camera roams through Istanbul; long-term Istanbul taxi driver Süleyman Fidaye; *çekçekçi* (or ragpicker) Dursan Saka; Turkish film actress Türkan Şoray; photographer Ara Güler; and ferry hand Alparslan Bulut. This constellation of narrators allows the film to explore the development of social mores, historical markers, both grand and personal, and the topography of the city of Istanbul. Their collected memories and perspectives, real and fictional, are equivalently channelled through Gee's strategy of 'laying' the past next to the present. As Corrigan has explained, 'essays tend willingly, and often aggressively, to undermine or disperse that very subjectivity as it becomes subsumed in the world it explores', in contrast to practices such as the novel, which, 'generally speaking, recuperate and organize public space through the finished frameworks of a coherent and determining subjectivity' (2011: 19).

The wider mix of narrators used by Gee in *Innocence of Memories* offers a dispersal of perspectives, and reflects the intersection between Pamuk's museum and literary project by blurring the boundaries of the real and fictional. Gee is on the record describing Pamuk's books as 'a kind of literary SimCity. He's setting up these characters that almost feel like documentary characters that he's experienced over his lifetime, and finding ways to set them operating in the fictional world' (in Allen 2016: n.p.). The narrator's function in *Innocence of Memories* is passed around like a baton between real and fictional characters, always returning to the principal themes: prized objects, landscapes and memories of Istanbul, and the constant, at times bewildering, metamorphosis wrought by time.

The film distinguishes between different types of narrator. Physically absent fictional characters Ayla and Kemal are represented by indexical signs such as museum pieces, Gee's images or Ara Güler's photographs. The camera floats when following the lead of these disembodied narrators' voice-over, in a manner consistent with an essay film tradition demonstrated in totemic works such as *Sunless* and Patrick Keiller's *Robinson* series. These films explore space through the experience of the *flâneur*; the assignation of a fictional identity to the narrator can lend an air of detachment, of observational precision, as well as a degree of irony to their perspective. *Innocence of Memories* is replete with factual detail, precisely presented, reinforcing a veneer of veracity perversely constructed from Pamuk's fictional narrative. We learn that Kemal and Füsun made love forty-four times, the first time being the afternoon of 26 May 1975 at about a quarter to three; Kemal's first visit to Füsun's matrimonial home came 339 days after he last saw her; he visited her home for supper 1,593 times over the next eight years; and he squirrelled away 4,213 of her cigarette stubs. This accumulation of detail creates an almost anthropological sense of Istanbul life.

Real-life narrators who currently work in Istanbul, such as Fidaye, Saka and Bulut, appear on-screen physically, in contrast to the disembodied fictional narrators. They observe and reflect from the position of working men who keep the contemporary city running by transporting or cleaning up after its citizens. In particular, the ragpicker Dursan Saka seems to channel Kemal: a self-confessed sensitive soul who is easily hurt and combs the city recycling its detritus. Among these narrators, the famous Turkish actress Türkan Şoray is the exception, bridging the past and the present as she reflects on her career as a leading actress, and we toggle between her image in the present day and images, places and films associated with the Istanbul of the past. As I want to examine in the next section, this juxtaposition between the past and the present is indicative of how *Innocence of Memories* uses the profound affective quality of the image as another means to summon the complex mix of loss, memory, comfort and escape attached to the items that are fetishised in Pamuk's novel and museum.

### The Indexical Impulse

Film and photography provide a visual analogue of the past, a veritable storehouse of images that can take on a distinct characteristic as the past is vivified, playing out in the present. In *Death 24× a Second: Stillness and the Moving Image*, Laura Mulvey argues that as cinema moves into its second century and digital modes of production and exhibition proliferate, the sense of cinema as a virtual museum gains momentum. While cinema can annihilate time, reanimate the past and resurrect the dead, images from earlier eras paradoxically also appear ghostly and emphasise the distance between the present and the past, effectively memorialising the moment captured. Even fleeting details that seemed marginal or banal can 'acquire the aura that passing time bequeaths to the most ordinary objects' (Mulvey 2006: 192).

Stylistic choices are central to the frequent switches between contemporary Istanbul and the ghosts of its past in *Innocence of Memories*. In particular, Gee constantly uses superimposition to layer one image over another. This technique melds and blends images of the past and present, museum exhibits and roaming streetscapes, archival footage and contemporary landscapes, old movies and interviewees. By judiciously matching this visual 'evidence' with the testimony of the film's broad range of narrators, Gee literally enacts the displacement of the past by the present that is the film's central theme. He also generates a strong sense of polyphony, probing the relationship between past and present in surveying the history and culture of Istanbul from a range of perspectives. A sequence featuring Türkan Şoray exemplifies this strategy, beginning with Ayla describing how Füsun loved both Turkish film and Türkan Şoray's eyes. The film then moves between images of Soray in the present day and footage from her films from decades ago, as she reflects in voice-over on how her memories are associated with different parts of Istanbul in which she shot 200 films over fifty years.

We witness the effect of film's powerful affective capacity to arrest and revive time through the images of Soray in the present day, illustrating the transformation wrought by time. Film theorists have long pointed to the indexical link between the medium of film and the pro-filmic reality. In his catalogue of signs, Charles Sanders Peirce described the indexical sign as physically connected to its object, like smoke from a fire, or a footprint (1987: 163, 245, 379). In the case of film, the image recorded by the camera derives from a trace left on light-sensitive film, providing a physical index of the reality that existed in front of the camera, generating a truth claim as evidence of the 'real' scene represented. Despite the differing mode of operation of digital media in contemporary times, prominent theorists continue to read an indexical connection into the photographic image (cf. Doane 2002: 231; Rosen 2001: 309). With the image being formed digitally through data about light, Tom Gunning states emphatically that it 'is encoded in a matrix of numbers', but that 'storage in terms of numerical data does not eliminate indexicality' (2004: 40).

In allowing traces of the past to continue to exist in the future, photography and film literally reproduce slices of time that have been spent, generating a complex relation to temporality through their ability to revive moments from the past. Film is the perfect medium for transporting objects, space and landscapes across time. Towards the end of *Innocence of Memory*, Kemal compares the spiral pattern in Füsun's earring on display in the first box in the museum with the design of the museum and the broader temporal dimension:

> we later realised that the line that connected Aristotelian moments, in other words time, was not a straight line, and that it could only be a spiral. Those who look down from the attic to the spiral of time at the museum's entrance three floors below will see that just as the line that links moments together forms time, so the line that ties objects together creates a story. This according to Kemal is the greatest happiness that a museum can bring: to see time turning into space.

*Innocence of Memories* is unique in the way it intertextually refracts the relationship between past and present on two further levels: Pamuk's novel's study of memory and past time, and his Museum of Innocence, which exhibits items physically redeeming reality in a complementary relationship to the novel. The film captures these objects as it roams through the museum and the city of Istanbul. It also incorporates Kemal's narration from the novel, recounting his tendency to see ghosts and apparitions of Füsun as he travelled around Istanbul after his engagement party. Ayla takes over the narration, stating that 'Istanbul was now a galaxy of signs that reminded him of her.' Orhan Pamuk's narration in the film completes this sequence, noting that these signs 'turn into an index – that's what westerners call it'.

Pamuk's explicit reference to the index in the film's narration conjures the notion of the indexical relationship between the image and the pro-filmic world. The medium's unique relationship to reality shares something with the fetishisation of physical relics connected to Füsun that Kemal takes without her knowledge in both novel and museum. One key item, mentioned at the beginning of the novel, is a gold earring in the shape of a butterfly with the letter F in its centre. Gee shoots it in the museum, where it is mounted in a display case accompanied by an inscription (also the novel's opening chapter title): 'The happiest moment of my life', which refers to Füsun's first sexual encounter with Kemal. The earring will become a recurring visual motif throughout *Innocence of Memories*. In Pamuk's novel Kemal describes how the items smuggled out of Füsun's flat in the aftermath of their break-up, such as a nutcracker or a watch with Füsun's scent on its strap, provide solace as he daydreams in bed (2009: 157).

One striking sequence in *Innocence of Memories* crystallises the way the film riffs on source material contained in the novel and the museum in a hall of mirrors relationship, creating an analogy for the filmic index. Comprising a series of shots highlighting a wall of cigarette butts 'pinned in a glass cabinet as if they were exotic butterflies' (Brooke 2016: 60), it begins with a relatively tight tracking shot focused on three cigarette butts. Each lipstick-smudged butt is pinned to the wall mount and accompanied by a handwritten explanatory annotation, including the date of consumption. Successive cuts gradually expand the viewer's perspective to reveal the true scale of this exhibit. With characteristic precision, the film's narration reveals that the sum of this display is a total of 4,213 mounted and annotated cigarette butts.

Immediately, we are alive to the disjunct between the ordinary denotation of the cigarette butt as an emblem of discarded, filthy detritus, and the loving attention to retrieval, collation, arrangement and display behind glass in an institution for exhibition to the public. These cigarette butts, like the image of an earring that recurs throughout the film and its source novel, are the physical remnants of an epic central love affair. The accompanying voice-over narra-

'TIME TURNING INTO SPACE'

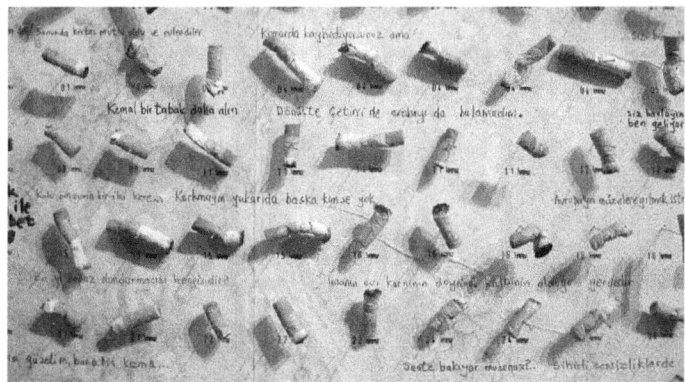

Figure 7.1  The wall of cigarette butts in *Innocence of Memories*, Grant Gee, 2015.

tion initially features Ayla saying, 'all those cigarette butts are now a sort of calendar for the museum, a timeline of Kemal and Füsun's love story', before switching to Kemal's loving account of the relationship between the cigarettes and Füsun's mouth. Kemal's subsequent narration, taken verbatim from the novel, identifies the discarded cigarettes as a form of index, evidencing a physical link to Füsun:

> During my eight years of going to the Keskins' for supper, I was able to squirrel away 4,213 of Füsun's cigarette butts. Each one of these had touched her rosy lips and entered her mouth, some even touching her tongue and becoming moist, as I would discover when I put my finger on the filter soon after she had stubbed the cigarette out; the stubs, reddened by her lovely lipstick, bore the unique impress of her lips at some moment whose memory was laden with anguish or bliss, making these stubs artefacts of singular intimacy.

In *Innocence of Memories*, Gee takes his lead from Pamuk's writing, connecting this idea of signs from the past to a distinctly Turkish concept of *hüzün*, roughly translated as a sense of collective melancholy. Ayla's voice-over comment 'we felt we were growing up in a black and white world' blends into Pamuk using the term when describing Istanbul's characteristic muddy, cobblestone streets and crooked houses as transmitting a feeling of melancholy and introversion. Just before this sequence, Kemal's narration, taken from the museum audio guide, reflects on the moment he waited forlornly for Füsun in the apartment in which they conducted their affair, after she had terminated it. To literally anatomise Kemal's melancholy, Gee focuses on a model of the human body that was in the window of every Istanbul pharmacy at the time. The combination of images and narration in this sequence typifies the way

*Innocence of Memories* links the affective dimension of the index across film, novel and museum. As Gee's peripatetic camera surveys Istanbul, it strives to evince the feeling so bound up with the city and Pamuk's work: 'To feel this *hüzün* is to see the scenes, evoke the memories, in which the city itself becomes the very illustration, the very essence, of *hüzün*' (Pamuk 2005: 84).

Working at a personal level to evoke a mixture of melancholy and romantic connection to the past through the description and visual illustration of the 'black and white world', this sequence connects memories to objects in order to demonstrate the broader idea of *hüzün*. The notion of *hüzün* pervades Pamuk's novel and is also examined at length in his account of the city that has shaped his life in *Istanbul: Memories and the City*. In this memoir he notes the inadequacy of the loose translation of *hüzün* into English as melancholy, noting:

> If I am to convey the intensity of the *hüzün* that Istanbul caused me to feel when I was a child, I must describe the history of the city following the destruction of the Ottoman Empire, and – even more important – the way this history is reflected in the city's beautiful landscapes and its people. The *hüzün* of Istanbul is not just the mood evoked by its music and its poetry, it is a way of looking at life that implicates us all, not only a spiritual state, but a state of mind that is ultimately as life affirming as it is negating. (Pamuk 2005: 82)

Grant Gee locates a visual corollary to Pamuk's 'black and white *hüzün*', evoking an Istanbul of the past through Ara Güler's photographs, snippets of old Turkish films and archival footage of Istanbul. Pamuk cites Güler as a key source of inspiration. His black and white photographs of the old city are prominent in *Istanbul: Memories and the City*. In this memoir Pamuk refers to the photographs as 'a superb record of Istanbul life from 1950 to the present day' (2005: 335). Güler's home studio and archive are located in Beyoğlu, where he spent most of his life, where Pamuk spent his childhood and where the Museum of Innocence is located:

> Ara Güler's photographs show Istanbul to be a place where traditional life carries on regardless, where the old combines with the new to create a humble music that speaks of ruin and poverty, and where there is as much melancholy in the faces of the city's people as in its views; especially in the 1950s and 1960s, when the last brilliant remnants of the imperial city – the banks, *hans* and government buildings of Ottoman Westernisers – were collapsing all around him, he caught the poetry of the ruins. In his *Vanished Istanbul*, with the marvellous photographs of Beyoğlu as I knew it as a child – its tramways, its cobblestone avenues, its shop signs, its tired, careworn, black and white *hüzün*. (Pamuk 2005: 234)

## What's in a Name? Memory, Modernity and 'Innocence' Unpacked

*Innocence of Memories* reflects Laura Rascaroli's dictum that the essay film form is transnational

> because it is the cinema of international filmmakers who programmatically experiment and explore new territories, not only spatial but existential, affective, aesthetic, communicative, political. The absence of rules in this field means that essayistic directors are in conversation with one another, rather than with established national and generic practices. (Rascaroli 2009: 190)

The film's English director responds to Istanbul as a global city, and Orhan Pamuk as an internationally garlanded author. Its indexical, affective component and engagement with disparate essay film narrative strategies aligns it with broader filmmaking currents. The treatment of sex, politics and Füsun's death in *Innocence of Memories* even more explicitly reflects its outward-facing aspect, its engagement with the west, modernity and questions of nationalism and freedom of expression.

While the title *Innocence of Memories* appears to underscore the purity or lack of taint attached to memories and the past, the film's portrait of tradition and modernity in Istanbul complicates this sentiment. Narrators from the novel such as Kemal and Ayla provide voice-over in the present in which their memories appear occluded or just beyond grasp, only accessible through indexical signs such as photographs, films or physical objects connected to the past. At one level, 'innocence' has an idyllic, positive connotation suggesting the prelapsarian moment preceding the acquisition of knowledge and inevitable subsequent fall or corruption. The film's dialogue around sex wraps up a lot of these issues. Ayla's voice-over describing the length of Füsun's hair and her long brown legs is juxtaposed with related images from the museum (shoes, handkerchiefs, comb), and comes before a shift to black and white images from an old Turkish film. Ayla then recounts: 'He told Füsun she was "modern" and "courageous" to give him her virginity' before noting that this comparison to secular, western European women was 'Kemal's first mistake'. Old images of bathing beauties accompanying this narration meld with newspaper images of women with black banners over their eyes, the Turkish media's customary method of depicting adulterers, prostitutes and other 'women of ill repute' in the 1970s. This dialogue juxtaposes innocence, purity and honour with female sexuality and shame. It also points to a city and culture in ferment, with a sharp divide between orthodox Islamic morality and the contemporary western counter-culture.

Reflecting Rascaroli's invocation of an interstitial, disjunctive practice, *Innocence of Memories*' treatment of concepts such as innocence, memory,

Figure 7.2   Condemnatory photographs of women in Turkish media in *Innocence of Memories*, Grant Gee, 2015.

tradition or modernity is never straightforward, demonstrating a distinctly ambivalent posture towards the concept of 'innocence'. Memory is associated with melancholy, *hüzün* and nostalgia, a distinct mental process, a way of parsing reality and dealing with loss, pain, guilt and remorse. With the passage of time, the easy dichotomies (virgin/scarlet woman, good/bad girl) give way to something more complex. Kemal's attachment to Füsun, initially fundamentally corporeal, shifts to become both platonic and obsessive. This shift challenges the notion of innocence inherently associated with a 'proper', culturally approved, platonic relationship. Indeed, Ayla's recollection in her narration of Füsun saying to Kemal that when they first made love, 'she was imagining a field of sunflowers', suggests another kind of disjunct, a form of cognitive dissonance, in the way she initially processes the taboo of lost virginity, indicating the friction between western and traditional Turkish attitudes to love, sex and marriage. Memories that appear innocent can shapeshift and deceive.

Another example of the way the film, taking a lead from its source novel, reads in complexity, is its parallel reference to Füsun's death in a car crash as she is about to travel to Europe and the demise of Grace Kelly, a movie star she adored. Calling back to issues raised throughout the film, the viewer is invited to make a wealth of connections: the struggle of these two women to straddle the modern world and the demands of tradition; the burden of their personal history; and their surrender to the straightjacket of conservative cultural convention, surviving and adjusting to a new equilibrium. What more appropriate metaphor than a car, the ultimate symbol of freedom, mobility and modernity, to unite them and close off their narratives?

Indeed, the reference to Grace Kelly chimes with the theme of cinema as a reflection of modernity, another running trope throughout *Innocence of Memories*, associating modernisation and movement away from the past in Istanbul with cosmopolitanism, globalism and modernity. The turn to modernity is linked to signifiers of westernisation such as the Hilton Hotel, which is described in Pamuk's voice-over as a talismanic building that became the location for new films and dances. While the film emphasises the Hilton's role in the transformation of Istanbul, Pamuk has also noted that 'the great drive to Westernize amounted mostly to erasure of the past' (2005: 27). It is

'TIME TURNING INTO SPACE'

Figure 7.3   Istanbul street dogs in *Innocence of Memories*, Grant Gee, 2015.

no coincidence that he links the Hilton to a watershed moment in his novel, Kemal's engagement party to Sibel, where the scales fall from Füsun's eyes and she determines to break off contact with Kemal. In Gee's film, contrasting the mid-twentieth-century images of the Hilton with contemporary footage paradoxically highlights how this erstwhile icon of modernity has become a heritage building. *Innocence of Memories* highlights the contrast between the Hilton and the Ballardian anonymous any spaces referred to earlier, reinforcing the rapid pace of change in a city where the population increased tenfold between 1950 and 2000.

Similarly, *Innocence of Memories* handles the politics of contemporary Turkey in oblique but recognisable terms, inviting the audience to 'think through' moments of transformation such as the fate of Istanbul's street dogs. What at first appears to be a playful digression with captivating images of dogs roaming Istanbul's streets at night moves into much darker terrain as Pamuk's narration broaches the disappearance of the packs of dogs that had dominated the city for 500 years, acting as 'guardians of the city'. He describes this development as 'a genocide' of dogs. This incident resonates at another point in the film, when Pamuk mentions being 'pulled into the political situation between 2004 and 2010'. This 'situation' that he obliquely refers to includes receiving death threats and being prosecuted in 2005 for the offence of insulting the Turkish Republic. According to Maureen Freely, he stated in an interview with a Swiss magazine that 'a million Armenians and 30,000 Kurds were killed in this country and I'm the only one that dares talk about it' (2005: n.p.). The danger of challenging the government in contemporary Turkey is also reinforced through Ayla's narration at the beginning of the film, which refers to needing to leave Turkey in 2001 because of her husband's political activity, and Kemal's reference to the 1980 coup, accompanied by archival newsreel footage.

## Conclusion

As an essay film, the way that *Innocence of Memories* examines change and transformation is protean. It addresses both personal experience and public debates – for example, in relation to sex and politics – in evaluating the culture and history of Istanbul. It employs both fictional and living characters as narrators in constructing a mosaic approach to storytelling, switching between modes while always returning to the project's fountainhead: Orhan Pamuk's creative role in writing the novel *The Museum of Innocence* and establishing the Museum of Innocence. Interview snippets with Pamuk, Gee's co-conspirator, co-creator and inspiration, pepper the film, along with the reflective voice-over narration of fictional characters and present day denizens of Istanbul. The film simultaneously celebrates the excitement of development in a burgeoning metropolis, and reflects on the inevitable sense of loss caused by destruction and change.

In all these senses, *Innocence of Memories* is characterised by a disjunctive process, switching between often seemingly incompatible strategies. Yet this restlessly inquisitive methodology allows it to fluidly chart the myriad links between the concrete and the physical (everyday items, the natural landscape and the built environment) and the subjective and chimerical (memory, nostalgia, *hüzün*). Analysing a city and a culture in perpetual transition from a range of perspectives, exploring the richness and complexity of memory, the clash between tradition and modernity, and the process of cultural transition, *Innocence of Memories* frequently refers to a sense of *hüzün*. As Pamuk notes, 'Istanbul does not carry its *hüzün* as "an illness for which there is a cure" or "an unbidden pain from which we need to be delivered": it carries its *hüzün* by choice' (2005: 93). True to the spirit of radical openness at the core of the essay film, *Innocence of Memories* harnesses the power of the visual image to store and reproduce traces of the past, augmenting the elaborate legend created by Pamuk.

## References

Allen, Joshua Bruce (2016), 'Innocence of Memories: Director Grant Gee in Orhan Pamuk's Istanbul', *The Guide Istanbul*, 5 February, <http://www.theguideistanbul.com/article/innocence-memories-director-grant-gee-orhan-pamuk-istanbul> (last accessed 18 June 2018).
Brooke, Michael (2016), 'Innocence of Memories: Orhan Pamuk's Museum and Istanbul', *Sight & Sound* (February), 60–1.
Corrigan, Timothy (2011), *The Essay Film: From Montaigne, After Marker*, Oxford and New York: Oxford University Press.
Doane, Mary Ann (2002), *The Emergence of Cinematic Time: Modernity, Contingency, the Archive*, Cambridge, MA: Harvard University Press.
Freely, Maureen (2005), 'I Stand by My Words. And Even More, I Stand by My Right to Say Them . . .', *The Guardian*, 23 October, <https://www.theguardian.com/world/2005/oct/23/books.turkey> (last accessed 18 June 2018).

Gunning, Tom (2004), 'What's the Point of an Index? Or, Faking Photographs', *Nordicom Review*, 25:1–2 (August), 39–49.
Hall, Duncan (2015), 'CineCity Hosts the UK Premiere of Brighton Filmmaker Grant Gee's Istanbul Fantasy Documentary Innocence Of Memories', *The Argus*, 20 (November), <https://www.theargus.co.uk/news/14092718.CineCity_hosts_the_UK_premiere_of_Brighton_film_maker_Grant_Gee_s_Istanbul_fantasy_documentary_Innocence_Of_Memories/?ref=arc> (last accessed 29 November 2018).
Mulvey, Laura (2006), *Death 24× a Second: Stillness and the Moving Image*, London: Reaktion.
Pamuk, Orhan (2005), *Istanbul: Memories and the City*, London: Faber & Faber.
Pamuk, Orhan (2009), *The Museum of Innocence*, London: Faber & Faber.
Pamuk, Orhan (2012), *The Innocence of Objects*, New York: Abrams.
Peirce, Charles S. (1987), *Writings of Charles S. Peirce: A Chronological Edition*, vol. 5, ed. Max H. Fisch, Bloomington: Indiana University Press.
Pulver, Andrew (2015), 'Innocence of Memories Review – Orhan Pamuk's Istanbul Rendered Strange and Beautiful', *The Guardian*, 10 September, <https://www.theguardian.com/film/2015/sep/10/innocence-of-memories-review-orhan-pamuk-istanbul-grant-gee-venice-festival> (last accessed 18 June 2018).
Rascaroli, Laura (2009), *The Personal Camera: Subjective Cinema and the Essay Film*, London and New York: Wallflower Press.
Rascaroli, Laura (2017), *How the Essay Film Thinks*, New York: Oxford University Press.
Rosen, Philip (2001), *Change Mummified: Cinema, Historicity, Theory*, Minneapolis: University of Minnesota Press.

# 8. *LOVERS IN TIME*: AN ESSAY FILM OF CONTESTED MEMORIES

## Thomas Elsaesser and Agnieszka Piotrowska

### 'Let's Call the Whole Thing Off'

Few film forms or genres have in recent years attracted as much attention or controversy as the essay film. Even as scholars agree that it can be many different things to many different parties, its saving grace would seem to be that it has something for everybody. Interrogative, discursive, ruminative, argumentative, subjective, affective, refractive, reflexive ... The essay film has given rise to such a plethora of adjectives, they conjure up the old Fred Astaire–Ginger Rodgers duet about 'you like to-may-toes and I like to-mah-toes, I say ei-ther and you say ee-ther, either/eether/nei-ther/nee-ther/', where 'things have come to such a pretty pass' that Astaire declares, 'let's call the whole thing off'.

With this chapter, we are not calling it off, and so – once more with Astaire – we can 'call the calling off off'. But neither will we make an attempt to add yet another definition of the essay film to the preceding contributions rich in such definitions, as well as rich in disclaimers such as this one. Instead, we declare as a possible extension of the essay film a certain complementary but also contrasting combination of elements, gestures, stances and activities: these range from high theory to artistic practice, from making a film about putting on a play, to writing in a book about the making of a film about putting on a play, while being disarmingly autobiographical as well as seriously self-reflexive, emerging at the end from a process that engenders a practice, with a practice that results in a product – or two.

It is one of these products that I first encountered at the *World Cinema Essay Film Conference*, when I saw Agnieszka Piotrowska's experimental documentary *Lovers in Time*. Asked to participate in a post-screening round-table discussion, I found myself intrigued by how provocatively and yet productively the film fitted into the situated framing it had received at this academic conference devoted to the topic of the essay film. I decided to write up my notes, which I take the liberty of reproducing here before adding a further layer of essayistic reflection that both amplifies my review notes and shifts them towards broader considerations of how to locate and legitimate within academia such an ongoing self-interrogation and reframing as Piotrowska conducts in her film work and her writing, where each mirrors – refracts and reflects, subjects and affects – the other, while also displacing each other, and thereby disturbing this very mirroring. This might indeed be a further definition of practice research and essayistic thinking.

From its opening scene *Lovers in Time* alerts us to the porous boundaries between documentary and fiction, using the device of 'putting on a play' as a lens through which to raise an impressive range of contemporary issues, intertwining colonialism, race, gender, identity with the 'return of the repressed', in a tale of love and retribution, forgiveness and the quest for justice, set in today's Harare, among Zimbabwe's educated younger generation. All of it makes *Lovers in Time* not only a timely political film, but an unusually riveting example of the 'essay film': here understood as a special kind of historical reflexivity, manifesting itself across several layers of subjectivity.

The film introduces perspectives of the subjective, first by highlighting the protagonists' different emotional, professional and political stakes, as the conflicts inherent in the topic of post-colonialism and race inescapably surface, as tensions increase and suspense tightens, mainly about whether the play will in fact be staged (or be shut down by the police and demonstrators), but also about how to interpret especially the male lead's ambiguous position, as both the most articulate political voice and yet seemingly the least reliable team player.

A subjective perspective is also palpably present insofar as the film features its director, Agnieszka Piotrowska, behind the camera, and in front of it, when directing the play and keeping track of an increasingly volatile situation. She is both a persona and a role, both an authority and someone struggling to stay in control: of an errant cast and of her inner turmoil, growing doubts and split feelings.

Although in some ways a classical documentary of both the participatory and observational kind, *Lovers in Time* exceeds and innovates the genre, in the way it weaves in a fictional plot line: a mixed-race couple mutually recriminate each other, hinting at sexual infidelities, jealousy, as well as professional rivalry. Since the lovers' quarrel is clearly a performance (and done with

Figure 8.1   Company of *Lovers in Time*, Agnieszka Piotrowska, The Harare International Festival of the Arts, 2014.

considerable gusto by the two actors concerned), this intrigue acts as both a distancing device and a seriocomic counterpoint, taking the more sombre and intractable conflicts (highlighted in the play and its production) into a minor key. In fact, *Lovers in Time* – its double entendre already present in the title – teases us with a number of possible plots and sub-plots that involve black and white characters, and the trans-ethnic love story that provides the fictional frame obliquely but unmistakably mirrors the central relations within the play: the unavenged death of a national liberation figure returns not just to haunt the laid-back Harare actors and musicians, but to inhabit their bodies, making them twist and turn in confusions of gender, transgender and other transgressive emotions and actions – in the hope that this might retroactively rewrite the past and thereby redeem some of its horrors.

Yet *Lovers in Time* ironically cites the 'putting on a show' plot device of Hollywood 1930s musicals also in order to give its topical themes a movie-history pedigree. Reminding us of the complications that are a mainstay of this genre, the film varies them (and provides them with further resonance), so that the old 'will the financial backer (who sleeps with the chorus girl) pull the plug on the production?' becomes 'will the police ban the play and arrest the director?' And 'will the leading lady break an ankle and finally give the pesky understudy her chance?' becomes 'will the leading man go missing on the opening night, and there is no understudy to replace him?' One could extend the tragic-comic echoes and mention other Hollywood films in this tradition, from Bob Fosse's *All that Jazz* (1979) to Alejandro González Iñárritu's *Birdman* (2015), but the cinephile spectator will surely also recognise in *Lovers in Time* another well-established genre, this time a French speciality of directors such as Jacques Rivette and Éric Rohmer. They tended to take a group (e.g. friends, colleagues, extended families) and either put them in exceptional circumstances, where friendships, loyalties and partnerships are tested (e.g. Rohmer's *Claire's Knee*, 1970, and *Pauline at the Beach*, 1983), or make them stage a play (as in Rivette's *Paris Belongs to Us*, 1961, and *L'Amour Fou*, 1969). In all these films – as in *Lovers in Time* – fictional roles get fatally entangled with actual lives, exposing the mechanisms of projection, transference and over-identification, which both blur and merge the conflicts, at the same time as they open them up to possibly more productive solutions.

As with these French films that so often sparkle with Gallic wit, *Lovers in Time* modulates its moods quite masterfully between humour and tragedy, real danger and farce. It finally leaves the viewer more pensive and thoughtful, but also more positive and hopeful than had the director opted for a racially less entangled and a politically more correct 'film of the play'. After all, what is more encouraging than seeing victory snatched from the jaws of defeat, or witnessing near-disaster and almost-failure transform itself into art before one's very eyes?

As a full-time academic Piotrowska would seem to be living proof that the higher education initiative which goes by the name of 'practice-based research' or 'practice research' is pedagogically sound and can fulfil its mission: to undertake original investigation in order to gain new knowledge by means of practice and the outcomes of that practice, which in this case is demonstrated through creative work in cinema and writing. The combination of producing a film (*Lovers in Time*) and writing a book (*Black and White: Cinema, Politics and the Arts in Zimbabwe*, 2017) extends the film work by reflecting on it critically and putting it in a broader context. It serves as a useful demonstration of how practice-based research can be mutually reinforcing, adding value to each endeavour. If parts of the *book* are a theoretically elaborated commentary on the making of the film, then the *film* is also a dramatised demonstration of some of the key theses of the book. Of course, *Black and White* is much more than a commentary and a reflection on the making of *Lovers in Time*. It ranges widely, covering topics in literature, filmmaking and theatre, and it delves into current post-colonial theory and its history, from Frantz Fanon to Edward Said. Frequent visits to Zimbabwe pay additional dividends, because they give the writing the texture of anthropological fieldwork, brought to life through interviews and vividly depicted encounters. What makes it pertinent to the practice based research concept is the unstable position of the filmmaker/author/researcher, which, despite *Black and White*'s disclaimers to be speaking from the position of non-knowledge, does produce knowledge of an unexpected kind.

While *Lovers in Time* impresses by its film historical echoes and fluid cinematographic idiom, what strikes one about *Black and White* is therefore the remarkable honesty in the author's account of the practice of 'learning by doing'. This necessarily proceeds by trial and error, is in constant dialogue with the (racial) other, but is also not afraid of risk and even of courting failure. Given the broader context of post-colonialism and the persistence of its legacy, 'performing failure' may even be seen as an achievement, the ethical consequence of risking the very encounter between 'black' and 'white'. In

Piotrowska's case the odds were daunting: *Black and White* documents what it means to be a feminist filmmaker in a male-dominated profession, what it means to be a white woman working in an African country, what it means to tackle a topic – Zimbabwe's colonial past in *Lovers in Time* – that is so raw and sensitive, so traumatic and so unresolved, that to this day it divides the people in Zimbabwe, even without someone from outside running the risk of appearing to interfere, especially when mixing philosophically inspired theory with the practical engagement of a documentary filmmaker.

Both book and film are prepared to take this risk of the author and the director being perceived either as a coloniser appropriating part of the national narrative, or trying to offer support and redemption from trauma, when it is neither wanted nor appreciated. Zimbabwe seems for many in the west a failed state, run for decades by a brutal dictator who portrayed the west to his people as united in behaving like colonisers, determined to punish Zimbabwe with sanctions and boycotts, while still trying to gain access to its raw materials and other valuable resources. Both *Lovers in Time* and *Black and White* deserve credit for letting us see another side of Zimbabwe, its artists and creative spirits, and to do so in a nuanced and by no means uncritical manner.

The particular irony of her position is not lost on Piotrowska. After all, she herself originally comes from a country that has a long history of being occupied and colonised. The fact that having a Polish name in Britain invites prejudice and may even include overt discrimination, nevertheless neither mitigates being perceived as 'white', 'privileged' and 'British' in Zimbabwe, nor protects from being treated with suspicion and distrust: on the contrary, the dilemmas of gender and race persist, as Piotrowska hints at when she writes (below): 'part sex object and part the embodied representative of the race and culture which is both hated and yearned for'.

*Lovers in Time* is therefore about several kinds and several layers of trauma. First, it confronts a colonial and post-colonial situation, which means displacing the reference from the Holocaust, the Balkan or US wars and 9/11, to centuries of colonialism in Africa and elsewhere. Second, it deals with a society whose sense of identity and nationhood is built on a traumatic event – the event that the play in *Lovers in Time* both revives and turns into a surreal comedy. Third, Zimbabwe is a country that has had its share of loss and traumatic memory: suffering that has been silenced, wounds that refuse to heal, hopes that have been dashed. After Independence, expectations of a better life have been disappointed, ideals betrayed, injustices gone unredeemed, and lost lives not accounted for: all the hallmarks of national and collective trauma. Yet, as Piotrowska once pointed out, the Shona language does not know the word 'trauma', and instead relies on other words, on other rituals of mourning, on other forms of 'acting out' to give body and voice to what I have here called national and collective trauma.

What therefore makes a scholarly and artistic intervention such as Piotrowska's especially valuable in the context of both the essay film and practice-based research, is to observe with what means (theatrical and filmic), by what strategies (scholarly and essayistic) and in what manner of embodiment (re-enactment, repetition compulsion, role reversal, gender-bending) *Lovers in Time* and *Black and White* make us 'experience (post-colonial) trauma' when there is no stable or established frame of reference, but only acting out, only near misses ('how we nearly got arrested') and only the courage of risking failure. If the essay film as an aesthetic practice, a political process and a pedagogical tool has a place and a task in an academic setting (as opposed to its role in the art world or on the film festival circuit), then those of us concerned with defining its meaning and refining its forms must surely recognise work such as Piotrowska's as belonging to the essay film: fitting its brief and deserving its name by helping to consolidate the scholarly legitimacy and ethical integrity of 'essaying', that is, of learning by doing, and of doing by never ceasing to try.

*Thomas Elsaesser*

### Lovers in Time as Essay Film and Practice Research

'Trauma', a wise woman once said, 'is like opening the kitchen cupboard, and everything falls out.' Europe's dealing with post-colonial Africa continues to be traumatic for all sides, and in many an encounter with the people and the societies shaped by this legacy, 'everything falls out': race, gender, black, white, Orientalism, self-exoticism, murder, silence, laughter, music, love, friendship, movie-making. Agnieszka Piotrowska is not afraid to open that cupboard, on her various actual and metaphorical journeys to Harare, when meeting with Zimbabwe's post-independence generation of gifted artists, self-assured intellectuals and brave journalists as well as literary works and cinema.

(Thomas Elsaesser, endorsements for *Black and White: Cinema, Politics and the Arts in Zimbabwe*)

*Lovers in Time or How We Didn't Get Arrested in Harare* (2015) previewed at the World Cinema Essay Film conference in Reading in May 2015. There, Thomas Elsaesser saw it for the first time and wrote the endorsement above. Eighteen months later, my monograph *Black and White: Cinema, Politics and the Arts in Zimbabwe*, was published, which is a collection of essays on Zimbabwe with a particular chapter on the film. In the spirit of treating the film and its making as an extended experiment – an 'essay' – an article by me focusing on the media reactions to the film was published in the *Journal of African Media Studies* in June 2016. Here I hope to add another dimension to these statements, still in view of extending and assessing a multidimensional set of processes, encounters and collaborative ventures, as to their implications for practice based research. It is my view that it is not possible to assess one's own work in the same way in which one would analyse that of somebody else. If subjective knowledge is, according to Michel de Montaigne, the hallmark of any essay, then the notes that follow of my subjective knowledge gained because of this film also contribute to the film as essay.

Because of the provenance of the film, and its origins as a practice based research exercise, I took a decision to give the film a chance of being discussed at various events, screenings and institutional collaborative encounters as well as submitting it to festivals. To date I have not sought to obtain a broadcast distribution for the film for a variety of reasons – one of them being my concern that people in it might be exposed to repercussions by the regime. Another reason is that to my mind the film is flawed and without my presence to discuss it, might not stand well enough on its own. The thoughts below, therefore, are a kind of 'behind the scenes' presentation, rather than 'autocritique'. The work is collaborative and one major research question of both the film and the book was whether creative collaboration can serve as a bridge and mediator in dealing with post-colonial trauma. What I discovered were some surprising challenges that emerged in my relationship with Joe Njagu, a key collaborator on this project – challenges to which I will return at the end of this essay.

As already hinted at in the first part of this chapter, both the film and the book are about trauma, post-colonial trauma and the near impossibility of

Figure 8.2 Performance of *Lovers in Time*, Agnieszka Piotrowska, The Harare International Festival of the Arts, 2014; Charmaine Mujeri (Kaguvi) and Michael Kudakwashe (Time Traveller Nehanda).

getting at it at all. The key research question of the book was whether a creative collaboration across cultures could help ameliorate problems inherent in a post-colonial era (Piotrowska 2016). *Lovers in Time* deals with a singular historical event but the underlying issues are precisely those of post-colonial trauma. As my foundational theory and practice is psychoanalysis and applied ethics, it is worth recalling briefly what post-colonialism means from a psychoanalytical perspective.

Stephen Frosh reminds us that 'colonialism not only oppressed its victims; it also stole their past, making it unmournable' (2013: 54). Judith Butler also discusses this sense of profound unconscious melancholia in which

> a loss is refused, [but] not for that reason abolished. [...] [M]ore precisely the internalization of loss is part of the mechanism of its refusal. If the object can no longer exist in the external world, it will then exist internally, and that internalization will be a way to disavow the loss, to keep it at bay, to stay or postpone the recognition and suffering of loss. (Butler 1997: 134)

Frosh adds further that

> colonialism has comprehensively destroyed the sources of value within the cultures that it conquered – left those subjects so unrecognized, one might say – that whilst there might be powerful *sensations* of loss at work in those cultures, there is little access to the actual things that were lost. [...] This could also forge a psychic response in which the unbearable nature of this loss is denied and replaced by a manic rush towards the colonial mode of being, for example in aping the structures of the colonial nation state. (Frosh 2013: 55)

He goes on to say:

> there is no actual lost object simply to be recovered, a presence that will return to lead everything to its satisfactory, integrated conclusion [...] This kind of melancholia understands the recovery of the lost object not as something that refers only to the past, but as a ghostly act troubling the present because of its *continuing* suffering. (Frosh 2013: 63; original emphasis)

This sense of confusion and pain regarding the furore surrounding the performance might have been, in some ways, due to the impossibility of the recovering the 'lost object' of the pre-colonial past which in some way the play was attempting to do. The film offers another chance to think through the trauma of the past as well as the trauma of what we all went through during the production of the film.

Another notion to consider in discussing *Lovers in Time* is the idea of metaphorisation (Piotrowska 2014a, 2014b). This is a good psychoanalytic term, which simply means an ability (or desire) to express something that can sometimes be hard, if not impossible, to express otherwise. Metaphorisation usually accompanies a sense of loss, conscious or otherwise, and extreme psychic pain, mourning and melancholia – in short: trauma. Ranjana Khanna, who uses the term in her influential book *Dark Continents* (2003), also appropriates another notion, that of 'an organic intellectual' taken from Antonio Gramsci and in particular from a reformulation of this notion in the famous essay on Hamlet by C. L. R. James. James identifies the split in Hamlet's mind as one that characterises all intellectuals caught between 'the communal change from the medieval world to the world of free individualisation' (1992: 244). The communal change manifests itself in Hamlet's mind as a ghost – as a haunting. Khanna reminds us that 'an organic intellectual' already in Karl Marx is a figure emerging 'from the people' rather than from the system. In *Dark Continents* she uses the concept freely to denote a person who has been subjected to colonial subjugation and melancholia (i.e. the inexpressible haunting) but can use it creatively to sublimate violent impulses.

By writing the play *Lovers in Time* the Zimbabwean author Blessing Hungwe is perhaps indeed 'an organic intellectual' of the kind Khanna has in mind: Hungwe attempted to get close to expressing post-colonial trauma through fiction and comedy, shying away from any factual account. Curiously, it was perhaps this move to humour (as well as a European directing his play) that created the controversy with the authorities and the conservative elements in society that my film both captured and amplified.

Hungwe wrote a surreal comedy about national icons Mbuya Nehanda and Kaguvi Sekuru. They were executed by the white colonisers at the end of the nineteenth century, as they struggled to incite an uprising against the white domination. The memory of this event has been used ever since by the authorities in the struggles for independence and as a tool of uniting the divided Zimbabwean population – not even a nation yet – against white domination. These characters have become an untouchable example of a strictly nationalist patriotism, fostered and enforced in order to align the country's different tribes behind the leadership of the Shona president and now autocratic dictator Robert Mugabe (see my elaboration of this in Piotrowska 2017). That narrative is a closed system and offers no possibility of an outcome that might carry the seeds of some form of reconciliation with the white population.

Hungwe, like many others, felt that the rigid worship of these historical figures was in the end a force that held the country back. He felt that the undoubted historical trauma, the betrayal surrounding their deaths and their transformation into untouchable national icons amounted to fatally blocking any black and white relationship. However, this organic intellectual abandoned our ship as soon as we began the rehearsals – perhaps the process of 'metaphorisation' was still more a fantasy on his part than a liveable reality: perhaps it was simply too hard and he, too, was fearful of seeing these national icons presented as comedy figures – when his writing came to life on stage. And so the film documents the theatre company struggling to populate the space his play had opened while the writer is nowhere to be seen.

In addition, if Blessing Hungwe attempted to get at the unspeakable colonial trauma then certainly, by asking a white European to direct it, he delegated authorship and provoked a situation in which some structural positioning of the colonial power relation was repeated and re-enacted – perhaps unconsciously.

There is something else to be added: whilst we tried together to redraw the lines of belonging – and create a space for a dialogue which was about artists working together, rather than a white European leading a black and white Zimbabwean theatrical troupe in Harare – in reality, old fears and anxieties were in some way re-emerging. When we grew scared of possible repercussions, it became a curiously phantasmic fear – as in reality the play was 'passed' three times by the Ministry of Information and the Board of Censors. In addition, the festival had a robust agreement with the government regarding the festival's time-honoured artistic freedoms. However, my actors felt scared and I felt scared and guilty too; something was re-enacted in the production of the play and it still seems too early to analyse it fully. To put this in context, there had been a case not so long before where a whole production had been closed down by the authorities and the whole cast was indeed arrested (see *The Zimbabwean* 2011).

In my book I talk about the body as a site of post-colonial trauma – in Zimbabwe and in my film it centres on the issue of touching and not touching (Piotrowska 2017: 34). Jean-Luc Nancy in his seminal text on the body and its significance in the history of philosophy points out that the body needs to remain an open system. He says that in reflecting on it he did not want to

> produce the effect of a closed or finite thing, because when we talk about the body we talk about something entirely opposed to the closed and the finite. With the body, we speak about something open and infinite, about the opening of closure itself, the infinite of the finite itself. (Nancy 2008: 122)

Whilst the film *Lovers in Time* deals with many issues, in part it also puts up for scrutiny our different bodies and focuses on voice and touch in colonial and post-colonial encounters. As a film essay it becomes a site of

Figure 8.3  Co-directors and co-producers Agnieszka Piotrowska and Joe Njagu.

loss, representing the non-representable collapse of ordinary human communications, reclaimed gradually and painfully in the de-colonial period. The staging of the play presented in the film was 'touching' something, which is indeed very difficult, if not impossible, to express clearly. *Lovers in Time or How We Didn't Get Arrested in Harare* presents the connections between the body, language and touching without exactly making clear what is going on – it avoids spelling out what is impossible to articulate: any attempt to issue a definitive statement would have been doomed to failure – a matter I discuss elsewhere around a re-reading of Jacques Derrida's essay 'Demeure' (Piotrowska 2014a, 2017).

Since the preview in Reading it has been interesting to note the ways in which audiences have responded to the screenings. In essence one could say, risking some generalisations, that people who expressed the greatest anxiety over the issues of my otherness in this context have been white Europeans themselves. Black Zimbabweans, including Winston Mano, Rufaro Kaseke, the cast and the crew usually find the film moving, hilarious and thought provoking. At the screening at Edinburgh University's Centre of African Studies in March 2017, the chairperson – the Zimbabwean and esteemed academic Francisca Mutapi – said, based on her experience of leading research groups in rural Zimbabwe, that she felt my approach was almost too democratic, with attempts at organising votes on important issues. Conversely, other screenings did produce attacks on me personally, which repeated the space of abuse that had been created by the authorities and the media in Harare.

I have recently been reflecting on the role of deception in Sarah Polley's *Stories We Tell* (see Piotrowska 2018, 2019: 65–85) – which of course is a narrative and not an essay film. In *Lovers in Time* the comedy sketches function in a way that is not dissimilar to the fake archive in Polley's film. The viewer may well feel a little deceived in the end (the sketches with the biracial couple are pure fiction), but the reward is that sense of getting a little closer to the actual trauma the film is attempting to portray: in Polley's film the profound family trauma, in mine the post-colonial trauma which in Zimbabwe appears to throw a long shadow over everything and everybody – and yet, nobody is allowed or expected to talk about it.

*Lovers in Time* is in a way, apart from being an essay film and the story of Zimbabwean politics, also a story of my position in these circumstances. The problem here goes beyond establishing and naming the position from which one speaks, as Edward Said ([1979] 2003: 25) insisted was necessary in any discussion of cultural politics, especially one that involves issues of culture, gender and race. Why this is important, according to Said, is that it helps us understand how we come to form knowledge, and how this knowledge is inflected by our subjectivity. Such knowledge can often be based on *prejudice* against the Other, not only because of the way this Other looks or behaves, but also, and perhaps primarily, because of the personal background and the *experience* that the one who studies the Other brings to this knowledge and its dissemination. Conversely, proponents of auto-ethnography (Muncey 2010) have called for the introduction of the first person experience in the academy as offering 'the missing story'.

In some way, the film is offering this missing story, although the questions persist: what are the lines between freedom of speech and respect for other cultures? Do we have the right to speak out if our stance and utterances might endanger our collaborators who live in difficult political systems? The experience has also taught me humility regarding my own position of perceived as well as actual privilege – the position I did not choose and which I, too, question in my own culture as a foreign woman struggling in the patriarchal world, but which, in the context of Zimbabwe, is still seen within the wider context of post-colonialism, where my whiteness is the key issue, because it challenges the rigid views of historical legacy as well as the local patriarchy, even as this patriarchy challenges me as a woman.

When the asymmetrical lines of power and belonging cross, collaborations bring a number of issues into sharp focus: how do you collaborate when you are considered both inferior as a woman, part sex object and part the embodied representative of the race and culture which is both hated and yearned for? Is it possible to circumvent the post-colonial position in race relations and if so, how? Are we stuck with the embodiment being such a dominant signifier – which Frantz Fanon ([1952] 1975) believed to be the case sixty years ago – or should we insist that things have changed during the intervening time? No easy answers are forthcoming, but in a globalised world of increasing interdependence and with Africa a continent poised to undergo momentous changes, it is especially important to pose these questions and to do so at a very local and specific level. Only with direct exposure and with case studies such as the ones documented and presented in *Black and White* can we hope to formulate answers and arrive at the processes of negotiation necessary for new ways of relating to each other, in spite of colour and gender, ethnicity and religion, colonial past and global present.

## What Has Been Left Out of the Film

I have since wondered many a time why Blessing Hungwe came up with the notion for the play and, when I questioned him, still felt he wanted to proceed, despite the obvious risks. Did he just want his work to see the light of day? Did he want to set me up against the regime? Did he not know himself what we were about to do? Did he unconsciously feel he was happy to provoke the regime with me being the silly white woman going towards an inevitable disaster naively and innocently? In short, did he use me as bait? There were moments when I was very angry about it all – but I am grateful now that we produced the play, as it was an extraordinary experience and also gave me the chance to make an essay film and collaborate with another Zimbabwean artist, filmmaker Joe Njagu.

I have talked in some detail about the press reactions to the play in my book (Piotrowska 2016, 2017). However, the controversy went beyond articles in the papers.[1] On the final day of the performance on 5 May 2014, an African traditionalist jumped onto the stage, calling the play sacrilegious: 'What kind of black people are you? Blasphemous! Blasphemous!', he yelled. In my film I do say that whilst we were half expecting it, it still came as a shock and we were genuinely scared. It was after the Danish cartoons of the Prophet Muhammad and a few months before the assassinations at *Charlie Hebdo* in Paris, but the general sentiment was the same: do not touch traditions through humour, if you are not part of the culture, or else dire consequences might follow. And I wondered then – as I wonder still – was the play in the end the right thing to do? Did we achieve anything beyond creating this controversy in the media?

## *Lovers in Time* – Post Production

One of the strengths of the film is that it is funny as well as sad, and yet I found the editing of this essay film incredibly difficult – traumatic even. Directing and producing the play was in itself an example of practice research (as opposed to practice-based research, that is, the practice is in itself the research) – so much was learnt about how to collaborate across boundaries of history and race; but it is also true that there was a simple necessity of putting on a difficult play very quickly for the festival opening. The film was a different matter entirely, as the process of making it went on a long time after the actual festival. Joe Njagu, a Zimbabwean filmmaker, was my co-director, co-producer, the director of photography and later the film's editor. His creative contribution to the film was extensive – almost as significant as mine. In truth, as he co-directed the film with me, he made many creative decisions on his own, as I was busy directing the lay whilst he was capturing on camera the proceedings – filming a lot of my difficulties whereas I would have perhaps chosen a greater focus on the performers. We made the film together, and there is no doubt in my mind that I would not have been able to get through the *Lovers in Time* furore without Njagu's support. However, it was not a straightforward relationship.

First of all there is an issue of the credit. Joe Njagu refused the co-directing credit for reasons of the political situation at the time. We have subsequently discussed it and he has asked me to keep the credits the way they are. But this was only one of many issues. As a way of interrogating further the white/black and gender dilemmas, Charmaine Mujeri and the white actor who played executioner Shane Stockhil came up with the comedy sketches throughout the film. Their marital spats were often hilarious but also quite close to the bone: in one of them Mujeri's character recalls the incident of her parents-in-law shooting at her with a gun. She shows the scars: 'Look at this, look at this!' The sketch is in the film; however, Joe Njagu prevailed in excluding another sketch in which Mujeri accuses her parents-in-law of setting their dogs on her and her daughter Melody. I actually thought it was a very successful and funny sketch but Njagu said, 'No, it's too much. It is not just funny – it's too painful. This is what happened here. This is what happens still – we must not use it.' And so we didn't. I still remember looking at the screen at the edit and feeling a shame rising through my very bones. This was perhaps the key moment in which I understood what was meant by the white privilege and white shame. I was ashamed then, as I am now, that my own whiteness is a marker of the historical abuse vis-à-vis black Africans.

Another moment when Njagu influenced the film's final shape was also connected to the editing of the comedy sketches. We wanted to be as outrageous as possible during these scenes, so we included scenes in which the couple discuss their sex life. One improvisation produced an unexpected accusation from Mujeri to Stockhil that he 'had a frigging orgy', to which Stockhil's character responds: 'Orgies are very impersonal and we used protection.' I felt a little taken aback at this as the underlying suggestion was that white people were ludicrously immoral – but I let it go; it was funny and Mujeri talked me into keeping it in – as did Njagu: while whites chasing blacks with dogs was too close to the bone, the idea of whites having orgies was deemed to be satire. Conceptually, we were keen that these conversations really pushed the boundaries of the safe and the acceptable, thus dislodging the expectation that any narrative or discourse dealing with race always either had to deploy tragedy in some way or needed to be careful to stay politically correct; however, there were clearly limitations to what we could do.

Towards the end of the shoot, we filmed a scene in which Stockhil, playing the fictional husband of Mujeri, confesses to another member of the cast,

Anthony Mazhetese, that he has developed strong feelings for Michael K: strong, homosexual feelings. At the time, we all thought it was a fantastic turn in the couple's relationship – an unexpected and radical gesture. However, Njagu in the edit absolutely refused to include that scene in the film. It was one of those occasions when I felt we bumped into walls which were simply not to be crossed – either because they had to do with a historical pain, which was still too raw to be laughed at, or because their inclusion would simply be too dangerous. In a country where homosexuality, if not outright illegal, is still looked at very dimly by the authorities, it felt too risky to include references to it in the film. But perhaps there were other considerations, too: Njagu, a practising Christian, may have felt that he could not be associated with a project that somehow implicitly condoned homosexuality. And so the scene was dropped.

In the edit, I left certain things the way Njagu cut them – although I now feel unhappy that the financial arrangements are left unclear in the film. The fact that every cast member got paid well, and even very well by Zimbabwean standards, is far from evident in the documentary – on the contrary: there is a scene in which I appear to be arguing about money with one of the musicians, Discord Makalanga, also known as Lovedale Mafriq. In the wider context, the exchange and the money stood for something that could never be enough, the signifier of white privilege and of a debt that cannot be repaid. During the many screenings of the film in the past two years, this sequence has caused painful discussions, because it seems as if I had short-changed the crew and expected him and others to work hard for $5 a day – which was emphatically not the case. And yet I have decided to leave it the way it is. In truth, if one listens carefully to the dialogue, one can glean the actual circumstances of the matter, namely that the musician in question was paid $700 for his role in the production and was asking for additional travel money over and above the $5 a day he was getting in order to facilitate his transportation. Why I left the sequence uncorrected, I do not know – perhaps I wanted to let Njagu express his sense of the unfairness of life itself, rather than our personal circumstances. Perhaps I did feel guilty – even if there was no need from a factual point of view

Figure 8.4  Writer and co-director Agnieszka Piotrowska (middle) with musicians Pauline Gungidza (left) and Discord Makalanga (right).

– that relatively speaking, the asymmetrical power structures in this encounter were shameful, and that not much could be done to correct the balance, and that this possibility should also be 'on the record'.

## Concluding Remarks

Charmaine Mujeri says at the end of the film, 'You cannot please everybody so you might just as well please yourself! If you don't like what we have made, make something that you like!' As a result of the experience, I have decided to carry on with my research in post-colonial race relations through art. I am involved in various initiatives in Zimbabwe – not really being an observer any more but in some ways part of the arts scene there. My Zimbabwean friends and I set up a creative partnership called Thinking Films in Zimbabwe in later 2015. We have made a number of short fiction films since, as well as a feature film, *Escape*, in late 2016, and a new fiction work written by the notable Zimbabwean writer Stanley Makuwe and directed by me, to be finished in 2019 and called *Repented*. In it we deal with the issue of post-colonial trauma differently, through a love story between two Africans. In November 2017, the Mugabe regime fell in Zimbabwe to ecstatic reactions. On 18 November, during the joyous march on the streets of Harare, I was receiving happy texts from my artistic friends there urging me to join them, which indeed I did do a few weeks later. 'Down with the fear!' they texted.

The filmmaker and feminist thinker Trinh T. Minh-ha observed more than a quarter of a century ago that 'a conversation of "us" with "us" about "them" is a conversation in which "them" is silenced' (1989: 67). She too, like Donna Haraway ([1985] 2008), criticises the patriarchal 'detached "us" discourse' (Trinh 1989: 67), including the attempts of anthropologists to enter other cultures' intimate lives, thereby violating them. Clearly, my engagement in Zimbabwe has been far from detached for better or worse, and I hope that despite my 'otherness' there, there were at least moments when we stopped being 'them' and 'us' and were just a bunch of artists trying to get things done.

Will I change the commentary on the infamous money discussions in the film so that it can stand on its own without me discussing it at screenings? I think not. My long television training taught me to call a piece of work finished when it begins to have a public life. Will I attempt to have the film broadcast on television despite its flaws? Possibly. Perhaps with writing this essay and claiming my film as an essay film, the time has come to let go of it and let it have a life of its own.

*Agnieszka Piotrowska*

## Note

1. For a selection of press responses, see Cheru (2014), Three Men On a Boat (2014), Kangondo (2014), Marunya (2014), Mushawevato (2014), Phiri (2014), Samukange (2014).

## References

Butler, Judith (1997), *The Psychic Life of Power: Theories in Subjection*, Stanford: Stanford University Press.
Cheru, Monica (2014), 'When Paymaster Calls Wrong Tune', *The Herald*, 5 May, <http://www.herald.co.zw/when-paymaster-calls-wrong-tune/> (last accessed 1 March 2018).
Fanon, Frantz [1952] (1975), *Black Skins, White Masks*, London: Pluto Press.
Frosh, Stephen (2013), *Hauntings: Psychoanalysis and Ghostly Transmissions*, Basingstoke: Palgrave Macmillan.
Haraway, Donna [1985] (2008), 'A Manifesto for Cyborgs: Science, Technology, and Socialist Feminism in the 1980s', in Neil Badmington and Julia Thomas (eds), *The Routledge Critical and Cultural Theory Reader*, Abingdon and London: Routledge, pp. 324–55.
James, C. L. R. (1992), 'Notes on Hamlet' (1953), in C. L. R. James, *The C. L. R. James Reader*, ed. Anna Grimshaw, Oxford: Blackwell, pp. 243–6.
Kangondo, Fanuel (2014), 'Nehanda Assassination Dramatised', *The Herald*, 12 April, <http://www.herald.co.zw/nehanda-assassination-dramatised/> (last accessed 1 March 2018).
Khanna, Ranjana (2003), *Dark Continents: Psychoanalysis and Colonialism*, Durham, NC: Duke University Press.
Marunya, Kundai (2014), 'Nehanda as a White Man? "Lovers in Time" Historical Comedy Set for HIFA', *HarareNews*, 14 April, <http://www.hararenews.co.zw/2014/04/nehanda-as-a-white-man-lovers-in-time-historical-comedy-set-for-hifa/> (last accessed 1 March 2018).
Muncey, Tessa (2010), *Creating Autoethnographies*, Portland: Sage Publications.
Mushawevato, Evans (2014), 'HIFA: The Good and Bad', *The Patriot: Celebrating Being Zimbabwean*, 1 May, <http://www.thepatriot.co.zw/old_posts/hifa-the-good-and-bad/> (last accessed 1 March 2018).
Nancy, J. L. (2008), *Corpus*, trans. R. Rand, New York: Fordham University Press.
Phiri, Brenda (2014), 'Producer Seeks Ban on HIFA Play', *The Herald*, 29 April, <http://www.herald.co.zw/producer-seeks-ban-on-hifa-play/> (last accessed 1 March 2018).
Piotrowska, Agnieszka (2014a), 'Mourning and Melancholia at the Harare International Festival of the Arts', *Journal of African Media Studies*, 6:1, 111–30.
Piotrowska, Agnieszka (2014b), *Psychoanalysis and Ethics in Documentary Film*, London: Routledge.
Piotrowska, Agnieszka (2016), 'Lovers in Time – Practice Research in the Times of Patriotic Journalism', *Journal of African Media Studies*, 8:2, 219–38.
Piotrowska, Agnieszka (2017), *Black and White: Cinema, Politics and the Arts in Zimbabwe*, London: Routledge.
Piotrowska, Agnieszka (2018), 'Replacement and Reparation in Sarah Polley's *Stories We Tell*', in Jean Owen and Naomi Segal (eds), *On Replacement*, London: Palgrave Macmillan, pp. 231–41.
Piotrowska, Agnieszka (2019), *The Nasty Woman and the Neo Femme Fatale in Contemporary Cinema*, London and New York: Routledge.

Said, Edward W. [1979] (2003), *Orientalism*, New York: Vintage Books.
Samukange, Tinotenda (2014), 'Hungwe "Zimpunk'd" into Apologising', *NewsDay*, 17 June, <https://www.newsday.co.zw/2014/06/17/hungwe-zimpunkd-apologising/> (last accessed 1 March 2018).
*The Zimbabwean* (2011), '"Rituals" Team Arrested . . . Again', *The Zimbabwean: A Voice for the Voiceless*, 19 February, <http://thezimbabwean.co/2011/02/qritualsq-team-arrestedagain-2/> (last accessed 29 November 2018).
Three Men On a Boat (2014), '"Lovers in Time" Director Pens Open Letter to the Herald Editor', 3-MOB.COM, 30 April, <http://www.3-mob.com/?p=15635#.VYkymVXBzGc> (last accessed 1 March 2018).
Trinh, Minh-ha T. (1989), *Woman, Native, Other: Writing, Postcoloniality, and Feminism*, Bloomington: Indiana University Press.

# PART FOUR

# LANDSCAPES OF TRAUMA

# 9. *NO MAN'S ZONE*: THE ESSAY FILM IN THE AFTERMATH OF THE TSUNAMI IN JAPAN

## Marco Bohr

### Introduction

Produced in the immediate aftermath of the tsunami and earthquake that hit Japan on 11 March 2011, Toshi Fujiwara's film *No Man's Zone* (*Mujin Chitai*, 2012) is a portrait of a country coming to terms with the nuclear fallout in Fukushima. In the feature length documentary film, interviews are interlaced with long takes of the post-apocalyptic landscape and subtle observations that signify the suffering and trauma of the people living in, or uprooted from, the area near the Fukushima Daiichi Nuclear Power Plant. In parallel to these images of a new ecological reality in Fukushima, the film intermittently questions the role of images of the disaster and indeed it questions the role of the filmmaker creating these very images. As such, Fujiwara's film is not just about the nuclear meltdown in Fukushima and how it affected the citizens living in close vicinity of the power plant, but it actually interrogates the legitimacy of the camera in this context. In this chapter I will highlight how the philosophical debate about the role of images produced in a disaster zone is primarily facilitated through the aesthetic, formal and structural device of the essay film. Fujiwara's cinematic journey through the 20 kilometre exclusion zone thus not only feeds into a wider cinematic genre, but it actually utilises the self-reflexivity and subjectivity of the essay film to provoke the viewer in seeing the disaster and, perhaps more importantly, seeing representations of the disaster in a new light.

It is important to note that as Fujiwara embarked on filming *No Man's Zone*, the scale and scope of the nuclear disaster was scarcely apparent.

Relayed in a chronological order, in the first instance the film focuses on the destruction caused by the earthquake and tsunami. However, as Fujiwara commences on his journey through the area around Fukushima, his focus markedly shifts from the natural catastrophe to the manmade disaster of the nuclear fallout. Here, Fujiwara develops an eco-critical perspective that runs counter to the official narrative by the Japanese government that the situation in the Fukushima power plant is contained and under control. One remarkable aspect in *No Man's Zone* is Fujiwara's foresight to identify the severity of the crisis long before it became known to the general public.

Fujiwara's cinematic intervention in Fukushima evokes comparisons to what Anil Narine has defined in psychoanalytical terms as 'eco-trauma cinema' (2015). Narine's term – although it is mostly applied to major studio film productions in his study – is useful here because it adequately describes a self-inflicted and therefore also deeply contradictory trauma which ultimately also endangers mankind. Fujiwara explores this trauma primarily vis-à-vis local citizens in a series of interviews. The impact of the nuclear disaster on the local community is therefore an aspect that is emerging through the narrative structure as the film develops. As I will argue in this chapter, Fujiwara's journey in a physical sense, but also the emerging eco-critical perspective on a conceptual level, is explored through specific visual, aesthetic and narrative devices borrowed from the essay film.[1]

### Setting the Scene

*No Man's Zone* begins with an epic long shot panning across a landscape littered with debris and rubble. The shot functions as a quasi-survey of this new environment, painfully establishing the level of destruction on a scale so large that it is difficult to express in words or indeed images. Filmed with a long telephoto lens, it takes a full three minutes before the camera finally completes this near 360 degree journey across a landscape that has changed beyond recognition. The shot sets the scene for the film in a number of important ways: first, it physically locates the film in the centre of the disaster where the destruction of the tsunami is the most 'visible'. Second, the shot foreshadows a consistent theme, which is explored throughout the film: critiquing and questioning the role as well as the veracity of images of disasters. On the one hand, the 360 degree shot is an attempt to provide the viewer with a visual totality of what has happened on 3.11 – as the disaster is commonly referred to in Japan – yet on the other hand, the slowness of the panning shot as well as the tight crop facilitated by the long telephoto lens allows the viewer to see only a very deliberate framing of the landscape.[2] Last, the shot establishes that Fujiwara is concerned with symbols and visual metaphors that are frequently emphasised through the devices of cinema. The scale of the destruction is not

Figure 9.1 *Opening sequence of No Man's Zone,* Toshi Fujiwara, 2012. © trigon-film.org.

only incidentally mirrored by the monumentality of the panning shot, but it is emphasised through specific cinematic methodologies. A tree, seemingly unharmed by the carnage of the tsunami, appears totally out of place at the beginning of the sequence, whereas the shot ends by focusing on a utility pole, bent and crooked from the destructive forces of the tsunami. In this single take Fujiwara metaphorically explores the tension between a *natural* disaster, as signified by the tree, overtaken in both size and scope by a *manmade* disaster, the nuclear meltdown in Fukushima as signified by the utility pole.

In spite of its apparent simplicity, the shot depicts a remarkable degree of foresight since the utility pole as a visual reference to the Fukushima power plant is in fact a recurring motif throughout the film. Interviews with survivors, the representation of the landscape and the lives of people are, on many occasions, 'framed' by electricity. For instance, Fujiwara depicts a number of interviewees who have become increasingly aware of the fact that the electricity produced by the Fukushima power plant was in fact destined for Tokyo and not for the local area. Without saying as much, local residents feel exploited by the energy company TEPCO, which has received much criticism for how it handled the nuclear meltdown. The social dissent, as subtle as it may be in the context of Japanese culture, is relayed like a series of sometimes surprising discoveries that Fujiwara comes across in the weeks after 3.11. The very methodology of the opening shot thus symbolically relates to this sense of journey, or quest, visually explored in the film. The pan of the camera across the landscape thus foreshadows Fujiwara's own physical movement through the debris and rubble later on in the film, but it also illustrates the gradual process of local citizens recognising that they have been deceived by TEPCO and the official state narrative that nuclear power is a clean and safe energy.

The long and symbolically laden opening scene visually and structurally relates to a number of recent art house films where long takes have been explored to a comparable effect such as Jia Zhangke's *Still Life* (2006), Apichatpong Weerasethakul's *Syndromes and a Century* (2006) or Steve McQueen's *Hunger* (2008).[3] In all of these films the boundaries between narrative and documentary cinema are tested, whereas the long take is one of the primary methods to blur and undermine oversimplified cinematic genres. In these films the long take provides moments of contemplation or indeed a type of visual confrontation, it produces ruptures within the structure of the film, and it functions as an antithesis to the quicker editing favoured by mainstream studio cinema. Pioneered by Russian avant-garde filmmakers such as Mikhail Kalatozov in groundbreaking films such as *I am Cuba/Soy Cuba* (1964), the long take must therefore also be seen as an implicit political act that is meant to question cinematic orthodoxies. *No Man's Zone* mainly differs from these examples in the sense that it is more closely oriented towards the documentary genre and, consequently, the long take provides a more sustained spatiotemporal coherence or a simulacrum of wholeness. Monica Dall'Asta argues that the long take, or what is commonly referred to as *plan-séquence* in Bazinian terms, 'can put the spectator in a condition to assess the authenticity of what is shown on screen' (2011: 62; see also Schoonover 2012: 26). In doing so, Dall'Asta argues, the *plan-séquence* 'allows us to witness not just the visible scene developing before the camera, but the invisible side of the event, the living presence of the look onto the scene from *behind* the image' (2011: 62; original emphasis). On the one hand, the opening scene to *No Man's Zone* thus deeply implicates the viewer in the visual experience of the film; on the other hand, it also provokes the viewer to question the authenticity and veracity of the film from a distance. The tension between these two modes of enquiry is continuously revisited throughout the film via essayistic methods.

## The Presence of the Filmmaker

In his seminal analysis on the essay film, Timothy Corrigan writes that one of the key formulations of the genre is 'a testing of expressive subjectivity' which can most commonly be 'seen in the voice or actual presence of the filmmaker or a surrogate [. . .] sometimes quite visible in the film, sometimes not' (2011: 30). Accordingly, this testing of expressive subjectivity can be explored on a visual level such as by incorporating shots of the filmmakers in the process of producing the film. In *No Man's Zone* this is primarily the case in scenes where Fujiwara can be seen interacting with local residents during interviews or when he is depicted traversing the ravaged landscape. In that sense Fujiwara is physically as well as verbally present in the sense that his body and his voice are intermittently part of the film. These scenes that include or at least allude to the corporality of the filmmaker further highlight the notion of a journey or quest: the film is less about a disaster than it is about a filmmaker making attempts to comprehend the disaster via the medium of cinema. Fujiwara attempts to do this through fairly frequent engagement with local citizens and how their relationship to the land has now dramatically changed: how they cannot pick flowers in their own garden, how they are prohibited to enter certain areas or indeed how they are forced to leave the area altogether. The story that he tells through cinema is that the ecological balance of the region near the power plant was pushed to its limits and now that disaster has struck, the balance is totally out of kilter. The bleakness of the long opening shot thus also foreshadows the bleakness of this growing realisation. All these elements further contribute to the impression that Fujiwara uses the language of cinema very deliberately to create a discursive structure where the spectatorial experience of the film is put into question.

The essayistic dimensions of *No Man's Zone* are further emphasised via the presence of a female voice that partly describes Fujiwara's actions, while partly also questioning his actions. Importantly, this voice – narrated in the English language by the female actor Arsinée Khanjian in a gentle Canadian-Armenian accent – refers to Fujiwara in the third person.[4] The opening shot described above is accompanied by the following voice-over:

> Images of destruction are always difficult to digest. While facing them we become desperate to find a clue to understand, to decode, to measure the size of the damages, maybe as an excuse to cover our secret fascination with them. They become stimulants, often consumed as drugs. Today, perhaps, we have become simply addicted to all images of destruction. (Fujiwara 2012: n.p.)

Treading through the debris and the rubble left behind by the tsunami, Fujiwara strategically applies this voice to continuously question why he is there, and whether or not he should be there in the first place. In this context the voice thus fulfils a quasi-split personality that incorporates both elements: as a surrogate of the filmmaker while also as a critic of the filmmaker at the same time. With regards to the latter, it is important to stress that Fujiwara chose a voice spoken by someone who is quite literally the total opposite in terms of gender, cultural background and accent. Fujiwara uses the Otherness of the voice-over to highlight the philosophical confrontation with regards to his very own presence in the disaster zone. Rachel DiNitto, in her analysis of *No Man's Zone*, writes that the voice-over 'recognizes the film's complicity in the morbid consumption of disaster images' (2014: 344).

The voice-over also fulfils the important function of further situating *No Man's Zone* in the essay film genre. For Laura Rascaroli the essay film requires a single authorial 'voice' that 'approaches the subject matter not in order to present a factual report (the field of the traditional documentary), but to offer an in-depth, personal and thought-provoking reflection' (2008: 35). Perhaps one of the best-known cases where the essayistic voice is explored with a powerful effect is the film *Sans Soleil* (1983) directed by the French artist and filmmaker Chris Marker.[5] Yet not just through the presence of a voice, *No Man's Zone* also appears to reference *Sans Soleil* with regard to the subject matter as Marker's classic film – considered by both Rascaroli and Corrigan as a key benchmark in the genre – primarily focuses on Japan's futuristic consumer culture in the early 1980s (Rascaroli 2009: 27). More specifically, in *Sans Soleil* the voice makes a rather specific statement about Japan and its relationships to frequent disasters that eerily relates to Fujiwara's cinematic project nearly three decades later:

> Poetry is born of insecurity: wandering Jews, quaking Japanese; by living on a rug that jesting nature is ever ready to pull out from under them they've got into the habit of moving about in a world of appearances: fragile, fleeting, revocable, of trains that fly from planet to planet, of samurai fighting in an immutable past. That's called 'the impermanence of things'.

Seen in a post-3.11 context, Marker's acute observation on Japanese attitudes towards the fragility of nature is rather poignant. Fujiwara appears to have borrowed from Marker not just by including an omnipresent, all-seeing and all-questioning voice, but also in what the voice tends to subjectively and self-reflexively observe. For instance, in *No Man's Zone* the voice can be heard observing the body language of interviewees, analysing the fact that while they will not express their resignation about the disaster in words, they do this in a more dignified way through silence.

Silence can also be applied in a more aggressive way, however. In August 2011, footage of a security video emerged on the Internet which depicted an anonymous Fukushima worker fully covered in a protective suit and gas mask pointing his finger at the camera for a prolonged period of time. Through this simple but also confrontational gesture, the footage represented an act of defiance and subversion. It later turned out that this was a performance art piece by Kota Takeuchi, an emerging artist, whose pointing gesture was meant to reference Vito Acconci's work titled *Centers* (1971). This type of direct confrontation against corporate or state structures is rare, or at least it rarely receives much media attention in Japan, and it is for this reason that the pointing man video caused widespread consternation – even amongst art critics frustrated by the fact that Takeuchi never actually fully admitted to being the man in the video (Sawaragi 2012). *No Man's Zone* is more subtle in the sense that interviewees express their dissatisfaction through long pauses in speech, restrained facial movements or discomfort signified by body language to indicate a sense of resignation. This is where Fujiwara's film indeed becomes a portrait in the true sense of the word – a portrait of a people quickly giving up hope.

These partly ad hoc and partly staged instances where Fujiwara asks locals questions about how the disaster has affected them bears a resemblance to theatre, whereas the voice provides an additional commentary about what has been unfolding on the metaphorical stage. In the first instance, the voice in *No Man's Zone* situates the film within the international essay film genre, referencing very prominently the work of Chris Marker and his mesmerising depiction of Japanese image culture in the early 1980s. Like in *Sans Soleil*, in *No Man's Zone* the voice functions as an epistemological nodal point between the film-maker, the image and the viewer. Beyond that, however, in *No Man's Zone* the voice continuously questions the role of images as well as the role of those producing images in the aftermath of the disaster. By doing so the voice actually attacks the very structure within which it operates. It is the voice, therefore, that makes *No Man's Zone* a deeply self-referential and also self-critical cinematic journey into notions of ecological trauma, memory and 'truth'.

## The Journey

One of the key elements in *No Man's Zone* is the overriding theme of a journey. This is established with the very first shot, which in itself mimics the physical act of a journey signified by the camera panning across the rubble. The theme is further emphasised by the narrative structure, which broadly follows a chronological order: the journey begins within the 20 kilometre exclusion zone where local residents struggle to deal with the ecological trauma in the immediate aftermath of the tsunami, and it ends outside of this zone after the government shuts down all access to the area as the nuclear crisis worsens. The chronological depiction of the journey thus also has topographical implications as Fujiwara and his team are pushed further and further away from the epicentre of the nuclear meltdown in Fukushima. Several shots depicting Fujiwara as he crosses from one side of the frame to the other allude to this very process of increasingly being pushed further afield as the nuclear crisis worsens.

Yet in addition to the journey in a physical sense, Fujiwara also undergoes a psychological journey, which becomes more complex the more time he spends near the stricken nuclear power facility in Fukushima. At the beginning of the film it seems that Fujiwara was primarily interested in the effects of the earthquake and the tsunami. His focus, therefore, was on the physical level of destruction caused by the natural disaster. Yet as the situation in Fukushima worsens, Fujiwara is increasingly drawn to the nuclear crisis. In doing so, Fujiwara confronts an important contradiction, which is also being addressed by the voice-over: how can images visually capture a disaster which is caused by invisible radiation? Nicholas Vroman describes this ambitious aim as follows: 'Fujiwara attempts to film the unfilmable' (2015: 18). The invisibility of the nuclear disaster that Fujiwara attempts to record with his camera evokes Rob Nixon's (2011) influential concept of 'slow violence', which he defines as a type of violence wrought on the Earth by climate change, toxic drift, pollution and so forth. In contrast to spectacle-driven environmental disasters, Nixon argues that our current capitalist system, which is dominated by corporate interests, ignores the gradual and often invisible dangers of these disasters to our ecology.

Fujiwara's strategy to represent this type of slow violence in spite of its apparent invisibility is to focus on visual metaphors. In one scene he comments on the beauty of a bed of flowers planted by an elderly woman living not too far from Fukushima. For fear of radiation poisoning, the government has requested that no organic material be physically handled, and all this woman can now do is to watch her garden deteriorate. Via metaphors such as these, Fujiwara makes a powerful argument in his film: it is perhaps not the disaster in itself but the subsequent helplessness that is causing the most pain to local residents. Yet the aesthetic appreciation of the elderly woman's garden is creating another apparent contradiction that needs to be emphasised here: on the one hand, the film is concerned with the ugliness of the disaster signified by endless rubble and debris; on the other hand, the film is intermittently concerned with subjects that signify beauty. In his series of daguerreotypes 'Here and There', the Japanese photographer Takashi Arai created a similar visual dichotomy by photographing flowers that, although beautiful and visually attractive, are now poisoned. Like Arai, Fujiwara strategically uses this visual binary between the beauty and the poisonousness of a flower to emphasise the ugliness caused by nuclear radiation.

These visual binaries, however, not only are created through what is being depicted, but also show *how* it is being depicted from a cinematographic and indeed optical perspective. It is quite apparent that Fujiwara and his team paid acute attention to framing the landscape through mise-en-scène and a clear focus on rich textures and colours. Combined with careful observations, which are emphasised by long takes, *No Man's Zone* is a surprisingly beautiful film, consistently drawing the viewer into the subject matter. The image of Fujiwara traversing the rubble creates a powerful image that finds its origins, amongst other historic and visual precedents, in German romanticist painting. The figure in the landscape was a visual trope tackled by artists such as Caspar

Figure 9.2 The framing of natural beauty in *No Man's Zone*, Toshi Fujiwara, 2012. © trigon-film.org.

David Friedrich whose works alluded to the subliminal beauty of nature as experienced by man. To emphasise the awe elicited by looking at the landscape, Friedrich incorporated in his paintings a single figure, or what is commonly referred to as *Rückenfigur* (literally 'back figure'), a subject whose back is turned to the viewer of the image (see Koerner 2009). By looking at the back of the figure, the viewer is asked to focus not so much on the beauty of nature, as on the visual and awe-inspiring experience of *looking* at nature. The figure in the landscape, a visual technique previously explored by filmmakers such as Alexandr Sokurov, thus emphasises a spectatorial as well as phenomenological experience of the natural environment (Panse 2006). A similar effect is created in *No Man's Zone*, because it is only through Fujiwara actually walking through and being situated within the landscape that the viewer is able to appreciate the magnitude of the disaster and its effects on the surrounding area. In other words, the viewer looks at the landscape via Fujiwara physically experiencing it. The figure in the landscape motif also fulfils the function of repopulating the barren landscape. In doing so, Fujiwara actually embodies a sense of hope for the region that would be missing if he himself were absent from the frame.

## The Presence and Absence of the State

The depiction of a lone figure traversing a post-apocalyptic landscape is one of the most powerful motifs consistently explored in *No Man's Zone*. This motif strongly alludes to Andrei Tarkovsky's fantastical depiction of a post-nuclear event in *The Stalker* (1979). On a visual level both films share the same focus on an individual figure traversing a scarred landscape sealed off from the outside world by the state. 'The zone', as it is referred to in both films, thus relates to a totally new form of space where the normal rule of law is suspended. As Fujiwara documents, even long after the disaster, the bodies of the deceased remain uncollected and access to private property is tightly controlled; in some cases, properties are seized or destroyed. On this journey through the *No Man's Zone*, Fujiwara thus becomes increasingly aware of the role of the state: not necessarily that of helping victims or survivors, but rather in many cases trying to control their movements or limit their access to their homes. The visual style of following the director on a surreal journey fulfils the important purpose of representing the post-nuclear landscape as a metaphor for psychological trauma.[6]

In this space where the rule of law is suspended, inversed or at the least perverted, Fujiwara's only contact with 'the state' is via a brief encounter with what the voice describes as the 'ghostly figures': men dressed in white protective suits combing through the landscape looking for the deceased. In one short scene these ghosts confront the filmmaker and ask him what he is doing in the exclusion zone. These figures are represented as anonymous, from a distance, almost inhuman and operating in a team or a pack – thus signifying the anonymity of the state as a bureaucratic apparatus that lacks compassion and empathy. It is in this context that *No Man's Zone* becomes a deeply political film, consistently questioning the role of the state and its actors. Midway through the film, the voice in *No Man's Zone* relates the state's decision to close off access to the zone to images of the disaster produced and further disseminated by this very film: 'Because cameras rarely came here, its destruction went unnoticed as if it never happened. What is not recorded as an image goes by as if it never existed' (Fujiwara 2012: n.p.).

Following this line of thought, Fujiwara reveals that the decision to seal off access to the zone was partially related to stopping or, at the very least, to controlling what type of image could be produced in this area. As recounted by the voice, Fujiwara implicates himself and other filmmakers in the government's decision to do so: in order to remain in control of the narrative that the nuclear crisis is contained, all access to images, and thus also the production of images, needed to be tightly controlled. Since he was operating outside of press journalist unions or state-controlled media companies, the authorities had, up until the area was sealed off, virtually no control over Fujiwara's film project. The access, or the lack thereof, to produce images of a disaster thus has very powerful implications with regard to the reading of the film: are disasters becoming part of our collective memory only once they have been represented in images? *No Man's Zone* raises the very problematic possibility that the state actively hinders the production of images of the zone in order to avoid the disaster becoming part of a nation's collective memory.

In his reading of *No Man's Zone*, Joel Neville Anderson argues that Fujiwara 'grounds his sharp critique of the state-corporate complex in a natural setting. He thereby raises the stake for asserting a personal appreciation of images and their creation' (2015: 227). Anderson argues that this politicisation of the landscape is historically located in the 'landscape theory' or *fūkei-ron* of Japanese experimental films of the late 1960s. According to the director Masao Adachi, the basic principle of this theory centres on the notion that all representations of landscapes are 'essentially related to the figure of a ruling power' (in Sharp 2007: n.p.). This position against the state can be similarly found in the so-called Provoke Era of photographers from the late 1960s and early 1970s, whose work questioned the media's biased representation of the student uprisings in Japan at the time (Bohr 2011). This level of criticality towards representation and media representation, in particular, surfaces to a similar degree in *No Man's Zone* where the very fabric of the image is consistently questioned. Indeed, this self-awareness about the image and its ideological power functions itself as a metaphor for the growing dissent emerging in Japan in the wake of the Fukushima disaster. As William Andrews (2015) has argued, the Fukushima disaster saw the re-emergence of social dissent and anti-government protests that can be traced to Japan's turbulent post-war years. Fujiwara's explicit focus on a landscape now poisoned by the nuclear meltdown seeks to reveal the structures of oppression that underpin and perpetuate a political system that stood for economic growth at all costs, and one that is increasingly reaching its limit.

From a transnational perspective Winnie Lai Man Yee (2013) situates *No Man's Zone* within the context of a new generation of documentary East Asian filmmakers concerned with what she describes as 'eco-consciousness', highlighting the state's implicit involvement in the destruction of our ecosystems. One of the most powerful aspects of the film is that the methodology of this critique via the medium of cinema is itself the subject of that critique as well. Midway through the film, almost as if to question the very purpose of not just making but actually watching the film, the voice can be heard saying, 'for the last hour we were watching images – just images' (Fujiwara 2012: n.p.). *No Man's Zone* thus emerges as a type of meta-cinema, or a cinema about cinema, which makes itself the subject of the critique.

## Conclusion

*No Man's Zone* is a film that questions the role of the production of images, the attempt to control images as well as the consumption of images in the context of the nuclear crisis in Fukushima. Fujiwara thus engages in a constant push and pull: on the one hand, he is trying to justify the presence of his camera but, on the other hand, he is questioning whether it fulfils any real purpose other than sensationalising the event. This struggle is most apparent in the attempts to depict the disaster in visual terms such as via the motif of the lone figure traversing the post-apocalyptic landscape. Yet Fujiwara also deals with invisible or hidden subjects: not least the fact that nuclear radiation is invisible to the eye, but also the hidden hand of the state apparatus in promoting nuclear energy throughout much of the post-war period and failing to manage the meltdown now that disaster has struck. Fujiwara tackles these subjects via metaphors and visual allegories and thus raises the visibility of these subjects in cinematic terms. Essayistic methods such as self-reflexivity and subjectivity do not just provide the viewer with a deeply personalised investigation into the aftermath of the nuclear disaster, but they actually critique the political and ideological structures within which these images operate.

Fujiwara's film provides a powerful subversion of the official state narrative that tends to focus on the recovery or the rebuilding of the disaster-stricken area. In reality, however, and Fujiwara already alludes to this even in the early days of the nuclear meltdown, the crisis is far from resolved and it will likely be several decades before the area becomes habitable again – if indeed it will ever be. Yet unlike Kota Takeuchi's pointing finger, Fujiwara delivers his criticism of the corporate–political nuclear complex with great subtlety and introspection. This critique is mainly facilitated through the aesthetic, structural and formal devices borrowed from the essay film. By using the essayistic format, Fujiwara has not just made a film about a complex, surreal and often contradictory crisis, but he actually relates the crisis – its visibility and indeed invisibility – back to the viewer.

## Notes

1. The potential convergence between essay film and eco-cinema or eco-critical cinema is a yet underdeveloped area of academic research. One reason for this is that the essay film usually evades cinematic conventions and classifications. Werner Herzog's critically acclaimed *Grizzly Man* (2006) is one of only a small handful of films that has been analysed in relation to both the essay film (Corrigan 2012) and eco-cinema (Brereton 2013). Though as I want to make clear in this chapter, the essay film provides a significant opportunity to explore eco-critical issues from a new and sometimes self-critical perspective.
2. As recounted in an interview with the film critic Chris Fujiwara, Toshi Fujiwara had a considerable dispute with the cameraman who was opposed to using such a long telephoto lens for this shot for fear he might capture dead bodies (Fujiwara 2012).
3. Weerasethakul's and Fujiwara's artistic practice is also connected more concretely: Weerasethakul provided the voice-over for Fujiwara's short experimental film *Walk* (2003).
4. Arsinée Khanjian is the wife of the Canadian film director Atom Egoyan.
5. Similar to Fujiwara's film, the voice in Marker's *Sans Soleil* is female. The pace, accent and softness of the voice are all comparable to Marker's groundbreaking work.
6. A post-nuclear landscape similarly coalesces with personal psychological trauma in Alain Resnais's film *Hiroshima, Mon Amour* (1959).

## References

Anderson, Joel Neville (2015), 'Cinema in Reconstruction: Japan's Post 3.11 Documentary', in Alan Wright (ed.), *Film on the Faultline*, Bristol: Intellect, pp. 215–32.

Andrews, William (2015), *Dissenting Japan: A History of Japanese Radicalism and Counterculture, from 1945 to Fukushima*, London: Hurst Publishers.

Bohr, Marco (2011), 'Are-Bure-Boke: Distortions in Late 1960s Japanese Cinema and Photography', *Dandelion*, 2:2, 1–15.

Brereton, Pat (2013), 'Appreciating the Views: Filming Nature in *Into the Wild*, *Grizzly Man*, and *Into the West*', in Stephen Rust, Salma Monani and Sean Cubitt (eds), *Ecocinema Theory and Practice*, New York: Routledge, pp. 213–32.

Corrigan, Timothy (2011), *The Essay Film: From Montaigne, After Marker*, Oxford and New York: Oxford University Press.

Corrigan, Timothy (2012), 'The Pedestrian Ecstasies of Werner Herzog: On Experience, Intelligence, and the Essayistic', in Brad Prager (ed.), *A Companion to Werner Herzog*, Oxford: Blackwell, pp. 80–98.

Dall'Asta, Monica (2011), 'Beyond the Image in Benjamin and Bazin: The Aura of the Event', in Dudley Andrew and Hervé Joubert-Laurencin (eds), *Opening Bazin: Postwar Film Theory and Its Afterlife*, Oxford: Oxford University Press, pp. 57–65.

DiNitto, Rachel (2014), 'Narrating the Cultural Trauma of 3.11: The Debris of Post-Fukushima Literature and Film', *Japan Forum*, 26:3, 340–60.

Fujiwara, Toshi (2012), 'A Conversation with Toshi Fujiwara about No Man's Zone. Interview by Chris Fujiwara', <http://www.docandfilm.com/pdf_press/2012_02_InterviewToshiFujiwaraFullVersion.pdf> (last accessed 21 August 2015).

Koerner, Joseph Leo (2009), *Caspar David Friedrich and the Subject of Landscape*, London: Reaktion Books.

Narine, Anil (2015), 'Introduction: Eco-Trauma Cinema', in Anil Narine (ed.), *Eco-Trauma Cinema*, London: Routledge, pp. 1–24.

Nixon, Rob (2011), *Slow Violence and the Environmentalism of the Poor*, London: Harvard University Press.

Panse, Silke (2006), 'The Filmmaker as *Rückenfigur*, Documentary as Painting: Alexandr Sokurov in "Elegy of a Voyage"', *Third Text: Critical Perspectives on Contemporary Art & Culture*, 20:1, 9–25.

Rascaroli, Laura (2008), 'The Essay Film: Problems, Definitions, Textual Commitments', *Framework*, 49:2, 24–47.

Rascaroli, Laura (2009), *The Personal Camera: Subjective Cinema and the Essay Film*, London: Wallflower Press.

Sawaragi, Noi (2012), 'Criticism "Points Its Finger": Kota Takeuchi and the Finger-Pointing Plant Worker', *Bijutsu Techo* (Special Edition distributed at Art Hong Kong) [originally published in *Bijutsu Techo*, December 2011], n.p.

Schoonover, Karl (2012), *Brutal Vision: The Neorealist Body in Postwar Italian Cinema*, Minneapolis: University of Minnesota Press.

Sharp, Jasper (2007), 'Masao Adachi', *Midnight Eye*, 21 August, <http://www.midnighteye.com/interviews/masao-adachi/> (last accessed 30 November 2018).

Vroman, Nicholas (2015), 'No Man's Zone', in John Berra (ed.), *Directory of World Cinema: Japan 3*, Bristol: Intellect, pp. 17–19.

Yee, Winnie Lai Man (2013), 'Of Ruins and Silence: Topographical Writing of Nature and Urban in Three Asian Documentaries', *The 8th International Convention of Asia Scholars* (ICAS 8), Macau, China, 24–7 June.

# 10. 'IMAGE-WRITING': THE ESSAYISTIC/ SANWEN IN CHINESE NONFICTION CINEMA AND ZHAO LIANG'S BEHEMOTH

## Kiki Tianqi Yu

### INTRODUCTION

*Yingxiang xiezuo* (影像写作), literally meaning 'image writing', is an independent nonfiction film practice of experimenting with, and 'writing' through, moving images as artistic expression and intervention in the politics of contemporary mainland China.[1] As a concept, it is similar to the *caméra-stylo* advocated by Alexandre Astruc in 1948 (Astruc 1992), but its motivation and aesthetic features are rooted in China's cultural, social and political reality. The aesthetic form associated with *yingxiang xiezuo* is influenced by a Chinese literary essay tradition, cultural expression and the socio-political conditions in China. The essay film in the west is usually closely linked with the French *Rive Gauche* filmmakers, or *Nouvelle Vague* filmmakers such as Chris Marker, Alain Resnais or Agnès Varda (Elsaesser 2017: 243). As a mode of filmmaking the essay film has become increasingly popular on the documentary film festival circuit and has caught increasing academic attention, yet specific Chinese traditions of the essayistic in nonfiction filmmaking have not been sufficiently acknowledged yet. Non-western films, including those from China, are usually thrown in the category of 'world cinema' or specific national context art exhibitions, and their distribution and circulation are largely subject to the changing politics and economics of programming and curating such films in the western world.

Essayistic nonfiction film could be seen as more explicitly literary and linguistically linked than other forms of cinema. The core of essay film practice is to create a subjective expression or impression of the world. Hence, the complexity of such an expression based on the on-going interaction between the audio-visual and the verbal deserves nuanced consideration. Current criticism and theorisation around the essay film, however, is largely rooted in western cultural and social contexts. Features of the essayistic and the 'screen-writing' process in cultures with different socio-political contexts, distinctive cultural, philosophical and literary traditions, as well as unrelated linguistic structures require alternative methods of interrogation. I am not arguing here for a completely unique set of aesthetics of these films, but I do aim to draw readers' attention to the literary, socio-political, linguistic and artistic traditions these films inherit from their culture, whilst also benefiting from transnational 'contaminations'.

'Screen-writing' for essayistic cinema includes a complex on-going process of filming or collecting, (re)writing and (re-)editing moving image materials. In the following, I seek to unpack how this process is practised as 'image writing' by a group of Chinese independent filmmakers. First, I contextualise the act of 'image writing' in contemporary Chinese socio-political reality and demonstrate how this act is similarly motivated by a form of intellectual social engagement known from ancient China. I also show how 'image writing' inherits the aesthetics of the scattered vision and ideographic expression of the Chinese language essay, *sanwen* (散文), literally meaning 'loose text' or 'scattered writings' (Handler-Spitz 2010: 113). Then I provide a detailed analysis of Zhao Liang's *Behemoth* (*Bei Xi Mo Shuo*, 2015) in order to show how Zhao's thoughts are 'written' on the screen, both explicitly and implicitly, through rhetoric techniques such as *paibi* (排比) or 'parallelism' and *hongtuo* (烘托) or 'juxtaposition'. Admittedly, the very fact that I am writing this essay and addressing issues of Chinese essayistic moving image practices *in English* reflects the complexities of expression beyond translation. A closer look at Zhao's filmic work may shed light on the ways the essay film can be understood internationally.

## 'Image Writing' and Personal Voice

The discourse around creative artistic expression in contemporary China is inevitably a political one. Although the search for an original voice in cinematic aesthetics and narrative strategies is a desire among many Chinese filmmakers – and this is the case irrespective of whether their work is market-oriented, politically safe or made to explicitly resist mainstream ideology – independent cinema has been more tightly controlled since Xi Jinping's leadership in 2012. Returning to China in 2013 to live there until 2017 gave me an immersive ethnographic experience to understand the changed and continuously changing cinema culture. In 2013, independent film festivals or *yingzhan*

(影展, film exhibition),[2] including the 5th Yunfest, the Visual Anthropological Documentary Biennale[3] and Beijing Independent Film Festival (BIFF),[4] were repeatedly forced to close down as a result of a wider national crackdown on independent cultural activities. China Independent Film Festival (CIFF) in Nanjing was also warned to 'go quiet'.[5]

Parallel to the diminishing of the independent filmmaking community[6] is the rise and proliferation of state-supported youth film festivals across different regions and provinces in China. It is a typical response to the call for developing China's creative industries and strengthening cultural confidence. Many filmmakers, especially the younger generation, embrace the new environment, which means no political risk, more financial support from the government and private investors, more exposure, possible theatrical release and online streaming, but also more self-censorship, even before state censorship is applied. The notion of independence has also changed from a political position alternative to the mainstream ideology to a production mode which means independently seeking funding, including state grants. Some documentaries produced recently in this mode have received domestic theatrical release and surprising box office success, and they also match the themes of promoting Chinese heritage or nationalist sentiment.[7] However, not all formerly independent filmmakers can quickly reorient themselves and many are reluctant to adapt. Political and economic constraints on the one pole of what Pierre Bourdieu regards as 'the field of power' in the field of cultural production (1993) have become overwhelmingly heavy.

Having been making film in that context and researching the changing cinema culture in China myself, I noticed the idea of *yingxiang xiezuo* or 'image writing', which is advocating filmmaking as a form of personal writing with a camera. This form of audio-visual writing is cherished especially amongst an older generation of independent filmmakers in China. At a Yunfest special event in Hunan in 2012, filmmakers including Cong Feng, Gui Shuzhong, Hu Xinyu, He Yun, Lin Xi, Li Xiaofeng, Mao Chenyu, Qiong Jiongjiong, Wu Wenguang and Ma Li (as the only female voice) gathered together and founded the quarterly journal *Dianying Zuozhe* 电影作者 – *Film Auteur*, conceptually influenced by the French New Wave. These filmmakers consider themselves *auteurs* or 'film *zuozhe*', that is, persons who 'write' with images, and many of them practise essayistic nonfiction. Apart from these filmmakers, artist-filmmakers such as Zhao Liang, Gao Shiqiang and Kang He also deploy essayistic image writing, including in experimental installation works.[8]

Image writing maximises the creative autonomy of a filmmaker and puts the filmmaker-self at the centre, hence celebrating the 'voice' of the creator. I discuss the rise of subjective first person cinema and its motivations in an individualising China in my monograph *'My' Self on Camera* (Yu 2018), highlighting both artistic experimentation in nonfiction cinema and ethical tensions surrounding this practice. Image writing practice continues the essence of first person nonfiction cinema, but expands artistic expression. The self in image writing is not necessarily the focal point; instead, the subjective commentary on the socio-political reality is given more attention, which is addressed through either direct first person narration, or implicit personal critique. In other words, image writing not only stresses the filmmakers' ambition to experiment with innovative forms of filmmaking, but also foregrounds their desire to expand a space of personal expression in the political and industrial context of China of the 2010s as described above. When verbal language is inadequate to this task, writing with images can be more expressive. Image writing, in this sense, is a political act, allowing the filmmaker to critically comment on issues that are too sensitive to openly discuss under oppressive or adverse conditions.

Aesthetically, image writing inherits the seemingly 'loose' structure and 'scatteredness' (Handler-Spitz 2010: 113) of the literary essay or *sanwen* in Chinese, which refers to nonfiction writings that express an author's subjective thoughts with less rigid structures.[9] Chinese prose forms such as *sanwen* (scattered writings), *suibi* (the brush follows) and *xiaoping* (small appraisals), which were well established in the Tang and Song dynasties (c. 618–1279), proliferated in late Ming China (1573–1644), when Montaigne's *Essais* also emerged as a new form of prose writing in late sixteenth-century France (Handler-Spitz 2010: 110). Montaigne's essays and Chinese versions of this form share many similarities, such as their scattered quality, inclusiveness, spontaneity and temporary mode, aiming to raise thoughts and provoke questions rather than offer conclusions (Pollard 2000; Kafalas 2007; Handler-Spitz 2010). In early modern France and Ming China, essays were seen as a response to 'large-scale transformations occurring in both societies' (Handler-Spitz 2010: 114). Such an intellectual reaction to the social change through literature continued when the modern form of the essay emerged in early twentieth-century China.

Late Qing political reformer, intellectual and writer Liang Qichao (1873–1929) put forward a concept of 'new style' writing or *xinwenti*, and emphasised the emancipation of thoughts and writing with emotions in more vernacular language (Wang 2007). This concept was further developed by early Republican intellectuals, writers and reformists such as Chen Duxiu, Lu Xun, Zhou Zuoren and Hu Shi during the New Literature Movement (1917–19). Vernacular essay practice, expressing one's thoughts in the vernacular as opposed to the classical literary language, flourished from 1919 onwards (Wang 2007; Zheng 2009).[10] Image writing as a personal vernacular expression also highlighted socio-political engagement in China of the 2010s.

Filmmaker Cong Feng sees image writing primarily as a social engagement and advocates the concept of *pinfa dianying* or 'poor cinema', a filmmaking practice with little financial, human or technical resources, presenting ordinary, everyday life stories and events. Images are kept in a 'rough', rather than exquisite, state, and the main objective is social criticism. In his 'Pinfa Dianying de Renwu' ('Tasks of Poor Cinema'), he states:

> Writing is an inevitable overflow of the things society cannot digest – an expression of those things that are difficult to express but must be expressed. In a world overwhelmingly dominated by image media, the responsibility of image writing must be to digest such a reality, using writing 'bacteria' to infect everything that needs to be examined. (Cong 2016: 115; originally written in Chinese, my translation)

This engagement with the society echoes a long tradition of male intellectuals showing concern for national fate and social change. It is worth mentioning that 'image writing' as an intellectual practice is still very male dominated, mirroring the scene of independent cinema in China, or Chinese society at large, which is still very patriarchal.[11] It also reflects the 'cultural fever' (Wang 1996; Zhang 1997) during the relatively liberal period of the mid to late 1980s, when public debates on the nation's fate, culture and political system in the wake of China's opening up became a national concern. This nationwide intellectual debate eventually led to the violent Tian'an men crackdown and, consequently, the shifting focus on furthering economic developments as well as de-emphasising the political reform and ideology. The filmmaker Sha Qing comments, 'the problem of expression to a great extent comes from our history, as there has been a fear of expression' (Sha, author's interview, 2017). Through cinema this fear is contested: first, through the observational style that emerged in the late 1980s, and, second, through the first person filmmaking practice that emerged during the DV-wave at the turn of the twenty-first century. Image writing continues in that same spirit.

Capturing images is similar to taking notes or making *suibi*, that is, letting 'the brush follow'. Wu Wenguang reveals, 'the mode of image writing is that no matter who you are, where you are, you can always take a camera and film' (in Huang 2013: n.p.). Later filmmakers, such as Cong Feng, Mao Chenyu and Kang He, frequently compare editing to writing, albeit on a timeline where the writer needs to deal with both duration and space (Kang 2017). Writer, theatre director and filmmaker Kang He understands image writing to be a continuation of the writer's identity. In his more than six-hour-long *Nihao Yuandian* (*Hello, the Original Point*, 2017), Kang starts with a sequence that presents him 'writing' on the screen. He is seen smoking and sitting with his back to the camera in front of a computer screen, in what looks like a personal space. Then the scene cuts to a close-up of the computer screen, revealing that he is 'writing' on the timeline of an editing program. Another filmmaker, Mao Chenyu, approaches the world through an ethnographic lens, deploying materials from his familiar paddy fields in rural China for his socially oriented image writing.

Given its stress on personal subjective expression, its aesthetic heritage from the literary *sanwen* and its emphasis on vernacular expression and social engagement, image writing resonates with the European notion of the essay film. Timothy Corrigan argues that 'an expressive subjectivity, commonly seen in the voice or actual presence of the filmmaker or a surrogate, has become one of the most recognizable signs of the essay film' (2011: 30). Examining the textual commitments and the spectatorial pact, Laura Rascaroli states that in essay film, it is '"I", the author, [. . .] reflecting on a problem, and shar[ing] my thoughts with you, the spectator' (2009: 15). For Rascaroli, 'The essay, is always subjective, but is not necessarily autobiographical' (16).

Expression in image writing or essay film practice is strongly linked to the expressivity of language in correlation with other audio-visual elements. Commenting on Marker's *Letter from Siberia* (*Lettre de Sibérie*, 1958) as 'an essay documented by film', André Bazin emphasises that 'the primary material is intelligence, that its immediate means of expression is language, and that the image only intervenes in the third position, in reference to this verbal intelligence' (2017: 103). Rascaroli argues that the verbal register is not the only place where the thinking occurs; instead, she focuses on the role of narration where the verbal is a part. For her, the essay film is 'a specific form of textuality, and narration is a constitutive element of its epistemological and signifying strategies' (2017: 144). Reflecting on art's relation to linguistic difference, T. J. Demos emphasises that 'the essay film creates a space of heterogeneity', 'a space of multilingual construction', where the language and the visual continually interact and modulate each other, as its 'very fundamental basis' (in Mamula 2016: 65). As a tool for forming, acquiring, analysing, interpreting, theorising and communicating our knowledge, language has a strong impact on the formation of culture and vice versa; language constructs thoughts, which could be expressed through or as moving image. What is usually emphasised is the structure or the style of an argument or narration that delivers these thoughts. I argue that the nature of language itself should also be noticed, as should the culture in which it is uttered.

Different languages and cultures have different rhetorical devices to mirror and structure thought; the ideographic Chinese language character also influences the construction and expression of meaning.[12] How do the literary and the linguistic *write* themselves into the moving image? And how does the expression of a particular language signify the cultural and social traces? The provocativeness of the language is often emphasised as postmodern and poststructuralist critique that originates in the west. As Christa Blümlinger argues, the essay 'seek[s] to prevent documentary images from drifting into the picturesque or spectacular, and cast[s] doubt on the univocity of photography'

(2016: 177). In transnational essay films, that is, works by artists outside of their cultural origins or by diasporic artists, the choice of language(s) should also be given attention, as emphasised in 'accented cinema' (Naficy 2001). For example, in Trinh T. Minh-ha's *Surname Viet Given Name Nam* (1989) and *Forgetting Vietnam* (2016), which explore female repression in Vietnam, modernity and problems of representation, the language of narration and the filmmaker's play on words to interpret and interrupt the images is predominantly English. Made for international and often western intellectual audiences, these films indicate her position as a transnational intellectual, placing postmodern thoughts onto the seemingly more distant culture of Vietnam, the other side of her 'self'. Similar cases can also be found with transnational Chinese artist-filmmakers.[13]

Undeniably, the circulation of films and theories from the so-called west and neighbouring countries in China also plays an important role in forming ideas of film practice locally. Chinese filmmakers have benefited from access to pirate DVDs and online downloading since the 1990s, as key sources of cinema education. Alternative nonfiction films and moving image art, such as those by Chris Marker, Jean-Luc Godard, Agnès Varda, Isaac Julien and Apichatpong Weerasethakul, have also been disseminated in China recently. In addition, Robert Bresson's philosophical notebook *Notes on Cinematography* (1975) has been translated and shared, especially his idea of cinema as a form of writing. Chinese translations of recent theories on essay films, such as Rascaroli's *Personal Camera* (2009; see Yu et al. 2014), have also gained popularity among Chinese readers and filmmakers. Appropriation, pastiche and homage to foreign films and art can be recognised in Chinese filmmakers' works, but image writing is foremost a specific response to the Chinese reality and is fundamentally a socially and culturally rooted intellectual practice.

The essayistic expression in such films inherits Chinese literary and art aesthetics and the rhetorical styles that filmmakers are familiar with. Meanings are scattered through various expressive methods and ideographic descriptions. Conventional rhetorical techniques of literary writing, such as *paibi* (parallelism), *hongtuo* (juxtaposition or contrast), *jiedai* (metonymy) or *fanyu* (irony), can be identified in these films in the way moving image materials are assembled. In the following, I focus on Zhao Liang's *Behemoth* (2015) to illuminate how image writing employs techniques from the Chinese literary essay, on the one hand, and recurs on Dante's *The Divine Comedy* (1308–20), on the other hand, to document and reconfigure conditions of labour and oppression that are socially and historically specific to mainland China but express global concerns.

EXPRESSING THE IMPOSSIBLE THROUGH SILENCE AND THE IDEOGRAPHIC:
ZHAO'S *BEHEMOTH*

*Behemoth* (2015) is an experimental nonfiction film by the internationally acclaimed filmmaker, moving image artist and photographer Zhao Liang.[14] The film has won several awards, including the Venice Film Festival Green Drop Award 2015.[15] Zhao is well known for his politically engaged documentaries, including *Paper Airplane* (*Zhi Fei Ji*, 2001) on drug addicts, *Crime and Punishment* (*Zui Yu Fa*, 2007) about a police station in Northeast China, near the border with North Korea, and *Petition* (*Shang Fang*, 2009), a twelve-year, long-term production depicting petitioners in a suburb of Beijing. These documentaries often take an intimate, *vérité* approach, reflecting what Cong regards as 'poor cinema'.

In *Behemoth*, which signifies an artistic turn for the filmmaker, Zhao aims for more artistic freedom and experimentation beyond the conventional reportage-style documentary (in Xue and Zhang 2015). He calmly and overtly writes his subjective vision through a *san* view, a loosely connected, scattered perspective. Always trying to retain autonomy in his work, Zhao's international fame now means that he can also attract funding from highly regarded international institutions, including National Audiovisual Institute France (INA), Arte France, IDFA Bertha Fund, Asian Cinema Fund and Hong Kong Asian Film Finance Forum (HAF). The film has two versions. One is the feature-length film, which is circulated in film festivals and cinemas and distributed through DVDs. The other is a three-screen film installation, exhibited in art spaces.[16] The impressionist nature of this film presents itself well in the gallery, which gives the audience a more immersive experience.

Although the film is, strictly speaking, no longer part of what Cong advocates as poor cinema, Zhao still had to work against political constraints. He worked on his own, sometimes with a camera assistant and a sound recorder, *writing* his thoughts through camera, in the large mining fields and steel factories of Inner Mongolia, an officially designated 'autonomous region' of the People's Republic of China.[17] The production was kept extremely low-key in order to not arouse the attention of the local authorities. Zhao was physically filming under very harsh conditions, both above the ground and hundreds of metres below the ground, which is shown through a two-minute long take going underground. Zhao puts himself in the position of the workers, writing his physical experience into the film and providing viewers with a vernacular perspective.

Thematically, the film continues Zhao's provocative as well as distinctly political way of looking at the world. This is done not by means of verbal advocacy, but through impressionistic and ideographic cinematic imagery that seeks to express the unspeakable. As a nomadic observation of the former nomadic land, *Behemoth* presents Inner Mongolia's natural landscape, wounded and maimed by excessive mining in recent years. Named after a mythical beast from the Old Testament, *Behemoth* implicitly mirrors the structure of Dante's *Divine Comedy*. The film starts with broken pastureland invaded by the expanding quarry and the deep coal pit, which signifies hell; then it moves to steel factories, portraying human living conditions that suggest purgatory; and the last part shows a large, uninhabited residential area notoriously identified as a 'ghost city' – a typical example of China's real-estate bubble, in an Inner Mongolian city called Erdos, which ironically means 'heaven' in Mongolian. As a transcultural appropriation of Dante's poem, the work is relocated to a different time and space and addresses the clash between modernity and human desire, adding a thick layer of syncretic absurdism.

The opening sequence consists of three static long shots presenting the massive quarry and opencast fields where continuous explosions take place. This sequence is followed by a slow motion of shrapnel raining down from the sky, accompanied by the haunting sound of Mongolian throat singing. The title '悲兮魔兽' (*Bei Xi Mo Shou*, which literally means 'Tragedy of Warcraft') appears in traditional Chinese calligraphy. The English title 'Behemoth' appears below the Chinese title. 'Behemoth' and '悲兮魔兽' translate each other homophonically; both indicate the human being as monster and the devastating anthropogenic effects. A quotation from Dante emerges on a title card: 'God created the beast Behemoth on the 5th day. It was the largest monster on earth. A thousand mountains yielded food for him.' In the next sequence smoke rises from the land, followed by a static long shot of scarred pastureland in which we can see a male nude lying curled up in a foetal position in the foreground. The three-part image is then reassembled, like reflections in a shattered mirror. Shot in a bluish tone, this surrealistic image provokes us to ask what is actually being presented. Zhao's personal narration starts with a description of a dream, echoing the visuals of broken landscapes, smoky and polluted air. As the film continues, 'Behemoth' metaphorically stands in for the expanding mining factories, which hire workers for coal mining, leaving big scars on the land. For Zhao, this figure also indicates the never-satisfied human desire.

Throughout the film, only two recurring figures are recognisable: one is a male nude who is seen as either lying on the edge of the mining field or standing with his back to the camera in a field. He appears to represent the filmmaker and is also emblematic of Dante. The man also signifies the purity of humanity, in contrast to the cruelty of the machine and of modernity's darker desires. The other figure is a mineworker, who acts as a mute guide taking the filmmaker and, by extension, the audience on a journey – like Virgil in Dante's *Divine Comedy*. The guide appears a few times in the massive, broken landscape, carrying a big mirror on his back, reflecting the scene behind him. He

'IMAGE-WRITING'

Figure 10.1   Man curled up in a foetal position in *Behemoth*, Zhao Liang, 2015.

also reappears later in the uninhabited 'ghost city'. The guide breathes heavily, as if affected by lung disease. Set against the larger scene's quietude, his inhalation and exhalation sounds are amplified, emblematic of the struggling 'body' of the wounded landscape. Zhao's voice-over comments: 'He doesn't know how to write poetry. Yet the eloquence his heart exhales is no less powerful than the Divine Comedy.' Though the film hints at Dante's work, this is the only time when *The Divine Comedy* is verbally mentioned in the film. The heavy breathing also suggests the imperilled body of the workers, who suffer long hours of heavy labour in coalmines and steel factories; and the silencing of their death, as they sacrifice their health and lives in the process. Their petitions for compensation are, however, often repressed, a subject tackled in Zhao's earlier film *Petition*.

The absence of the human voices is a noticeable feature of the soundscape, which is dominated instead by overbearing machine noises. The aesthetic decision to not include any subject as a recognisable speaking character, but to use silence and sound rhetorically instead, is intended to reflect upon and bring into 'visibility' the social position of these voiceless workers as well as the damaged landscape through industrial exploitation. Different machinery, technical and non-human sounds (such as the sounds of earth shaking, earth-changing drilling, swinging, and shovelling) occupy most of the first two-thirds of the film's soundscape, creating an unsettling psychological impact on the audience. Collecting interviews was a key process for Zhao to further his understanding of the mineworkers' situation; however, despite producing hundreds of hours of interviews with workers and families, Zhao eventually decided not to use any of these sources.

Figure 10.2  Guide carrying a mirror on his back in *Behemoth*, Zhao Liang, 2015.

Zhao's own narration in Chinese is also kept to a minimum. About three-quarters of his monologue is adapted from Dante's poem, complemented by his own accounts to fit the Chinese context (Zhao, in Guarneri and Wang 2016). Using Chinese words to reinterpret Dante and to situate *The Divine Comedy* in twenty-first-century China – a country that claims socialism with Chinese characteristics yet, notoriously, adopts the most exploitative aspects of capitalism – distances the viewer and suggests that this seemingly otherworldly and absurd place is precisely a contemporary condition.

Some Chinese phrases in the film have meanings that are very different from their original contexts. For example, after a sequence in which male and female workers pick up coals in an opencast mine, Zhao's voice-over comments, 'the crew spends all night daubing on dusky make-up'. By means of *paibi* or parallel editing, three workers' faces are shown in close-up. Zhao continues, 'what decides they are "*nongzhuang danmo*"' (translated as 'caked with powder or getting a light touch-up' in the film's English subtitle) 'depends not on their mood, but on how fast the wind blows'. The Chinese four-word idiom *Nongzhuang danmo* (浓妆淡抹) is originally a phrase taken from a poem by Su Shi, a well-known Song Dynasty poet. *Nong zhuang dan mo zong xiang yi* originally describes the famous West Lake in the centre of Hangzhou city through the metaphor of a woman, who is always charming: with or without make-up, well dressed or in simple clothes. The irony of using this phrase evokes bitterness. What viewers see is not what they conventionally may regard as beauty: it is the workers' emotionless faces and messy hair, covered unevenly by black coal. Highlighting the fact that the workers have no control over their daily appearance, the commentary also suggests that it is their fate to

'IMAGE-WRITING'

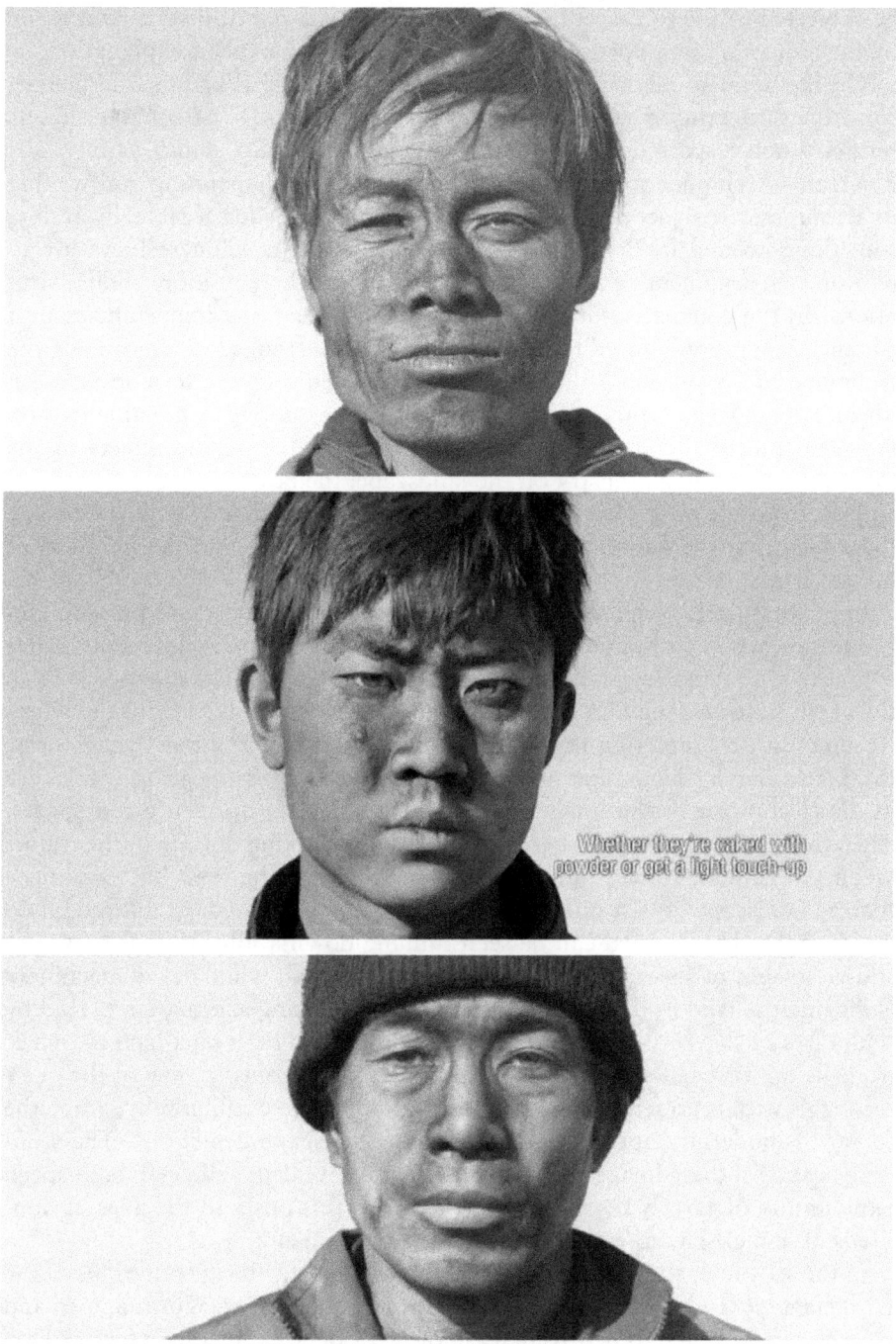

Figure 10.3  Faces of three workers covered by dust in *Behemoth*, Zhao Liang, 2015.

be subjected to the forces of the environment. It is a political statement made by the filmmaker in a poetic way, rather than through explicit explanation.

The literary also influences the assemblage of the verbal and moving image, sometimes to reinforce certain latent messages. Zhao's personal vision is refracted and dispersed through *hongtuo* and *paibi* in *Behemoth*. *Hongtuo* is a narrative technique in traditional Chinese calligraphic painting and writing to accentuate an object or a character, or to render a feeling 'visible' by adding something around it. *Paibi* or parallel is often used in Chinese literature to reinforce an argument or a meaning through listing three or more similar situations. In the cinematic context, these techniques become important as part of cinematography and editing when images are arranged. By means of the technique of *hongtuo* and the ideographic *paibi* editing, the tension between life and death is underpinned. Zhao does this, for example, by creating tension between the rapidly shrinking green pastures and the deadly effects of the massive toxic mining industry on the landscape; the beauty of the burning red embers from the steel factories and the heavy labour that is required to run these factories; the amount of dust that blurs the vision and the lightness of human lives.

In the first part, *hongtuo* is also deployed to contrast past and present, and to indicate what is disappearing on account of the rapid developments. After a sequence that nostalgically depicts traditional Mongolian nomadic life in the green pastures, the film cuts to a point-of-view shot taken from the windscreen of a lorry, entering the massive opencast mines. The noisy machinery, the black, smoky landscape and the uniformed workers wearing masks are in direct contrast to the images of nomads and sheep in open green spaces. Then the film cuts to a small herd of white sheep walking outside of the frame; when the camera slowly pans back, it reveals that the field has become a scarred landscape of vast opencast mines stretching hundreds of miles with no end in sight. Then a herd can be seen running down a hillside, before we are shown images of sheep eating grass in the foreground while heavy machinery is digging the land in the background. Gradually, living sheep are replaced by sculptures of sheep and a sculpture of a Buddha head built by a factory owner to make up for what was done to nature. An impressionistic view of the place resonates with representations of landscapes in Chinese calligraphy, while the forces of modernity appear to disrupt these landscape depictions. The stunning beauty of these images accentuates what is revealed: hell, 'evil' high-speed exploitation of earthly resources and the threat this poses to the lives of hundreds of nameless workers and the fragile environment.

In the second part, 'purgatory', which focuses on the living conditions of the workers, *paibi* is deployed in the organisation of the images. Working men and women can be seen to repetitively wash their dusty faces; a woman tends to her injured leg; a man sits quietly on the bed with breathing tubes covering his face.

Figure 10.4 Sheep running down a scarred hillside in *Behemoth*, Zhao Liang, 2015.

Flying dust blurs the view for over a minute. As it gradually dissipates, a Monet-style impressionistic landscape is revealed, and only the big lorries passing by remind the viewer of the location of an industrial mining field. With a man on a motorbike holding a drip infusion, the film cuts to the operating theatre in a hospital. Shots of bottles of black water lying on the floor, indicating what has been extracted from human lungs, point viewers to the pollution inflicted on the workers by black coal. This sequence is followed by shots of workers lying exhausted on a bed, inhaling and exhaling heavily. Their emotionless faces are covered by dust that has become part of their skin. A woman is seen standing in front of the camera, holding a portrait of her husband who recently died, before the scene cuts to a group of workers standing in rows holding placards in front of a local authority building, asking for an explanation and compensation for the deaths of their family members. Numerous tombs can be seen lying in the foreground, with big industrial chimneys and lorries in the background. This is followed by a gigantic sculpture of a Mongolian woman standing in the shrinking pasture, sarcastically revealing that what used to belong to here, the nomads and their families, has been crystallised into a motionless sculpture. Zhao collects these images and arranges them in parallel edits, allowing the subjects to tell their own 'Divine Comedy'. Without any verbal expression, these images are formidable yet terrifying evidence of lives being wrecked by highly exploitative capitalist systems as well as human greed.

This theme is further magnified in the final part, 'heaven'. Ironically, 'heaven' is represented by images of literal 'ghost cities', referring to the newly constructed yet vacant residential buildings in endless rows. As the camera travels from the 'hell' of the mining fields through the brutal imagery of the 'purgatory', the suddenly emerging high-rises occupy the landscape like a mirage, surreal and absurd. Although these industrial activities supposedly signify human success and the fruits of modernisation, the film also draws attention to the costs of this modernisation process: countless lives and irrevocable destruction of the natural environment. 'Behemoth', the monster, now becomes more obvious: 'We are the monster, monster's minions', Zhao's voice-over reveals. The stillness of the moving images and the 'silence' of human voices open up an immense space for viewers to reflect and form their own thoughts and comments on the 'unspeakable'.

## Conclusion

While China is seeking recognition for its creativity, independent artists, filmmakers and innovators have also been trying to express their autonomous creative voices in various ways.[18] However, individual expressions are not always in line with the official discourse. To maintain an alternative space outside the growing political and economic constraints, a group of filmmakers deploy the practice of image writing to keep their creative autonomy. Yet these films, including *Behemoth*, would never pass the state censorship for public screenings, and most would not even be submitted for consideration. Filmmakers like Zhao still manage to write their subjectivities, which would otherwise be muted. Works made through image writing practices often address poignantly personal feelings and concerns filmmakers have towards individuals, culture and society. Essayistic nonfiction films like *Behemoth* express themes central to the current social climate in China and are influenced by Chinese literary strategies and aesthetic traditions to express the impressionistic and the ideographic. Multiple cultural exchanges are also in evidence, addressing transnational concerns. Image writing in mainland China draws our attention to varying screen-writing practices and urges us to look for different methods to interrogate the interactions between language and the audio-visual in essayistic nonfiction cinema, especially in non-western contexts.

## Notes

1. Hereafter, 'China' refers to mainland China.
2. Most independent film festivals took the name *yingzhan* (film exhibition), rather than *dianying jie* (film festival), because in order to convene a film festival one needed to obtain official authorisation, whereas *yingzhan* offered more freedom. For example, BIFF in Chinese is Beijing Duli (independent) Yingzhan, while CIFF in Chinese is Chinese Duli Yingzhan.
3. Established in 2003 in Yunnan Province, with the support of the Ford Foundation and Yunnan Social Science Institute.
4. BIFF has taken place in Songzhuang since 2006, an artist district in the suburb of Beijing, led by influential Chinese artist and critic Li Xianting. The process

undergone by local authorities, forcing the festival to shut down, is recorded in the documentary *Film Festival without Film* (Wang Wo, 2015).
5. Arguably the oldest independent film festival, CIFF started in 2003. I learnt about the current situation through an informal conversation with the former festival director Zhang Xianmin. Quietly growing alternative public spaces, as mentioned in the anthology *The New Chinese Documentary Film Movement: For the Public Record* (Berry et al. 2010) and Dan Edwards's *Independent Chinese Documentary: Alternative Visions, Alternative Publics* (2015), have also been suppressed recently.
6. Screening events in big cities have continuously been forced to cancel. Through my observation and informal interviews with filmmakers, I have come to know that there were also problems within the former independent film community, which heavily relied on friendship networks, nepotism and lack of candid criticism. Thus, there has also been a tendency within the community to seek a reconfiguration of a healthier autonomous space, if it could still exist.
7. Examples are *Masters in Forbidden City* (*Wo Zai Gugong Xiu Wenwu*, Liang Jianjun and Xiao Han, 2015), featuring Forbidden City's cultural relics and their restorers, and *Twenty Two* (*Er Shi Er*, Guo Ke, 2016), on the life of China's 'Comfort Women' survivors.
8. Artist Gao Shiqiang borrows the concept of 'retreat' from ancient intellectuals as the artistic strategy in his ideographic multi-screen moving image practices (Gao 2011).
9. Many literary scholars and writers observe that Chinese prose forms such as *sanwen*, *suibi*, *xiaopin* and *xiaopingwen* have all been used to translate the English and French words 'essay' and 'essai' in different historical periods, with different emphases (Zhou 1937; Lin 1984; Rivi Handler-Spitz 2010). In modern Chinese literature, *sanwen* is more of an umbrella classification including various forms of nonfiction writing (Zheng 2009).
10. Especially Chen Duxiu was among those who had promoted the Vernacular Language Movement from its beginnings in the first two decades of the twentieth century.
11. The gendered aspect of this film practice deserves a more thorough exploration, which needs to be addressed elsewhere.
12. Due to space constrictions, I cannot elaborate on the ideographic nature of Chinese language and its relation to cinematic expression here. Relationships between the ideographic languages and cinema have been discussed previously in *Eisenstein, Cinema, and History* (Goodwin 1993), *Language and Cinema* (Metz 1974) and *Movement as Meaning in Experimental Cinema* (Barnett 2017), among others.
13. These include works by London-based Chinese filmmaker Guo Xiaolu, New York-based filmmaker-artist Wang Bo and Wang Nanfu.
14. Zhao has received numerous awards, including International Nuremberg Human Rights Film Award 2009; Best Director Award at One World International Human Right Documentary Film Festival 2008; the Marek Nowicki Prize, the Roman XI International Film Festival WATCH DOCS 2011; Humanitarian Awards for Documentaries at the 34th Hong Kong International Film Festival 2010; the Jury Award at the Festival International du Film des Droits de l'Homme de Paris 2010; and the Merit Prize at the 3rd Taiwan International Documentary Festival 2002.
15. *Behemoth* was the first Asian film to enter the competition section at the Venice Film Festival; it also received the Special Jury Prize at Tokyo FilmeX Japan 2015 and the WATCH DOCS Award for the best film in competition in 2015.
16. In the feature film version the narration is addressed through Zhao's voice-over, whereas in the gallery version narration is not heard but inserted on screens as captions.

17. Only since *Together* (2012), the only government-approved film, did Zhao begin working with a crew.
18. The theme of searching for creative and original voices is presented in my feature documentary *China's van Goghs* (2016).

## References

Astruc, Alexandre (1992), 'The Future of Cinema', *La Nef*, 48 (1948), reprinted in *Trafic*, 3 (Summer), 151–8.
Barnett, Daniel (2017), *Movement as Meaning in Experimental Cinema: The Musical Poetry of Motion Pictures Revisited*, London and New York: Bloomsbury Academic.
Bazin, André (2017), 'Bazin on Marker', in Nora M. Alter and Timothy Corrigan (eds), *Essays on the Essay Film*, New York: Columbia University Press, pp. 102–5.
Berry, Chris, Lu Xinyu and Lisa Rofel (eds) (2010), *The New Chinese Documentary Film Movement: For the Public Record*, Hong Kong: Hong Kong University Press.
Blümlinger, Christa (2016), 'Reading Between the Images', in Erika Balsom and Hila Peleg (eds), *Documentary across Disciplines*, Cambridge, MA and London: MIT Press, pp. 172–91.
Bourdieu, Pierre (1993), *The Field of Cultural Production*, Cambridge: Polity Press.
Bresson, Robert (1975), *Notes on Cinematography*, New York: Urizen Books.
Cong, Feng (2016), 'Tasks of Poor Cinema', *New Arts*, 10, 15–18.
Corrigan, Timothy (2011), *The Essay Film: From Montaigne, After Marker*, Oxford and New York: Oxford University Press.
Edwards, Dan (2015), *Independent Chinese Documentary: Alternative Visions, Alternative Publics*, Edinburgh: University of Edinburgh Press.
Elsaesser, Thomas (2017), 'The Essay Film: From Film Festival Favorite to Flexible Commodity Form?', in Nora M. Alter and Timothy Corrigan (eds), *Essays on the Essay Film*, New York: Columbia University Press, pp. 240–58.
Gao, Shiqiang (2011), 'Retreat into Images – a Strategy of Moving Image Practice in the Society of the Spectacle', *CAFA Online*, 1 November, <http://www.cafa.com.cn/c/?t=543079> (last accessed 25 January 2018).
Goodwin, James (1993), *Eisenstein, Cinema, and History*, Champaign: University of Illinois Press.
Guarneri, Michael and Jin Wang (2016), 'ND/NF Interview: Zhao Liang', *Film Comment*, 17 March, <https://www.filmcomment.com/blog/interview-zhao-liang-behemoth/> (last accessed 18 January 2018).
Handler-Spitz, Rivi (2010), 'Short Prose Forms in a Global Sixteenth-Century Context', *Prose Studies*, 32:2, 110–21.
Huang, Xiaohe (2013), 'Wu Wenguang Writing with Images, Beyond Conventional Documentary', *East China Morning Post*, 24 April, <https://ent.sina.cn/tv/tv/2013-04-24/detail-iavxeafr6723913.d.html> (last accessed 3 December 2017).
Kafalas, Philip (2007), *In Limpid Dream: Nostalgia and Zhang Dai's Reminiscences of the Ming*, Norwalk, CT: EastBridge Books.
Kang He (2017), 'Image Writing Declaration', 26 September, <https://site.douban.com/106812/widget/notes/129566/note/643636467/> (last accessed 5 January 2018).
Lin Yutang (1984), 'Lun Xiaopinwen Bidiao' ('On the Style of Essay'), *Ren Shi Jian (Human World)* (1934), p. 6, reprinted in *Zhongguo Xiandai Wenxue Ziliao Xuanbian (Selections of Chinese Modern Literature Archives)*, Huanan: Huanan Normal University Correspondence Department, pp. 423–6.
Mamula, Tijana (2016), 'Post-anthropocentric Multilingualism in Contemporary Artists' Moving Image: An Interview with T. J. Demos', in Tijana Mamula and Lisa

Patti (eds), *The Multilingual Screen: New Reflections on Cinema and Linguistic Difference*, London and New York: Bloomsbury Academic, pp. 57–68.
Metz, Christian (1974), *Language and Cinema*, Ghent: Mouton.
Naficy, Hamid (2001), *An Accented Cinema: Exilic and Diasporic Filmmaking*, Princeton: Princeton University Press.
Pollard, David (2000), *The Chinese Essay*, New York: Columbia University Press.
Rascaroli, Laura (2009), *Personal Camera: The Subjective Cinema and Essay Film*, London: Wallflower Press.
Rascaroli, Laura (2017), *How the Essay Film Thinks*, New York: Oxford University Press.
Sha, Qing (2017), Interviewed by Kiki Tianqi Yu, 1–28 November 2017.
Wang, Jing (1996), *High Cultural Fever: Politics, Aesthetics and Ideology in Deng's China*, Berkeley: University of California Press.
Wang, Zhaosheng (2007), 'On the Studies of Chinese Prose in the 20th Century', *China Writer*, 9 January, <http://www.chinawriter.com.cn/56/2007/0109/937.html> (last accessed 28 April 2018).
Xue, Feng and Han Zhang (2015), 'Zhao Liang: I Want to Find a More Comfortable Way of Expression Again', *Tiger Temple News Studio*, 30 July, <http://www.laohumiao.com/laohumiao/vip_doc/1311491.html> (last accessed 18 January 2018).
Yu, Kiki Tianqi (2018), *'My' Self on Camera: First Personal Documentary Practice in an Individualising China*, Edinburgh: Edinburgh University Press.
Yu, Tianqi, Ran Ma, Dan Wu and Jiachun Hong (2014), *Siren Shexiangji: Zhuguan Dianying he Sanwen Yingpian*, Chinese translation of Rascaroli's *Personal Camera: The Subjective Cinema and Essay Film*, Beijing: Xincheng Publisher.
Zhang, Xudong (1997), *Chinese Modernism in the Era of Reforms: Cultural Fever, Avant-garde Fiction and the New Chinese Cinema*, Durham, NC: Duke University Press.
Zheng, Mingli (2009), *Modern Essay*, 2nd edn, Taipei: Sanmin Publishing.
Zhou, Zuoren (1937), 'Zaitan Paiwen' ('On the Essay Again'), *Wenxue Zazhi* (*Literature Journal*), 1:3, 21–33.

# PART FIVE

# ARCHIVAL EFFECTS

# 11. INDIGENOUS AUSTRALIA AND THE ARCHIVE EFFECT: FRANCES CALVERT'S *TALKING BROKEN* AS ESSAY FILM

## Peter Kilroy

> The desire to appropriate [archival] material often involves a political commitment to drawing an audience's attention to the way films are constructed ... constructing meaning out of found-footage fragments and thereby inviting new readings of the original material.
> (Olivia Lory Kay, 'Gathering in the Orphans')

### Introduction

Paying heed to the film industry's trade magazines, websites, academic journals and institutions in recent years calls attention to the extraordinary rise in popularity of the essay film as a particular category of film practice. Canons have been drawn up, redrawn and debated, multilinear histories have been written and festivals have been launched.[1] However, despite the relative longevity of the essay film and the relative antiquity of the literary form from which it draws, extensive academic studies are relatively recent. Since Hans Richter, Alexandre Astruc and André Bazin's analyses, among others (Kay 2010; Rascaroli 2008), theoretical and historical surveys have included Laura Rascaroli's work (2008, 2009) and Timothy Corrigan's useful taxonomy (2011). Building on Aldous Huxley's anatomy of the literary essay, Corrigan lays out a schema for the essay film with three poles (subjectivity, experience, thinking)[2] and five modes (portrait films, travelogues, diary films, editorial films and 'refractive' or self-reflexive films) (8, 14). Unlike Huxley, Corrigan stresses the necessary overlap between these poles and modes (8, 14). The difference between essay films, therefore, is the balance of different elements, not their fixed position on an instrumental taxonomy.

Notwithstanding the obvious caveats in using such a taxonomy, Corrigan's model is a useful one, and the schema that I lay out in this chapter slightly reframes it. While clearly forming a complex and diverse body of texts, the essay film might be said to possess a number of key traits, notable among them being: a reflexive or personal authorial voice, a poetic and/or political focus, emphasising ideas or themes over narrative or events. Essay films are often also noted for an experimental or fragmentary structure, inviting or requiring spectatorial participation (Rascaroli 2008), and a citational use of source/archival materials, including personal and historical archives, still, moving and sound 'images' and multiple formats (Kay 2010). Needless to say, not all films that exhibit these characteristics might be deemed essay films and some essay films that do so may not be explicitly posed as such. Nevertheless, such a schema is a useful starting point.

In this chapter, I focus on strategic combinations of some of these 'building blocks' of the essay film in the directorial output of Frances Calvert (1950–2018). Calvert was a non-Indigenous Australian documentary filmmaker who, for the past thirty years, worked personally, politically, poetically and collaboratively with themes that bear upon Australia's 'other' Indigenous community, Torres Strait Islanders.[3] Her work includes a trilogy of documentary films that focuses on how Islanders negotiate the complex relationship between past, present and future. These are companion pieces exploring such themes as settler-colonial globalisation (*Talking Broken*, 1990), cultural repatriation (*Cracks in the Mask*, 1997) and mourning practices (*The Tombstone Opening*, 2013). Despite differences in approach, these films pay heed to Trinh T. Minh-ha's injunction in *Reassemblage* (1982) to 'speak nearby', and/or in collaboration with, rather than on behalf of (*Torres News* 1989). They make extensive use of historical archival material to do so, including still, moving and sound 'images' and multiple formats, and they eschew the merely evidential in their use of such material, emptying out any residual positivism that might persist (Tracy 2013: 48, 51). While not always explicitly posed as such, this usage forms a core performative element of the reflexive, rhetorical processes of the essay film. Focusing in particular on a close reading of Calvert's debut film *Talking Broken*,[4] I will argue that such citational archival practices, including what I will call 'archival tropes', generate fragments for a history of the present in Calvert's hands, highlighting and combining the processes of film grammar with the political performativity that such processes might enact.

## The Archive Effect and World Cinema

However, there are two points of emphasis that I would like to draw out first. One is the citational use of archival material. Following recent work in the field (de Jong 2012; Kay 2010; Kepley and Swender 2009; Seider 2013), I will argue that the appropriation of personal and historical archival material is a key element of the reflexivity of the essay film. Without wishing to labour the reductive literary metaphor of 'reading', the essay film can be said to perform a type of critical, citational reading of the source material, analogous to the citational practices of the literary essayist. Indeed, given the way in which early film absorbed or remediated other media – photography and theatre, for example (Bolter and Grusin 1998) – it is not a surprise that, by the middle of the twentieth century, film would remediate other forms, such as the literary essay, or rather that the essayistic would find new modes of expression (Corrigan 2011: 14–15). However, unlike the conventional literary essayist, the film essayist is able to make structural use not only of consecutive meanings and arguments (using archival material within linear montage sequences, for example), but also of meanings and arguments generated through parallelism, simultaneity or repetition (using archival material in split screen shots, in sound/image juxtapositions or in repeated 'readings' of the same material, for example).

Some scholars, such as Olivia Lory Kay (2010: 256), argue that the use of archival materials is not simply one attribute of the essay film, but the beginning of the essay film itself. This interpretation depends on which pre- or proto-histories of the essay film are considered, but one point is particularly well taken: the use of archive footage draws attention not only to how it functions or is constructed, but also to how the 'host' film functions or is constructed. It is therefore a fundamentally reflexive gesture and a key – if not determining – attribute of the essay film.

In following this strand, I take a lead from Jaimie Baron's work (2014) on what she calls the 'archive effect' in the cinematic repurposing of archival materials. Drawing on phenomenological accounts of cinema, one of Baron's key interventions is to focus on the archive effect as an *experience* of the past, thereby sidestepping either side of the 'truth claims' argument (whether or not archival film constitutes 'historical evidence') (8–13). For this effect to be felt, she argues, there is usually an experience of 'temporal' and/or 'intentional disparity', a perceived sense that the material is from another time in both content (different fashions, architectures, values and technologies) and form (black and white footage or decaying film stock), as well as a perceived sense that the material is being used against the grain of its originally intended use (17–30).

To this I would add the use of 'archival tropes', by which I mean intertextual references that allude to archival materials without directly deploying them as such. For example, ironically anachronistic intertitles and aerial shots (of which more later) and animated cinematic maps, or what Sébastien Caquard refers to as 'cinemaps' (2009). Maps in cinema – and particularly animated maps – often shift from a mere evidential function towards a broader symbolic or narrative function as, for example, 'a means of social control, a point of departure for journeys and adventure, a link between time and places, and a way of expressing untold memories' (Caquard and Taylor 2009: 6), or, we might add, a means of evoking another time, place or cinematic history. Clearly not all intertitles, aerial shots and cinematic maps function as archival tropes in this way, but, in the following context, I will suggest that such tropes simultaneously evoke another time, place or cinematic history and are often invoked against the grain of their originally intended use.

The other point to stress is that the discourse around the essay film tends to place a strong emphasis on American and European film. Thinking about the essay film in a transnational or 'world' context is relatively underdeveloped (hence this volume). However, the 'world cinema' category is complicated in the context of Australian film in general, and in the context of films with an Indigenous Australian focus in particular. Such films are often rendered peripheral in relation to American, European *and* to 'world' cinemas: not familiar enough in one context; too familiar in another. Indeed, there are a number of relationalities or layers of marginality at work here: Australian film in relation to American, European and 'world' cinemas; films made by, about or in collaboration with Indigenous Australians (both Aboriginal Australians and Torres Strait Islanders) in relation to other Australian films; and films made by, about or in collaboration with Torres Strait Islanders – such as Frances Calvert's *Talking Broken* (1990) – in relation to other Indigenous Australian films.

### *Talking Broken* as Essay Film

In the lead-up to Australia's bicentenary commemorations of 1988 – which marked 200 years since British colonisation, and which were accompanied by considerable Indigenous discussion and resistance (see, for example, Adrian Wills's *88*, released in 2014) – Calvert discovered that surprisingly little was known nationally or internationally about Australia's 'other' Indigenous community, Torres Strait Islanders.[5] This was all the more remarkable given that (a) there was a long film history in the region going back as far as 1898,[6] and (b) immediately prior to the bicentenary commemorations, the Torres Strait attempted to secede from the State of Queensland, bringing it to the attention of the United Nations Association of Australia (*Torres News* 1988). With this jarring gap between knowledge and potential cinematic narratives in mind,

Calvert set about conducting several years of research between the mid 1980s and the two-month shoot of what would become *Talking Broken* in July 1988 (Calvert 1991). Although an Australian filmmaker, Calvert was based in Berlin and, under the auspices of her own Talking Pictures Frances Calvert production company, managed to secure funding from a range of German cultural institutions and Channel 4 in the UK (Calvert 1991, 2016; McInerney 1991). The film was released in 1990, screened on the international film festival circuit and broadcast in 1991 in the UK and Australia (Calvert 2016). It is presently distributed on DVD by Ronin Films in Australasia and Icarus Films in the US.

While clearly very different films for different audiences,[7] the film is loosely analogous to Chris Marker's *Sans Soleil* (1983), insofar as it represents a layering of the different essay film modes that Corrigan (2011: 8) distinguishes. It is an essayistic travelogue, in this case shifting geographically, culturally and historically from mainland Australia (in Far North Queensland) to its Torres Strait Island margins south of Papua New Guinea. Indeed, the unresolved tension between these core/periphery relations is a key theme: this is a film in which Australia's margins offer a window onto its centre, and vice versa. It is a community portrait, in this case of marginalised and fragmented, but persistent and strategic, Indigenous communities facing the complex pressures of settler-colonial globalisation circa 1988. And it is a 'critical evaluation of film representation' (Corrigan 2011: 8), in this case repurposing elements from the long but 'stylistically conservative' (Calvert 1988) film history of the Torres Strait (circa 1898–1988). As Corrigan suggests, the travel motif has a particularly important place in the history of the essay film: 'essay films have emphasized travel and space as a central motif around which complex ideas and reflections have been put in play' (2011: 105).

Also loosely analogous to *Sans Soleil*, *Talking Broken* documents the subjectivities of filmmaker, spectators and cinematic subjects alike as displaced and decentred, particularly in the context of settler-colonial globalisation: 'the human experience as a struggle to understand itself in an increasingly smaller, fragmented, and accelerated global space' (Corrigan 2011: 36). Without being passive ciphers, Calvert's subjects are shaped by forces beyond themselves that they cannot control, and globalisation is presented as a series of centripetal and centrifugal forces: vortices pulling in outside influences and pulling out populations and raw materials. Although referring to a form of Torres Strait creole (also known as Yumplatok), this is part of what the 'Broken' of the title designates. Not broken versus fixed, but irreducibly fragmentary rather than whole in three overlapping senses: the irreducible instability and fragmentation of all subjectivity, of those forms precipitated by colonialism, and of cinematic meaning and form.

## The Tourist Gaze

*Talking Broken* opens with a sequence in the same conceptual terrain as Dennis O'Rourke's powerful study of the 'tourist gaze' in Papua New Guinea, *Cannibal Tours* (1988), a gaze whose power is often 'visually objectified or captured through photographs, postcards, films, models and so on' (Urry 2002: 3).[8] Shot in a seemingly conventional observational style intercut with talking head interviews, Calvert's film opens with images of Saibai Islanders performing a representation of Indigenous experience for tourists on the Australian mainland, while an American tour operator is interviewed discussing tourism and Torres Strait culture in awkward and halting terms:

> There is a great interest [in] tourism in California . . . discovering areas such as the Torres Islands . . . It's something so unspoilt. It's something so undiscovered. This is what people want to see; they want to experience life and cultures as it really is [sic] . . . It's just a step back in time . . . And this will do very well for the West Coast market, I think for the whole market in the States.

However, as with O'Rourke, what initially presents as a darkly comic mockery of the epistemological limitations, political partiality and cultural misrepresentations of the tourist gaze, this sequence establishes and destabilises a number of more complex and overlapping globalised subjectivities: the implied but marginal presence of the director as interviewer (by contrast, her enunciating position as director/author is very clear in this sequence); the various viewing positions of the tourists within the film; a type of Indigenous self-representation mediated by global socio-economic factors; as well as the various potential viewing positions of spectators with and without extra-textual knowledge of the Torres Strait. Indeed, this constellation of elements was part of the initial impetus for the film project: an attempt to contrast the Euro-American cultural and historical imagination of the Pacific (as a place of abandon, sexual licence, colourful performance and/or intoxicating danger, for example) with the globalised complexity of contemporary Indigenous lives (Calvert 1988).

This characterises the film as a type of 'inter-view' in Corrigan's terms (2011: ch. 3), not merely composed of a series of talking heads interviews, but an exploration of the relationships between and within different views that comes to thematise the fragmented, decentred nature of entangled subjectivities (Calvert 1997b: 190). The spectator is encouraged to compare these perspectives, not with a view to synthesising a coherent whole or with a view to ridiculing inaccuracies or discrepancies, but rather with a view to a type of 'Rashomon effect' where all the parts and perspectives do not add up to a coherent whole.

## Conjuring the Archive

In a move that further undercuts the seemingly linear, observational realism of the tourist gaze sequence, Calvert shifts into a reflexive mode via three 'archival tropes' or intertextual references that allude to archival materials without directly deploying them as such. In this case, an aerial shot (conjuring both general and particular colonial representations) overlaid with an animated cinematic map or 'cinemap' (Caquard 2009); a series of silent film-style intertitles (also conjuring general and particular colonial representations); and a recurring and surreal motif of a telephone booth hanging from a helicopter, intercut with recordings of Torres Strait Islanders literally 'talking Broken' on the telephone.

Although specifically requested by the broadcasters (Calvert 2016), the first can be read as an ironic intertextual allusion to the kind of colonial knowledge/power relations found, for example, in Frank Hurley's aerial shots and cinemaps of the Torres Strait and Papua New Guinea in films such as *Pearls and Savages* (1921) and *The Hound of the Deep* (1926) (Calvert 2016; Dixon 2001: ch. 2).[9] As I have written elsewhere, Hurley's aerial shots create:

> [a] panoptic, cartographic or God's-eye view that renders itself – and its technological mediation – invisible in the process of its deployment . . . [Calvert] literalizes the cartographic component within such a panoptic view by combining a zoom shot of a semi-transparent Torres Strait map and a dissolve as it transitions spatially from Cape York on the Australian mainland to the Torres Strait Islands. (Kilroy 2016: 142)

Calvert's intertextual allusion to Hurley levers open a rhetorical space between geography, history and identity (Corrigan 2011: 99), a point that is particularly heightened by the shot's appearance directly after the tourist gaze sequence. All of which distances the spectator from any naturalistic realism and – as with the tourist gaze sequence – places one into contact with an authorial subjectivity at work. As Paul Arthur notes, 'the manifestation or location of a film author's "voice" can shift from moment to moment or surface expressively via montage, camera movement and so on' (in Rascaroli 2008: 37).

However, as with Jaimie Baron's analysis of the archive effect, we also become acutely aware of the temporal disparity in using such an anachronistic convention (albeit at the behest of the broadcasters, Calvert 2016). This is particularly so in the post-1988 symbolic irony of using an 'empty' and featureless map. As I mentioned earlier, 1988 was significant for the Torres Strait for two key reasons. First, it marked the bicentenary commemoration of the first arrival of British colonial 'settlements', precipitating waves of discussion and resistance among many Indigenous groups. Second, the Torres Strait Islands

Figure 11.1   The politics of space in *Talking Broken*, Frances Calvert, 1990.

attempted to secede from the State of Queensland in the same year. In that context, an empty map reads more like a commentary on the doctrine of *terra nullius*, or no one's land, than an endorsement.

In addition, we become aware of the intentional disparity in using such a shot and map against the grain, ironically (Baron 2014: 17–30).[10] Following the work of the literary theorist Linda Hutcheon, Baron identifies two registers of such cinematic irony: antiphrastic irony, which stresses clear oppositional meaning (using archive footage of slain civilians intercut with an interviewee denying such deaths, for example) and inclusive irony (using archive footage in a new context to highlight the overlapping of multiple, sometimes contradictory, meanings, but without necessarily dictating a sole or preferred reading) (43). For Baron, such inclusive irony produces a kind of 'double consciousness' in which we become aware of – or are encouraged to participate in – different intentional registers at the same time, often held in tension with one another (27, 37, 43).

In this case, we are closer to the latter. We are challenged to add to the fragmented positionalities/subjectivities of the tourist gaze sequence, while also encouraged to make an associative connection between one history (settler-colonial globalisation in late 1980s Australia) and another (colonial expansion in the Pacific). On my reading, this is part of a building history of the present in the film, taking the present as the perspective from which to draw out associative but non-didactic historical links. Importantly, we are also encouraged to see that history as being, in part at least, a mediated cinematic history. Of

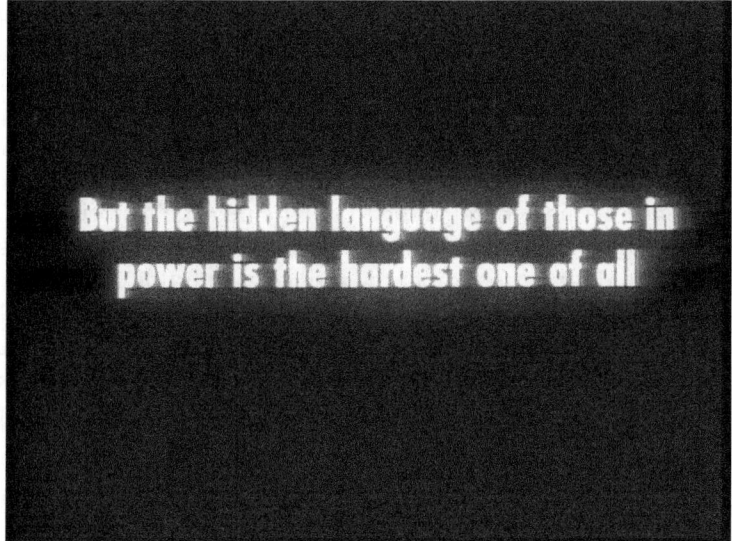

Figure 11.2  The language of power in *Talking Broken*, Frances Calvert, 1990.

course, as Baron makes clear (27–8), the extent to which archive effects are experienced depends in large part on the level of extra-textual knowledge about film history, colonial history and their coming together in the Pacific, but this was one of Calvert's trademark manoeuvres.

The second archival trope is the use of intertitles stylistically coded as being of the cinematic past, both in general terms (related to the history of silent cinema) and in particular terms (related to Frank Hurley's silent films from the region) (Calvert 2016). Just as Calvert rejects or ironically inverts the omniscient God's-eye aerial views of Frank Hurley, so too she rejects the voice-of-God narration that – in a broadcast context at least – she associates less with the elliptical and poetic narration of someone like Chris Marker or Patrick Keiller and more with a type of Griersonian didacticism (Calvert 1986b, 2016; McInerney 1991). Indeed, one of the reasons that Calvert (1991) gave for seeking funding and broadcasting from the UK's Channel 4 is that its audiences had become more accustomed to documentaries without didactic voiceovers. Such a voice is displaced into the pseudo-objectivity of the seemingly benign intertitles. The intertitles are playfully anonymous, masquerading as the omnipotent, omniscient voices of classic expository documentaries (Nichols 2010: 167–71, *passim*). However, such intertitles also play a double role of offering ostensibly neutral description while highlighting the core tension between the verbal and the visual, language and image (Corrigan 2011: 20–1). Calvert highlights this point by shifting from basic factual information to a wry suggestion that 'the hidden language of those in power is the hardest one of all'.

As an intertextual allusion to Hurley and others, the intertitles are also tied to the cinematic remediation of the book (Bolter and Grusin 1998). They literalise the essayistic element, albeit with varying degrees of self-reflexivity (Corrigan 2011: 55). However, the role of this style of intertitle is heightened in this context as a signifier of age, foregrounding Baron's temporal disparity (2014: 17–30). The intertitle goes far beyond any evidential function here and suggests its place within general and particular cinematic histories (i.e. intertitles in silent film in general and Hurley's use in particular). However, such an anachronism also draws attention to the artifice of intertitles, in this case with a wry sense of humour, foregrounding Baron's intentional disparity (17–30). Calvert's intertitles do not just repeat general and particular cinematic histories; they are an ironic commentary on them. Such a usage also addresses the spectator directly, pulling them out from any narrative immersion that might have been established in the tourist gaze sequence (Kay 2010: 260; Seider 2013: 148). In so doing, characters and narrative start to become supplemented by places and ideas.

The third archival or 'traveling trope' (Calvert 1991) is a surreal recurring image of a telephone booth hanging from a helicopter, filmed from a second helicopter and intercut with recorded fragments of Islander conversations on the telephone and other ambient sounds. Like the cinemap before it, this simultaneously denaturalises the aerial shot, highlighting the historical bonds of power between aerial photography, cinema and – in other contexts – war (Dixon 2001: ch. 2); but it also thematises the relationship between language, subjectivity, place and technical mediation. It is a dis-placement of place and subjectivity as well as a figure for the complexities of settler-colonial globalisation. Calvert links the settler-colonial dis-placement of subjectivity and land, in all its registers, with the globalised non-placement of media technologies, such as telephony and, later, video rentals, gaming arcades and satellite television (Corrigan 2011: 145–6). In this context, the telephone booth becomes a vortex of unstable, fragmentary and mediated subjectivities or 'contrapuntal voice[s]' (56). Like the intertitles, it displaces the didacticism of a Griersonian voice-over and foregrounds Calvert's desire to shift from 'explicatory' to 'revelatory' modes (1988). It also becomes a figure for the interviews to follow: snatched fragments of social conversation evoking the thinking processes of director and subjects alike.

However, the telephone booth sequences also play a key role in punctuating the fragmentary, 'mosaic' structure of the film (Malone 1999: 12), where ideas repeat and develop in a non-linear pattern (Kay 2010: 259; Seider 2013: 128–9, 147). They introduce the thematic sections of the film (tourism, politics, economics, sex, religion and media), forming a series of 'structural repetitions' (Corrigan 2011: 150). In so doing, they break the temporal and spatial linearity of the classic colonial aerial shot. They neither indicate an establishing

# INDIGENOUS AUSTRALIA AND THE ARCHIVE EFFECT

Figure 11.3 'Contrapuntal' voices in *Talking Broken*, Frances Calvert, 1990.

arrival scene ('we arrived by plane and then set out to explore the interior'), nor do they coherently join spaces ('now we are travelling from point A to point B'). They are the stitching of the cinematic patchwork, not realistic markers. Like the transitional black screens of Chris Marker and others, they are a form of punctuation, an audio-visual intertitle (Corrigan 2011: 92–4), engaged and expanded as cinematic editing and self-referentiality. In this context, they become an analogue of cinematic quotation itself, referring back to archival films without directly quoting from them. They are part of and produce an archive effect that will be enacted more directly later in the film.

## The Language of Power

It is significant, then, that Calvert's own direct presence (as cinematic subject) emerges only after these layered positions or 'contrapuntal' voices are established (the tourist gaze, self-representation mediated by socio-economic factors, representation mediated by technology, and so on), although, as I suggested earlier, Calvert's enunciating position or 'voice' permeates the film more generally through her cinematic choices. Despite many years as a researcher, a position she wanted to distance from journalistic and governmental positions (1988; 1997b: 190), Calvert, as cinematic subject, appears marginally, in the third person, as an outsider on the testing ground of the social. The scene is the build-up to an interview with the formidable Island Council leader, Chairman Mau, the homophonic irony of whose name resonates with the preceding intertitle: 'But the hidden language of those in power is the hardest one of all'.[11] Into the fragments of community subjectivity, an authorial subject is elliptically inserted.

Calvert is named by Mau, and is later seen arm in arm with him, performatively introduced in a jovial disagreement with her subject. This happens repeatedly in the film, where the filmmaker, although marginal or present only as a disembodied voice, is addressed by her subjects, sometimes confrontationally. Chairman Mau: 'Answer me Lindsey and Frances!'[12] She appears refracted through the lens of her subjects, which is offset by the literal reflections of the camera crew in Mau's television screen as they walk through his house in preparation for the interview, or the reflection of Islanders looking at representations of themselves on a television screen later in the film. There is a double play in these reflections: highlighting the crew and the partiality and positionality of the film, but also the relationship between globalisation and television, two core themes in the film.

This kind of loose, background material not only highlights the 'hidden language of those in power', in the Torres Strait and mainland Australia, but renders the film more self-reflexive, entangled in the same networks of language and power. Leaving in place some of the pre-interview contact that would normally be edited out is rather revealing of the limitations of the interview form. Calvert is setting up the complexity of intersubjective power up front, while also decentring her authorial subjectivity and foregrounding the inevitable failure of any kind of transparent face-to-face communication. In effect, she is interrogating the interview form itself as much as interviewing her subjects. This is also what the 'Broken' of the title conveys: not so much a mourning for loss as a commentary on the impossibility of transparent language and, by extension, coherent, centred subjectivities. Although this is heightened by focusing on seemingly asymmetrical moments of change (for example, where large, powerful historical and economic forces shape small communities and their individuals), the implication is that this is the fate of all historical subjects, albeit in subtler forms.

If the 'language of power' that pervades this sequence plays out inwardly in the intersubjective relations between filmmaker and subject, Calvert also folds it outwards and in so doing expands on the film's cinematic reflexivity. In a characteristic sound/image montage sequence, echoing the flying telephone booth motif – a montage 'forged from ear to eye' (André Bazin, in Rascaroli 2008: 29) – Calvert juxtaposes more Hurley-style aerial shots with a soundtrack of Mau discussing colonial power and land rights:[13]

> This is the lost paradise, Torres Strait. We've been used for years and years and we're fed up. Just like bloody tools. And by right it's ours. We want to see land and everything as ours. White people, they come and go. They take everything out.

This act of recontextualisation punctures some of the aerial shot's historical authority and explicitly politicises and historicises the aesthetics of the landscape. For those with sufficient extra-textual knowledge, it produces an archive effect, an intertextual relation. This can be read as another archival trope. Without directly using archival materials, such a juxtaposition invokes a kind of reflexive disparity: contemporary images are cast into film history and pushed against the grain of their ostensible aestheticism.

### Reframing the Archive

Such a signature manoeuvre becomes particularly heightened in the economy section of the film, through the use of carefully edited archive footage. This section is composed of interviews with turtle hunter and future political candidate Michaelangelo Newie, as he reflects on the economic realities and inequalities of contemporary Islander lives under a Capitalist world system:

> You know this system is moving into your area and you try to push it out, because you know what's going to happen . . . because it moved into all different countries around the world . . . where people have lived like us, especially Indigenous people, and they just destroy that race of people . . . for the sake of money . . . greed. Everything they look at they want to make money out of, even people's life [sic].

Repeating the sound/image juxtaposition of the Chairman Mau aerial shot sequence, Calvert intercuts Newie's discussion about settler-colonial economic inequality with footage of pearl shell diving from the 1930s government propaganda film *The Native Problem in Queensland*. The pearl shell industry had been a staple of Torres Strait economic activity since the middle of the nineteenth century, and it was one of the key ways in which Islanders were transformed from subsistence farmers to proletarian wage labourers (Beckett 1987: ch. 2). Although opinions differ (Calvert 2016), the film is claimed by some to have been made in response to a mass strike in the industry in 1936 (Sharp 1993: ch. 7), and it attempts to portray Island life and industry as one of social equality and meritocratic opportunity.

For those with sufficient extra-textual knowledge of the film or of the broader historical contexts, Calvert's 'dialectical' juxtaposition reframes Newie's subjectivity not only within the context of wider social, political-economic and historical forces, but also within that of film history in particular, or, rather, within the space between the two (Corrigan 2011: 89). Calvert suggests the fragmentation of subjectivity *per se*, and then uses archive footage as a cut to suggest the rupture of such subjectivities by colonial history. This is crucially without nostalgia; there is no pure or whole subjectivity against which this is set. However, the sequence attempts to navigate between two poles here: the one where the heroic, centred subject triumphantly shapes historical forces, and the other where the fragmented, decentred subject – particularly when that subject is affected by settler-colonialism – is passively shaped by such forces (86–9). Calvert confers an element of negotiated agency while paying full heed to the ultimate power of global historical/settler-colonial forces. That is one of the core tensions of the film, and it is left deliberately unresolved.

Using the footage in this way reframes not only the cinematic subject, of course, but the footage itself, which is being read against the grain of its original intention (Baron's intentional disparity, 2014: 17–30). Newie's commentary renders such footage ironic, but in an inclusive mode where multiple meanings coexist (Baron 2014: 37; Kay 2010: 254). We are encouraged to reflect critically on the harmonious image presented in the *Native Problem* and to make a link between the economic inequalities of the settler-colonial present and past, but the effect is not strictly didactic and each layer remains, inviting spectatorial participation in the process of meaning making (Seider 2013: 128–9, 145). This is characteristic of Calvert's particular history of the present. Implied historical arguments are associative and overlapping, rather than causal and linear, and historical analogies are drawn without filling in the gaps or reducing the excesses of meaning (Seider 2013: 128–9; Baron 2014: 25).

Calvert emphasises the artifice of the footage, not its transparency, and the difference between the two films creates a further archive effect, wherein we recognise the patina of age (Baron's temporal disparity, 2014: 17–30). The contrast between different film stocks, different colours, different rates of ageing, and so on, highlights the extent to which we are looking at opaque cultural representations, rather than an unmediated pastness. The very qualities that signpost that one is looking at archive footage (patina, colour, and so on) are the qualities that highlight that one is looking at a representation, albeit one filled with the desire of the indexical: an illusory transparency (Doane 2007). This is all contained within the concept of the archive effect. Implicitly at least, Calvert is making an argument not only about the relationship between 'then' and 'now', but about the capacity of film itself to generate alternate meanings. It is an argument about film and film grammar as much as it is an argument about history, and that is crucial to how the archive effect works in Torres Strait film: it foregrounds its own history and artifice as well as the place of contemporary film within that context.

There are a number of processes at work in this montage sequence, then. First, the realism and spatio-temporal continuity of the talking heads interview is being broken. Calvert is not simply 'illustrating' Newie's point (Tracy 2013: 48, 51; Seider 2013: 148). She is also making her own argument about the links between what he is actually saying ('now') and what is being shown on the screen ('then'). The subject is caught up and fragmented in a temporal disjunction between the two. Second, there is an appeal to the past through an archive source, a desire for a type of indexical transparency, but there is also an appeal to the opacity of the cinematic medium and its capacity for meaning making through montage. Calvert is playing on – and to varying degrees subverting – the expectation of the evidential (Tracy 2013: 48, 51). She is not obscuring the original meaning of the archive film, merely drawing out its polysemic qualities, particularly insofar as these play out over time. She is not sealing off the past either, using it as an evidential background for the heroic experiences of centred subjects (Corrigan 2011: 86). Rather, she is focused on sketching (a history of) the present: contingent experiences of decentred subjects entangled in wider political-economic forces and longer colonial histories.

## Conclusion

Despite the essay film's complex histories, canonical breadth and definitional imprecision, *Talking Broken* represents some of its most basic and overriding themes and patterns: the 'staging of an encounter between a "self" [or selves], filmed and/or archive images, and the world at large' (Corless 2016: n.p.). Touching on Corrigan's schema, the film pitches the personal into the public/political in such a way as to problematise both in an act of thoughtful, processual filmmaking. Calvert's point of focus is on multiple subjectivities (including her own) that do not cohere internally or as a collective whole. These are fragments of subjectivity, fragments of histories, fragments of ideas. She challenges the conventional ways in which authorial subjectivity is represented on screen, and replaces it with an intersubjectivity that is both a reflexive undercutting of her own enunciating position as well as a settler-colonial and cinematic theme. In that sense, there is a homology between the instability of the personal and social self and that of settler-colonial experience and cinematic meaning (Corrigan 2011: 144; Seider 2013: 128–9). However, this effect is doubled in an Australian or other settler-colonial context where the Indigenous 'other' within is often perceived as being as threatening to the majority as settler-colonial globalisation might be disorientating to Indigenous communities, particularly when it comes to land rights or other redistribution claims.

Within that context, the use of archival tropes (aerial shots, cinemaps and intertitles) and archival material becomes a key nodal point that links together the 'building blocks' of the essay film. While at first glance such tropes and material might appear to perform a conventional illustrative or evidential function, on closer inspection they perform a number of central roles: foregrounding the entanglement and displacement of multiple subjectivities across time and space; undercutting the seeming observational realism of the surrounding social milieu; and drawing attention to the specifically filmic quality of the histories in which both are embedded. In other words, we have a coming together of personal reflections, public encounters and multi-modal histories, including film histories. This combination is a broader figure for the essay film as a whole, not viewed as a site of loss (of personal, social, historical or representational wholeness), but viewed as a site of complexity, creativity and/or potential critical intervention.

#### Acknowledgements

At a very late stage in the development of this chapter, I learned of the tragic early death of Frances Calvert (1950–2018). Frances was a great source of inspiration, energy and support for the research represented in this chapter, and her insightful comments on this and other pieces of writing always sharpened their critical focus and accuracy. She will be greatly missed. I would also like to thank Michele Pierson and the editors of this volume for extremely useful comments on earlier drafts of this chapter.

#### Notes

1. The literature here is extensive, but histories include Rascaroli (2009) and Corrigan (2011), and festivals include London's Essay Film Festival, which has been running since 2015.
2. 'I return to my formulation of the essay film as (1) a testing of expressive subjectivity through (2) experiential encounters in a public arena, (3) the product of which becomes the figuration of thinking . . .' (Corrigan 2011: 30).
3. Torres Strait Islanders live between the Australian mainland and Papua New Guinea and in various diasporic communities across Australia. The islands were annexed by the State of Queensland in the 1870s and became part of 'Australia' upon federation in 1901 (Beckett 1987).
4. 1990, 76', colour, 16mm, DVD. Berlin: Talking Pictures Frances Calvert.
5. See above note 3.
6. I am referring here to the ethnographic film of the British anthropologist Alfred Cort Haddon (1855–1940), who produced the first moving images of Aboriginal Australians and Torres Strait Islanders in 1898. I also briefly discuss Frank Hurley's 1920s documentary films in the region later in the chapter. For a fuller filmography of the region, see 'Screening the Torres Strait', available at <https://ScreeningTheTorresStrait.Wordpress.com> (last accessed 26 March 2018).
7. Given the funding and broadcast contexts of the film, Calvert (1997b: 190) was clearly aware of a tension between a popular television audience and a desire to experiment with method and form.
8. Calvert (1986a) had earlier written an analysis of O'Rourke's work for a retrospective in Berlin in 1986. However, it should be noted that the opening sequence was filmed before *Cannibal Tours* was released (Calvert 2016).
9. Calvert has written about Hurley's work, but was critical of its not being seen through a 'colonial eye' (1997a).
10. On the broader figure of irony in Calvert's work, see Calvert and Purser (1998: 311).
11. The intertitle is intended to convey the difficulty Islanders have in negotiating governmental language and power (Calvert 1988), but it is open to multiple readings.

12. Producer, Lindsey Merrison.
13. This is in the context of the 1988 secession attempt.

## References

Baron, Jaimie (2014), *The Archive Effect: Found Footage and the Audiovisual Experience of History*, London and New York: Routledge.
Beckett, Jeremy (1987), *Torres Strait Islanders: Custom and Colonialism*, Cambridge: Cambridge University Press.
Bolter, J. David and Richard Grusin (1998), *Remediation: Understanding New Media*, Cambridge, MA: MIT Press.
Calvert, Frances (1986a), 'Dennis O'Rourke: A Retrospective', *Metro*, 70 (Winter), 8–12.
Calvert, Frances (1986b), Review of *The Gods Must Be Crazy*, *Metro*, 71 (Spring), 46.
Calvert, Frances (1988), Pre-production Documentary Synopses, Channel 4 Archives, London, n.p.
Calvert, Frances (1991), Post-production Documentary Synopses, Channel 4 Archives, n.p.
Calvert, Frances (1997a), 'Frances Calvert on Frank Hurley', *Metro*, 112, 13–15.
Calvert, Frances (1997b), '"Talking Broken": A Portrait of the Torres Strait Islanders', in Dieter Riemenschneider and Geoffrey V. David (eds), *Aratjara: Aboriginal Culture and Literature in Australia*, Amsterdam: Rodopi, pp. 189–91.
Calvert, Frances (2016), Interview with Frances Calvert conducted by Peter Kilroy, King's College London, 24 May.
Calvert, Frances and Emily Purser (1998), 'Moving Images, Making Meanings', in Marc-Olivier Gonseth, Jacques Hainard and Roland Kaehr (eds), *Derrière les images*, Neuchâtel: Musée d'ethnographie, pp. 307–36.
Caquard, Sébastien (2009), 'Foreshadowing Contemporary Digital Cartography: A Historical Review of Cinematic Maps in Films', *The Cartographic Journal*, 46:1, 46–55.
Caquard, Sébastien and D. R. Fraser Taylor (2009), 'What Is Cinematic Cartography?', *The Cartographic Journal*, 46:1, 5–8.
Corless, Kieron (2016), 'On Cinema's Nerve Ends: The Essay Film', *ICA*, 15 March, <https://www.ica.org.uk/blog/on-cinemas-nerve-ends-essay-film> (last accessed 26 March 2018).
Corrigan, Timothy (2011), *The Essay Film: From Montaigne, After Marker*, Oxford and New York: Oxford University Press.
De Jong, Wilma (2012), 'From Wallpaper to Interactivity: Use of Archive Footage in Documentary Filmmaking', *Journalism and Mass Communication*, 2:3, 464–77.
Dixon, Richard (2001), *Prosthetic Gods: Travel, Representation and Colonial Governance*, Brisbane: University of Queensland Press.
Doane, Mary Ann (2007), 'The Indexical and the Concept of Medium Specificity', *Differences*, 18:1, 128–52.
Kay, Olivia Lory (2010), 'Gathering in the Orphans: Essay Films and Archives in the Information Age', *Journal of Media Practice*, 11:3, 253–66.
Kepley, Vance and Rebecca Swender (2009), 'Claiming the Found: Archive Footage and Documentary Practice', *The Velvet Light Trap*, 64 (Fall), 3–10.
Kilroy, Peter (2016), 'Screening Indigenous Australia: Space, Place and Media in Frances Calvert's *Talking Broken*', *Ilha do Desterro*, 69:2, 139–49.
McInerney, Marie (1991), 'Germans Fund Australian's Torres Strait Islanders Film', *The Canberra Times*, 6 May, p. 24.

Malone, Peter (1999), 'Peter Malone Interviews Frances Calvert', *Nelen Yubu*, 71, 9–17.
Nichols, Bill (2010), *Introduction to Documentary*, 2nd edn, Bloomington: Indiana University Press.
Rascaroli, Laura (2008), 'The Essay Film: Problems, Definitions, Textual Commitments', *Framework*, 2 (Fall), 24–47.
Rascaroli, Laura (2009), *The Personal Camera: Subjective Cinema and the Essay Film*, London and New York: Wallflower Press.
Seider, Tanja (2013), 'Postcolonial Historiography in the Essay Film: Decolonizing Sound and Image', *InterDisciplines*, 1, 127–51.
Sharp, Nonie (1993), *Stars of Tagai: The Torres Strait Islanders*, Canberra: Aboriginal Studies Press.
*Torres News* (1988), 'UN May Support Independence Move', *Torres News*, 19 February, n.p.
*Torres News* (1989), '*Talking Broken* – A New Islander Film', *Torres News*, 24–30 August, n.p.
Tracy, Andrew (2013), 'The Essay Film', *Sight and Sound*, 8 (August), 44–52.
Urry, John (2002), *The Tourist Gaze*, 2nd edn, London: Sage Publications.

# 12. BETWEEN AUTOBIOGRAPHY, PERSONAL ARCHIVE AND MOURNING: DAVID PERLOV'S *DIARY 1973–1983* IN TEL AVIV

Ilana Feldman

### Openings: Arrival in Tel Aviv

In January 2015, I spent a month in the city of Tel Aviv, Israel.[1] I was there with my family with whom I shared an apartment in the north of the city. Our arrival in Tel Aviv was initially marked by disappointment: it was not the sunny and cloudless sky known from the images on Google Maps that greeted us, but rain, strong winds and a sandstorm that made it difficult for us to leave the apartment. My mother cursed the inadequacy of her clothes for the bad weather; my father, who remained, as always, calm and in good humour, attempted to make the heater work; I hurt myself, trying to open and close a window; and my sister made jokes about the absurdity of it all. I had booked myself on a tour of Hebron, on the West Bank, operated by an Israeli NGO. But due to the storm, which left the place in a state of alert, the tour was cancelled. Among a list of chores and other important information, I wrote in my notebook that being in Israel is always an experience marked by anguish, blindness and exhaustion. In the confinement of the apartment, between cancelled trips, banal as well as more heated family conversations, I also followed the recent world events on television. Perplexed by the images of the white storm that paralysed the country, I heard about the terrorist attack on the offices of *Charlie Hebdo*, a French satirical weekly newspaper, in Paris – the same city we had just passed through on our way to Israel from Brazil.

The bad weather ended, and I paid David Perlov's widow a visit. Mira Perlov lives in the central region of Tel Aviv. Without knowing how to speak

Hebrew, I made an effort to imitate the guttural accent of the local population, a strategy that did not always work out. *Ibn Gvirol*, one of the major streets in Tel Aviv, is difficult to pronounce in Hebrew. I met Mira again and we soon became closer friends. We had coffee and talked for hours below her windows, which allow for a beautiful overview of Tel Aviv. During the day, with the white buildings and the intense clarity, it was almost impossible to look at the landscape. Mira showed me the documents, passports, letters and postcards that she had exchanged with David during the 1950s, when he worked with Henri Langlois, the director of *Cinémathèque Française*, and was the assistant of Joris Ivens, the master of poetic documentaries. Mira herself milked cows at that time, in a *kibutz* near the Gaza Strip. In one of the letters she writes, with exclamation mark, 'I am waiting for you!'

Working with archives requires the constant problematisation and reinvention of a method. While I was investigating the relations between the private and the political in the autobiographical work of another, namely Israeli-born Brazilian filmmaker David Perlov (1930–2003), I was also affectively and intellectually deeply implicated in this research. But instead of ignoring my anxieties and anguish accompanying my research on Perlov, I tried to harness these feelings in order to self-reflexively problematise my position as researcher. I made a conscious decision to accept my anguish as a constituent part of my research, questioning my supposed neutrality as researcher. I am following here, among others, Georges Devereux in *De l'angoisse à la méthode* (*From Anguish to Method*, 2012), in which he argues for a dialectics between the subject and the object of the investigation in a prolonged process 'of becoming aware', which may have direct implications for the research. Applying also Marcio Seligmann-Silva's notion of the 'testimonial tenor' of culture (2002) to my own research methodology, I can safely say that there is no knowledge of the 'other' without recognition of the 'self'.[2] Problematising, in this way, academic research into the visual archive of another (Perlov), I argue for the significance of my own personal archives and the transformative power they had in the construction of this research.

As all essays, the following aims to be a little heterodox. Rather than providing readers with analyses of historical periods or cinematographic archives, it will question the role the researcher and her own methodology, analytical practice and private visual archive play in the encounter with Perlov's 'archive'. What in research affects and transforms the researcher's own life, like a meeting between archives? I will reflect in this chapter on the different materials and documents that made my investigation possible in the context of a work that uses various archives, including television images, photographs, newsreels, film frames, reproductions of paintings and shots from previous films, and that re-signifies – through the temporality of the narration – the very notion of the archive.

Figure 12.1  Chapter 1, São Paulo, 1973, in *Diary 1973–1983*, David Perlov, 1985. © Yael Perlov.

### David Perlov's Windows

Still in Israel, I return to the domestic images of the *Diary*, a work consisting of six chapters, each lasting six hours, filmed over ten years, between 1973 and 1983. In *Diary*, Perlov filmed the daily life of his family and the city of Tel Aviv through the windows of his apartment; the windows of the television which brought to the private space dramatic political events, such as the Yom Kippur War in 1973 and the rise of the right to power in 1977; and through car windows passing the affective geographies of cities such as São Paulo, Paris, Lisbon or Rio de Janeiro.

'May 1973. I buy a camera. I want to start filming by myself and for myself. Professional cinema does no longer attract me,' Perlov says in the first chapter of his documentary project, resisting a cinema of plots, intrigues and dramas, a cinema of cheats, tricks and mystifications – although later he admits that at various moments he drew on the dramas which *reality* offered him.

Considered the precursor of modern Israeli cinema, Perlov, son of an itinerant magician and an illiterate mother, was born in Rio de Janeiro in 1930, but spent his first decade of life in Belo Horizonte. At the age of ten, he moved with his brother to his grandfather's house in Vila Mariana in São Paulo, abandoning a painful, traumatic and not at all protected childhood. Between his studies in a state college and tram trips, Perlov dedicated himself to drawing and painting (he frequented the atelier of Lasar Segall), and became engaged in the Socialist-Zionist youth movement *Dror*, where he met Mira. She, a Polish Jewish survivor of the Shoah, would be the producer of *Diary 1973–1983* and his lifelong companion.

Living in a type of forced 'exile' in his own apartment, after bitter conflicts with the Israeli authorities, who desired a conventional documentary and official propaganda, Perlov relates the writing of his filmic diary to an act of war as well as of despair, giving the genre a radicalness that had not previously existed in Israeli cinema. In *Diary* the political gaze of the one filming becomes a cinematographic question in his work for the first time. Equally, the enunciation in the first person singular, situated in the embodied and rhythmic voice of Perlov himself, takes form for the first time. 'A stranger here, a stranger there, a stranger everywhere. I could go home, honey, but I am still a stranger there,' he states, citing a song by Odetta, while he observes through the car window, after twenty years of absence from Brazil, passers-by in a quiet street in São Paulo.[3]

Among the various films made by Perlov, *Diary 1973–1983* (1985) constitutes his most important and vigorous work, in addition to the also autobiographical *Updated Diaries 1990–1999* (2001) and his filmic essay and testament-film *My Stills 1952–2002* (2003). Added to these two works can be two other films which, although they do not directly deal with his own life, inaugurated in Israel the question of the witness in cinema, as well as the particularisation of the filmic enunciation through the insertion of the voice of the documentary maker *off-camera*, to the detriment of the 'neutral' enunciation of official and generic discourse of mainstream politics. These works are *Biba* (1977), Perlov's first film narrated by himself and the only one to have a proper name as a title, about the pain of a woman who had lost her husband in the Yom Kippur War; and *Memories of the Eichmann Trial* (1979), in which Perlov interviews in the living room of his house some of the witnesses (or the children of witnesses) of the emblematic 1961 trial, thereby joining the private and the political.[4]

## The Letter

My journey followed its course, and the investigation of the films and documents continued in parallel to other, more personal, investigations. In addition to an appropriate winter coat, my mother wanted to find in Israel the small part of the family who had survived the Second World War, of whom we had not received news since the last letter written in Yiddish, sent by her uncle from Israel to Recife, on 23 October 1974. But we, in addition to not speaking Hebrew, also could not speak Yiddish. My cousin who lived in Yafo, the oldest and most eastern part of the city, tried to help us. She searched on the Internet and in telephone directories, but the address did not exist. We looked in the search systems of the Yad Vashem Museum, dedicated to the Shoah, and Beit Hatfutsot, the Diaspora Museum. Nothing. If David or Moshe Feldman – my mother was not certain – was unreachable, what would his descendants say?

Figure 12.2  Letter by David Feldman, from Israel to Brazil. Personal archive.

The letter in Yiddish, like a relic to be deciphered and as impenetrable as a stone wall, waited to be translated.

### 'Batucada' (Beating)

During *Diary*, on more than one occasion, Perlov's focus migrates from the observation of his family and daily life to political and social commentary and the cultivation of a state of mind that is often marked by malaise, and then again to a formal radicalisation, in which language is shaken and convulsed through the editing process. The most intense moment is when, in the third chapter, a harmonious dance with friends in the living room to the sound of a Brazilian song, makes the filmmaker remember the moments of penury in his childhood:[5]

> This dance in my home is too sudden. How many moments of the past does it enclose? How many lost Carnivals? I feel the start of a long journey on my way home. My home, the house in the backyard in Belo Horizonte. Black beans with no rice. One or two bananas a week. What instead?

Based on this commentary, the editing contributes to the interweaving of the dance (enjoyed by Mira and their friends Julio and Fela) and the empty,

Figure 12.3  Chapter 3, Julio and Fela at Perlov's home, Tel Aviv, 1981–2, in *Diary 1973–1983*, David Perlov, 1985. © Yael Perlov.

silent house – a process that is further underlined through the sound of an intense beating that rhythmically resonates with the shaking of the photographs, postcards, paintings and newspaper cuttings stuck on the wall of Perlov's room. Camera in hand and agitated, Perlov then turns to the city: shot through the window, the city on the ground seems in convulsion, as if in a state of tremor, similar to that of an earthquake. The shots through the window onto the urban scenery also direct our attention to 1981, gesturing towards the fact that we are less than one year away from the start of the Lebanon War. Then the camera returns to the scene of the dance where Perlov's friends can now be seen waving goodbye to the off-screen filmmaker; the inclusion of this scene in the film highlights both the joyful and the ironic in the scenario. The chaotic, nearly 10-minute-long interlude between the beginning and the end of the dance, which is filmed with a highly subjective camera, symbolises Perlov's own vertiginous interior landscape; it can be compared to a stream-of-consciousness charged with agitation, anguish and deadlocked words.

In a talk I gave in November 2015, I called this scene 'Batucada' (Beating). Perlov's narration not only contextualises the moments of filming, but also sees in the memories invoked in this scene – including, most notably, those of his painful childhood in Belo Horizonte – affective 'bridges' to feelings, sensations and premonitions that now also inhabit his present and concern Israel's near future. One may argue, recurring to Walter Benjamin and his *Arcades Project* (*Passagenwerk*, 1927–40) that in this small, individual moment – the dance with his friends – Perlov found a subterranean anguish: the trace of an imminent tragedy or, as Benjamin writes, 'the crystal of the total event' (2006: 503). In this way two landscapes are fused or amalgamated: the visible

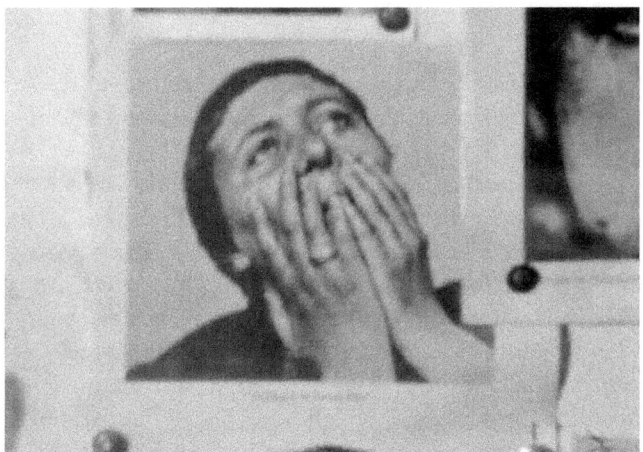

Figure 12.4  Chapter 3, still of *Passion of Joan of Arc*, Carl Dreyer, 1928, in *Diary 1973–1983*, David Perlov, 1985. © Yael Perlov.

exterior landscape of Tel Aviv, and the invisible interior or psychic-affective state of the filmmaker. The domestic space of house and family, neither protected nor separated from the outside through Perlov's window shots, becomes part of the urban chaos, the agitation of politics, the imminence of catastrophe and the waiting for a possible miracle. Traumatic personal past and intimate, domestic life in the present are linked through Perlov's cinematography and montage work to a collective and dramatic future that potentially awaits Israel.

Making use of his personal archive composed of photographs, paintings, postcards, newspaper cuttings and drawings, Perlov creates a form of 'Warburgian mural', an *Atlas Mnemosyne* for daily use: in a convulsive and trembling manner, he interlaces art and film historical references with his own biographical trajectory.[6] Among shots of newspaper cuttings with images of his wizard father, staging one of his magic numbers, viewers are also shown a shot of Carl Dreyer's image of the *Passion of Joan of Arc* (1928), which reappears several times, placing emphasis on the face and her gesture of supplication. Likewise, a reproduction of Vincent Van Gogh's lithograph *Sorrow* (1882), a homemade polaroid of a female nude and the magazine headlines 'My son, my son!', which appear to simulate someone's cry in fear upon the departure of their son for war, are shown.

This is what I also said in my November talk: my words in their search for organisation, meaning and coherence also make invisible the experience of being there, far from home, in Tel Aviv, blinded by a dazzling light, immobilised by a storm, deafened by the incomprehension of the language not understood.

## Stones

On 2 March 2015, hardly a month after we returned to Brazil, Nancy Rosenchan, a translator from Yiddish to Portuguese, wrote to my mother:

> On the envelope appears David Feldman. The address is Per 18-10 in the city of Hadera. I checked by Google but I did not find a street with this name. It could have changed or disappeared. There is no signature. The letter ends on the second page. On the top he makes use of the paper, turns over the page and asks to send him photographs soon. Irrespective of whether he could read or not, the letter is very short and his knowledge of written Yiddish is limited, which can be seen of the spelling of both Yiddish and Hebrew words, which he spells by their sound and not their original spelling. He is originally from Russia (he writes *gospital*, which is the Russian form for hospital).

While in Hebrew the word *bait* means 'house', 'religious temple' and 'body of a woman', the word *davar* means 'word' and 'thing'. In my great-uncle's letter, more than things, words seem like stones. Blue stones on a white tomb. Stones difficult to translate, whose possible transmission, painfully precarious, occurs between what is not written and what is inscribed, between what remains and what is lost.

It took me a long time to become courageous enough to read through the translation of the letter; if I am honest, it may have taken several months. It was difficult to reach the last lines where David Feldman says goodbye, begging for photographs. One of his phrases resonated with me: 'I do not know in which world I find myself.'

David Feldman survived the Nazi and Stalinist genocide, only managing to reach Israel in 1974, already elderly and with health problems. His documents were confiscated at the border and his address book nearly got lost. My grandfather, who probably received the letter from his brother at the beginning of 1975, when he was in Recife, never had time to answer it. The same year he discovered he had lung cancer, which brought him to Rio de Janeiro for treatment. It was his last journey. My grandmother did not speak Yiddish and did not understand what the letter said. After my grandfather's death, she kept the document as a treasure to be discovered one day. From what we know, David Feldman must have died in Israel soon after his brother's death in Brazil. He never received the photos, but he left us one of his.

ARCHIVE

More than a year and a half after our journey to Tel Aviv in January 2015, I found myself again in the situation of trying to decipher documents. Mira had entrusted me with David's diaries – this time his written work, consisting of three volumes, each around 300 pages long, in which he describes his everyday life and work in Tel Aviv. Opening Perlov's diaries with a certain reticence, I had no idea what I should do with these intimate documents; it felt, as if I was being encouraged to open a door that should not be opened.

On these pages depression is constant and on Thursday, 24 April (the year is probably 1980), Perlov writes in Portuguese, as always: 'I wake at 10 but I only get up a little after 11. A little anxious to have a day without something to do. I have breakfast, have my pills, get dressed, and shave. I am alone in the house.' At another moment, he says he is reading Brazilian Graciliano Ramos's landmark publication *Anguish* (1946). It could not be more appropriate.

I close the notebook and think that if we construct our present from the ruins of the past, as a single and gigantesque file (see Seligmann-Silva 2009b: 271–81; 2009a: 26), the personal file of Perlov, far from being a 'deposit which catalogues the traits of this to consign them to future memory', as Giorgio Agamben argues (2008: 145), occurs in an absence, like a hiatus between his mother tongue Portuguese, a lost language in a foreign country, and those who had lost it, his descendants – a language that no longer had much to say.

In this context it may be sensible to return to Perlov's visual work, the *Diary*. Anachronistic in the sense that it was constructed years after beginning the shooting in 1973, the film reconfigures a simple notion of the archive by means of montage and narration. The construction process of both montage and

Figure 12.5   David Perlov's notebooks. Personal archive.

commentary was sporadic until the beginning of the 1980s. In 1977 or 1978, a 45-minute pilot programme (composed of fragments from 1973 to 1977–8) was shown on Israeli television, as part of a programme called *Identities*, and in 1980 the same episode was shown on Channel 14 in New York.

According to what Mira told me in Tel Aviv, only in 1982 did she and David meet the director of the British Channel 4, Michael Kustow, who decided to fund the project based on the pilot he had seen (which corresponds today to parts of the third chapter). Thanks to Channel 4 funding, the fifth and sixth chapters (which involved journeys to London, Paris, São Paulo, Rio de Janeiro, Belo Horizonte and Lisbon) could be made. They were edited from 1981 to 1984–5. In 1988, over a period of six days, all six chapters were aired on Channel 4; only in the following year, they were screened in Israel, at the Tel Aviv Museum of Art, for the first time.

During all this time, David wrote the narration and commentary in Portuguese, while Mira worked as co-author, translating his writing into English for the Channel 4 production. The Hebrew version was only made a few years later. Strangely enough, in his written diaries, apparently composed at the same time that *Diary* was edited, Perlov spoke little about his cinematic creation and the editing process. His notebooks rather bear witness to what appears to be a lack of creativity, drawn-out hours and days, dull patches of time full of anguish, depression and finitude. They also gesture towards absence: to things we do not know and never will. Imagination is required, as Georges Didi-Huberman (2004) has argued many times: when we do not know the past, it is necessary to imagine it with the voices of archives.[7]

### Anna

In *Diary* Perlov begins his journey with the initially enigmatic epigraph: 'In the lands of poverty and illiteracy, those who couldn't sign their names had two crosses marked on their photographs: name and surname.' In a café in Paris (or was it a bakery in Vila Mariana?) I write on a napkin: where there is no name, there is no transmission. Where there is no name, there is no tomb, no remains, neither traces, nor ashes. Where there is no name, there can be no mourning.

Son of an illiterate mother, Perlov knew this cross like no one else. During the filming of his diaries, he captures some tombs and twice goes to the Israelite cemetery in Belo Horizonte, where his mother Anna, a figure little invoked and to some extent shrouded in mist, was buried. On the first visit, in the sixth chapter of *Diary*, Perlov notices that Anna's name has been spelt wrongly on her tombstone, Anna Perlof, with an 'f', instead of Perlov with a 'v'. This inscription of 'f', a letter which to Perlov is like the sign of the cross, functions in *Diary* as a shadow accompanying Perlov's search for the 'fatal image' of his mother who could not write her own name.[8] The illiterate mother who could not, due to misery or madness, inscribe herself in the symbolic order of language.

On the second visit, almost twenty years later, in the third chapter of *Updated Diaries 1990–1999*, Anna's name is finally corrected at the request of her son. In the place of 'f' Anna recovers the 'v' of her name, also regaining, against the flow of forgetfulness and anonymity, the inscription of her identity. Correcting his mother's name, inscribing her, in other words, correctly in the memory of those who live, constitutes a central objective of Perlov's autobiographic work.[9] It is precisely because Anna Perlov inhabits the place of trauma, of the irrepressible *par excellence*, that returning to the tomb and mourning constitutes the broadest meaning of David Perlov's journey over all these years. It seems as if it is necessary through mourning to abandon the origin of the moment, even when it is found, in order to guarantee the continuity of life. Survivors know well that 'where there is no tomb, the work of mourning never ends' (Klüger 2005: 87). It is for no other reason, as Jeanne Marie Gagnebin highlights based on the Hellenist Jean-Pierre Vernant, that the original meaning of the Greek word *sèma* was 'tomb' and only afterwards 'sign', since the tomb is the sign of the dead. Tomb, sign, written word, image: all struggle against being forgotten (Gagnebin 2006: 112).

### Crosses

On my journey to Tel Aviv in January 2015, I also brought with me a copy of Roland Barthes's *Camera Lucida*, his beautiful autobiographical essay. In this book, contemporaneous to the diaries of Perlov, Barthes tries to mourn his beloved mother through a hybrid form of narrating, including biographical details, images, aphorisms and critical reflection. Only through this form did Barthes feel able to voice his difficulty of sustaining his gaze at the photograph of his mother, whose image he could not, or was unable to, publish. 'Looking at the photograph of my mother as a child, I tell myself', Barthes writes, 'she will die. [. . .] Whether the subject is already dead or not, any photograph is this catastrophe' (1984: 142).

Benjamin argues that everything which disappears becomes an image; however, some photographs – such as 'the fatal image' of Perlov's mother or the image of Barthes at the age of five, pregnant with future, on a bridge in front of a garden – are real *dark cameras* and cannot be reproduced within the works which, in the negative, contain them. Therefore, to the aesthetic of presence, according to which photography is an apex of the real and the inscription of the reference, both Perlov and Barthes problematise the limits of the image and raise its impossibilities, proposing an aesthetic of absence, loss and disappearance. This is also an aesthetic of the 'impossible' – in the words of Alain Badiou (2004), maybe an 'impossible image' in the place of that 'fatal image'

Figure 12.6  Rue de l'Aqueduc, Paris, photograph by David Perlov, 1952–8. © Yael Perlov.

Figure 12.7  Chapter 5, Rue de l'Aqueduc, Paris, 1983, in *Diary 1973–1983*, David Perlov, 1985. © Yael Perlov.

of Anna – which can cope with the impotence of trauma, sustaining the necessity of struggle.

Perlov spent six years in Paris before he emigrated to Israel in 1958. When he began to photograph in Rue de l'Aqueduc, he encounters – as becomes visible in the fifth chapter of *Diary* – crosses everywhere.

I know now that mourning – for all those who have perished, for all that has disappeared or been lost – is what sets life in motion.

## Afterthoughts: Names

In November 2015, nearly a year after our trip to Tel Aviv and ten days after the terrorist attack of Friday 13 in Paris, I am back in Brazil. At a conference,

I show a sequence from Perlov's *Diary 1973–1983* (1985), made in Israel, through his windows.[10] I am, once again, exploring the ways the private and the personal, through film, are constantly being entwined with the public and the political. I also investigate the ways alterity is imagined, constructed and reconfigured through a singular autobiographical gesture. Having inherited a typically Israeli first name and a typically Jewish surname, I know that my talk can arouse suspicion and may be reduced to an identity stereotype. If a name is something received or inherited, however, it is also something invented and then appropriated. A name is a word that is carried, like a thing or a stone, between exiles and dislocations.

## Notes

1. A previous version of this chapter was published in 2018, in Portuguese with an English translation under the title 'Not Understanding: Archives, Documents, and Creation in the Meeting with *Diary* by David Perlov' in the bilingual book *Archives in Movement. International Seminar on Archive Documentaries*, ed. Adelina Novaes e Cruz, Arbel Griner, Patrícia Machado and Thais Blank, Rio de Janeiro: Fundação Getulio Vargas.
2. Seligmann-Silva has developed the 'testimonial tenor' of culture in some publications, most notably, in 'Literatura e trauma' (2002). After the linguistic and mnemonic turns of the 1970s and 80s, he argues, it is more productive to think of the traits of this testimonial content, now strongly present in cinema, literature, the visual arts and even theatre, than to try to restrict it to a specific genre, such as 'testimonial literature' or 'testimonial cinema'. The 'testimonial content' is what occurs between the fiction operated by linguistics and what we conventionally call the real, that is, between the literary and the factual.
3. The song *Stranger Here*, sung by Odetta Holmes (1930–2008), a type of adage of Perlov's journey, recalls a text by Georges Perec, which seems to illuminate the existential exile present in diaries: 'Quelque part, je suis étranger par rapport à quelque chose de moi-même; quelque part, je suis "différent", mais non pas différent des autres, différent des "miens"' (in Perec and Bober 1980).
4. Not by chance, the trial of the Nazi official Adolf Eichmann in Israel, in 1961, inaugurates, according to Annette Wieviorka, an 'era of testimony' in countries such as France, the United States and Israel, when the witness (especially of a genocide) comes to demand a privileged place in the public space and in the construction of individual and national identities (see Wieviorka 2009: 81).
5. I know from Mira Perlov that the original music played in the sequence was *O que será que será?* by Chico Buarque, but due to copyright problems, it was replaced in the editing.
6. Aby Warburg's *Atlas Mnemosyne* (1924–9), which remained unfinished, constitutes for all art historians a reference work today, as it transformed the way images are understood. *Atlas Mnemosyne* was his paradoxical masterpiece and his methodological testament: it brings together all the objects of his research in a device of 'moveable panels', which are constantly mounted, dismounted or remounted. It is also a response to the experience of psychic instability and war. It can thus be seen as a documental history of the western imagination (heir in these terms to Francisco Goya's *Los Disparates*, 1815–23, and *Los Caprichos*, 1797–8), and as a tool for understanding political violence in the image of history (comparable

in this respect to a compendium like *The Disasters of War*) (see Didi-Huberman 2013).
7. According to Arlette Farge, the archive is always singular and anonymous, absolute and lacking; it is survival, but above all it is the sign of finitude. In Farge's formulation, 'using archives today means translating this absence into a question' (2009: 58).
8. In the second chapter of *Diary 1973–1983*, Perlov refers to the photograph of a girl, which appeared a little before in a half-opened drawer, as 'the fatal image'. Only at the end of the work do we understand, through allusions and two Xs marked on the photograph, that this photograph was the only image of Anna, his mother, in the entire film.
9. It is interesting to note that in the Jewish New Year, after Yom Kippur, the Day of Atonement, which is a tribute to mourning, people wish each other in Hebrew 'Gmar chatimá tová', in other words: 'May we be inscribed in the book of life with a good signature.'
10. The *Diary* makes me think of Chantal Akerman's claustrophobic and autobiographical *Là-Bas* (2006), a film also made in Tel Aviv and behind windows. In relation to *Là-Bas*, see Feldman (2009).

## References

Agamben, Giorgio (2008), *O que resta de Auschwitz*, trans. Selvino J. Assmann, São Paulo: Boitempo.
Badiou, Alain (2004), 'Por uma estética da cura analítica', in *A psicanálise & os discursos*, trans. Analúcia Teixeira Ribeiro, Rio de Janeiro: Escola Letra Freudiana, ano XXIII, no. 34, pp. 237–42.
Barthes, Roland (1984), *A câmara clara*, trans. Júlio Castañon Guimarães, Rio de Janeiro: Nova Fronteira.
Benjamin, Walter (2006), *Passagens*, trans. Cleonice Paes Barreto Mourão, Belo Horizonte: Editora UFMG.
Devereux, Georges (2012), *De l'angoisse à la méthode*, Paris: Flammarion.
Didi-Huberman, Georges (2004), *Images malgré tout*, Paris: Minuit.
Didi-Huberman, Georges (2013), *A imagem sobrevivente: história da arte e tempo dos fantasmas segundo Aby Warburg*, trans. Vera Ribeiro, Rio de Janeiro: Contraponto.
Farge, Arlette, (2009), *O sabor do arquivo*, São Paulo: Edusp.
Feldman, Ilana (2009), 'Lá: do lugar que não existe à entrevista que deixou de existir', *Revista Cinética* (May), <http://www.revistacinetica.com.br/chantalilana.htm> (last accessed 5 July 2018).
Gagnebin, Jeanne Marie (2006), *Lembrar, escrever, esquecer*, São Paulo: Editora 34.
Klüger, Ruth (2005), *Paisagens da memória: autobiografia de uma sobrevivente do Holocausto*, trans. Irene Aron, São Paulo: Editora 34.
Perec, Georges and Robert Bober (1980), *Récits d'Ellis Island. Histoires d'errance et d'espoir*, Paris: P.O.L.
Seligmann-Silva, Márcio (2002), 'Literatura e trauma', *Pro-Posições*, 13:3 (September/December), <https://www.fe.unicamp.br/pf-fe/publicacao/2165/39-dossie-silvams.pdf> (last accessed 1 March 2016).
Seligmann-Silva, Márcio (2009a), *A atualidade de Walter Benjamin e Theodor Adorno*. Rio de Janeiro: Civilização Brasileira.
Seligmann-Silva, Márcio (2009b), 'Estética e política, memória e esquecimento: novos desafios na era do Mal de Arquivo', *Remate de Males*, 29:2 (July/December), 271–81.
Wieviorka, Annnette (2009), *L'Ère du témoin*, Paris: Hachette.

# AFTERIMAGES:

# A PHOTO-ESSAY

# STRANGELY REAL: A REASSEMBLAGE FROM THE FILM *FORGETTING VIETNAM*

## Trinh T. Minh-ha

Vietnam in ancient times was named 'the land of ten thousand springs'. One of the myths surrounding the creation of Vietnam involves a fight between two dragons whose intertwined bodies fell into the South China Sea and formed Vietnam's curving, 'S'-shaped coastline. Legend also has it that Vietnam's ancestors were born from the union of a Dragon King and a fairy, Âu Cơ. Âu Cơ was also a mythical bird that swallowed a handful of earthly soil and consequently lost the power to return to the 36th Heaven. Her tears formed Vietnam's myriad rivers and the country's recurring floods are the land's way of remembering her. In her geo-political situation, Vietnam thrives on a fragile equilibrium between land and water management. A life-sustaining power, water is evoked in every aspect of her river-born culture.

Shot in low and high technology – Hi-8 video in 1995 and in HD and SD in 2012 – the images of *Forgetting Vietnam* (90', digital film, 2015–16) unfold spatially as a dialogue between the two elements – land and water – that underlie the formation of the term 'country' (*đất nước*). In conversation with these two (ancient and modern) parts is a third space, that of historical and cultural re-memory – or what people remember of yesterday's stories to comment on today's events. Touching on a trauma of international scale, *Forgetting Vietnam* is made in commemoration of the fortieth anniversary of the end of the war and of its survivors.

Making films so as to make real, to persist and to resist what has come to be accepted as real. To show I-real while questioning who, what, how that real-I could be. Digital technology offers the possibility of working intensely with time in its liquidity and with indefinitely coexisting layers of temporalities, as ancient and modern meet on the light canvas. But in times of coercive politics and transnational terror, slowing down so as to learn to listen anew is a necessity. This is particularly relevant as one turns to digital systems in filmmaking, for the digital is here a *way* (of living) rather than a mere technology and the question is not so much to produce a *new image* as to provoke, facilitate and solicit a *new seeing*. In the interplay of hear and see, silence and sound, stillness and movement, the hearing eye and the speaking ear are constantly solicited, and form and formless are the two facets of a single process – or of life and death.

*it
all
began
with
two*

*sea and boat*

ancestral dragon's body

water of legends

Hạ Long

descending dragon

memory of a vast origin

thousands islets and islands rise
from the water

a fragile equilibrium between land and water

high and low technology

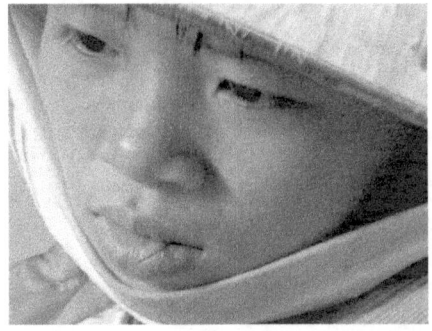

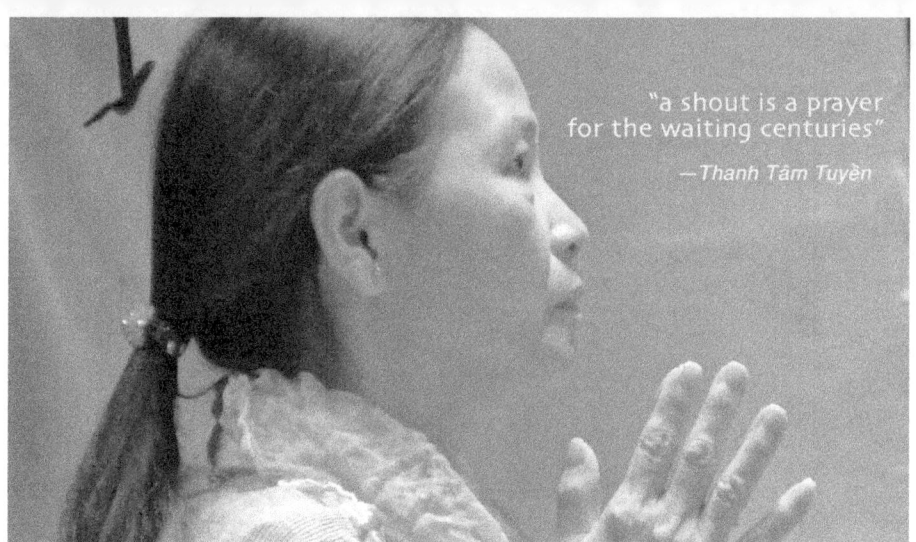

# INDEX

*88: The True Story of the March That Changed a Nation*, 196

*À Propos de Nice*, 7
accented cinema, 10, 55–68
Acconci, Vito, 164
Adorno, Theodor W., 1, 8, 14, 39, 40
aesthetics, 72–3, 85, 101, 108, 205
affinities, 12, 39–40, 117–19
Agamben, Giorgio, 219
Ahmedabad, 11, 70–2, 75–80
Akerman, Chantal, 34, 63, 224n10
Akomfrah, John, 3, 10, 56, 63, 66–7, 85
Alea, Tomás Gutiérrez, 34
*Algerian Dreams*, 63
*All that Jazz*, 140
allegory, 5, 97–8, 113
Alonso, Lisandro, 36, 42, 50n9
Alter, Nora, 1, 2, 15, 40, 50n3, 62, 63, 85, 92, 107, 119
ambiguity, 2, 28, 61
*Amour Fou, L'*, 140
Amsterdam, 2, 6
anachronistic, 2, 195–6, 199, 202, 206, 219
analogy, 5, 130
*Ananas see Pineapple*
anguish, 131, 211–12, 216, 220
*Anguish*, 219

Anthology Film Archive, 43, 48
anthropology, 70, 78–81
Antonioni, Michelangelo, 27–8, 29
anxiety, 31, 93, 97–9, 148
appropriation, 28, 91, 178, 180, 195
Arai, Takashi, 166
archival tropes, 13, 194–6, 199, 207
archive, 5, 10, 13, 26, 43, 48, 64, 66, 72, 77–8, 80–1, 85, 90, 119, 132, 148, 193–208, 211–24
*Archives de la Planète*, 90
Armenian, 63, 135, 163
*Arrival of a Train at La Ciotat Station, The*, 44
Astruc, Alexandre, 6, 9, 60, 83, 172, 193
atlas, 90–1
*Atlas Mnemosyne*, 217, 223n6
*auteur* theory, 6–8, 174
authenticity, 28, 67, 162
authorship, 10, 11, 12, 56, 59, 61, 81–2, 123–5, 141, 147, 174–5, 177, 204
autobiographical, 31, 56–7, 59, 61, 67, 70–1, 102n6, 138, 177, 212, 214, 221
avant-garde, 2, 4, 5–7, 37–8, 39, 40, 45, 73, 162

*Babel*, 102n9
Badiou, Alain, 9, 221–2

Baillie, Bruce, 117
Balázs, Béla, 90, 99
Ballard, J. G., 126, 135
*Baraka*, 102n5
Barriga, Susana, 3, 10, 32–5
Barthes, Roland, 46, 221
Bauman, Zygmunt, 1
Bazin, André, 6, 37–8, 46, 162, 177, 193, 204
*Behemoth*, 12, 13, 172–87
Beijing, 3, 28, 174, 179, 186n4
Belo Horizonte, 3, 213, 215–16, 220
belonging, 61–2, 67, 99, 116, 143, 147, 149
Benjamin, Walter, 8, 35, 216, 221
Benveniste, Émile, 40
Berlin, 2, 3, 6, 197, 208n8
*Berlin, Symphony of a Great City*, 7
*Berta's Motives see Motivos de Berta*
*Beyond the Mountains*, 63, 64
*Biba*, 214
Biemann, Ursula, 9, 62
Bing, Wang, 36, 41
*Birdman*, 140
Black Audio Film Collective *see Handsworth Songs*
*Blissfully Yours*, 109, 111
body, 46, 58, 76, 96, 109, 131, 147–8, 163–5, 181, 218
Bohinc, Nika, 43, 46
Boorman, John, 118
border, 1, 3, 10, 14, 49, 62, 64, 76, 111, 113, 179, 218
border-thinking, 62, 68n5
Brazil, 8, 56, 63, 64, 211, 214–22
bricolage, 78–9
British Empire, 72, 84, 86
*Brother Sharp Arrives Home*, 29–30
Buddhism, 114, 120n4
Burch, Noël, 3, 11, 38, 96–7

*Cahiers du Cinéma*, 6
Calvert, Frances, 3, 13, 193–208
*Camera Lucida see* Barthes
camera pen *see caméra-stylo*
*caméra-stylo*, 6, 60, 83, 172; *see also media-stylo*
*Cannibal Tours*, 198, 208n8
*Capital see* Marx
capital(ism), 5, 8, 9, 89, 97–9, 182, 205
*Caprichos, Los*, 223n6
Cartier-Bresson, Henri, 71, 76
Cassirer, Ernst, 114, 118

Cavalcanti, Alberto, 7
censorship, 10, 25, 26, 174, 186, 186
*Centers*, 164
Channel 4, 197, 201, 220
Chaplin, Charles, 44
*Charlie Hebdo*, 150, 211
Chen, Duxiu, 175, 187n10
childhood, 41, 109, 111, 132, 213, 215–16
China, 9, 13, 22, 26–31, 39, 86, 172–87, 226
*China Concerto*, 27–9
chronotope, 74
*Chung Kuo, Cina*, 28
*ciné-club*, 6, 7
*cinécriture*, 6, 9, 83
*Cinema Novo*, 8
Cinemã of Prayōga, 73
Cinémateque Française, 212
*Claire's Knee*, 140
colonial, 10, 12, 61, 66, 68n5, 73, 91, 98, 102n5, 119, 139, 141–9, 153, 208n9
colonialism, 95, 139, 143, 146–7, 196, 199–200, 205–7
commemoration, 13, 45, 107, 113, 196, 199, 226
commentary, 1, 25, 28, 60, 81, 120n3, 141, 153, 165, 175, 182, 200, 202, 204, 206, 215, 220
commercialisation, 30, 93
commodity, 72, 95, 102n9
community, 14, 25, 79, 124, 160, 174, 187n6, 194, 196, 197, 204
*Cómo construir un barco*, 32
*Complete Letters, The*, 36–7, 45, 48
Cong, Feng, 174, 175, 176, 179
*Contagion*, 102n9
correspondence project, 10, 36, 38–50
Corrigan, Timothy, 2, 6, 37–8, 40, 42, 60, 63, 74, 81–3, 92–3, 100, 107, 125, 127, 162, 164, 170n1, 177, 193–5, 197–9, 201–3, 205, 207, 208n1
cotton aesthetics, 77–9
cotton manufacture, 11, 70–2, 78–9, 82–6
Cottonopolis, 70–87
*Cracks in the Mask*, 13, 194
*Crime and Punishment*, 179
crisis, 1, 5–9, 26, 31, 56–7, 100, 102n6, 160, 165–70
crosses, 165, 220–4
Cuba, 9, 22, 32–5
Cultural Revolution, 28–9

239

Dante (Alighieri), 178–82
*Darwin's Nightmare*, 98
Demos, T. J., 177
Derrida, Jacques, 148
desire, 11, 22, 24, 25, 34, 41, 46, 63, 92, 94, 110, 123, 146, 173, 175, 180, 193, 202, 206, 207, 208n7
destruction, 132, 136, 160–9
Di Tella, Andres, 63
dialogue, 6, 9–10, 13–14, 21–50, 60, 72, 73, 81, 133, 141, 147, 152, 226
*Diary 1973–1983*, 13, 211–24
diary (film), 8, 13, 24, 44, 57–60, 63, 65, 67–8, 82, 193, 211–24
diaspora aesthetics, 10, 62, 70, 214
diasporic, 3, 10, 55, 58, 61, 62, 64, 70, 72–4, 80, 85, 178, 208n3
Didi-Huberman, Georges, 220, 223n6
dislocation, 56, 62, 66, 100, 223
*Disparates, Los*, 223n6
displacement, 10, 56–9, 64, 72, 100, 126, 129, 139, 142, 197, 201, 202, 207
*dissensus*, 5, 108, 118
distance, 24–6, 29, 39–40, 46, 128, 162, 168, 182, 199, 203
*Divine Comedy, The*, 178, 180–6
*Doctor Mabuse*, 46
dogs, 135, 151
*Domov*, 63, 64
Dorsky, Nathaniel, 117
*Double Steps, The*, 42
Dreyer, Carl, 217
Dwoskin, Steve, 39
*Dziga Vertov Group*, 7

earthquake, 24, 159–60, 165–6, 216
economy, 72, 75–6, 94–5, 97, 99, 204–5
editing, 6, 9, 30, 31, 42, 43, 46, 59, 64, 76, 78, 80, 82, 94, 111, 150, 151, 162, 173, 176, 182, 184, 203, 205, 215, 220, 223n5
Eichmann, Adolf, 214, 223n4
Eimbcke, Fernando, 36, 41–2
*Eleven Men*, 23, 25
emotion, 57, 67, 75, 83, 109, 139, 140, 175, 182, 185, 216
Engels, Friedrich, 72, 85–6
Enlightenment, 21
entanglement, 4, 11, 108, 114, 140, 141, 198, 204, 207
enunciation, 45, 49, 50n7, 95, 108, 207, 214
Erice, Víctor, 36, 42, 43, 50n1

*Escape*, 153
*Essais*, 37, 40, 50n8, 60, 175
essay film
 ability of, 22–3
 argument, 5, 195, 206
 as conceptual field, 3, 5–7, 14, 15n9, 21, 22, 27, 42, 50, 68n5, 73, 91, 109, 110, 118, 120n4, 131, 133–4, 141, 160, 166, 172, 175, 198, 206
 as counter-practice, 2, 5, 6, 8, 116, 205
 audience address, 40, 49, 50n7, 59, 65, 92, 95, 202, 204
 citational, 194–5
 epistemological, 11, 56, 68n5, 76, 165, 177, 198
 experimental *see* form
 festivals, 1, 2, 21, 22, 23, 32, 39, 43, 44, 47, 73, 79, 120n7, 140, 143, 147, 172, 173–4, 179, 186–7, 193, 197, 208n1
 form, 1–9, 11–12, 14–15n1, 21–35, 40–1, 56–7, 60, 62–3, 65, 68n5, 73–4, 80–1, 86, 89, 92–3, 95, 102n6, 107–8, 112, 123, 124–5, 133, 138, 172–5, 177, 193–5, 215, 221, 227
 fragmentary, 59, 61, 114, 194, 197, 202
 heresy, 2, 5, 8, 123, 125
 heterogeneity, 7, 59, 66, 177
 hybridity, 22, 24, 61, 107–8, 119, 175, 193, 221
 in-between-ness, 10, 23–7, 30, 62, 67, 74, 123–4, 198
 indeterminacy, 24, 59, 197
 literary, 6, 7, 9, 11, 13, 21, 23, 27, 30, 36, 62, 122, 124, 127, 143, 172–8, 184, 186, 187n9, 193, 195, 202, 223n2
 personal as political, 56, 193, 211–24
 personal vs social, 33, 207
 refractive, 38, 42–9, 138, 193; *see also* reflexivity
 taxonomy, 193–4
 thinking, 3–5, 11, 14n1, 25, 30, 40, 60, 62, 68n5, 74, 123, 125, 139, 177, 193–4, 202, 208n2
 utopian potential, 2, 9, 83, 90
 world, 1–14, 24–5, 32, 37, 61, 80, 85, 89–101, 116, 127, 130, 145, 196
essayfication, 1
essayism, 7, 13, 60
ethnographic, 3, 24, 41, 70–87, 102n6, 149, 173, 176, 208n6
*Evening Shoot, An*, 113, 120n8

# INDEX

*exagium*, 108
exile, 9, 11, 33, 59, 60, 62, 66, 125–7, 214, 223
experience, 80–2, 143, 149, 179, 193, 195, 211, 217
exploitation, 30, 91, 95, 101, 181, 184

fable, 5, 111, 120n5
*Fall of the Romanov Empire*, 7
family, 41, 56, 60, 64, 70, 72, 84, 148–9, 185, 211, 213–18
Fanon, Frantz, 141, 149
fantasy, 99, 101, 108–17, 147
*fanyu* see irony
*Far from Poland*, 63
*Far from Vietnam*, 25
Farrokhzad, Forough, 8
Farsi, Sepideh, 63
fiction, 4, 11, 13, 24–5, 32, 41, 62, 73, 74, 80, 107–11, 113, 118, 123–8, 136, 139–41, 146, 148, 151, 153, 223n2
*Film Auteur*, 174
*Film Culture*, 44
Fisher, Mark, 9
Flaherty, Robert *see Nanook of the North*
*flâneur*, 126, 127
fluidity, 29, 34, 82, 136, 141
food, 93–6
Ford, John, 44
*Forgetting Vietnam*, 13, 178, 226–37
*Forgotten Space, The*, 11, 96–7
Fosse, Bob, 140
*Fotografías*, 63
*Four Passports*, 63
freedom, 9, 24, 32, 34, 39, 86, 133, 134, 147, 149, 179, 186n2
French New Wave, 6, 8, 43, 172, 174
Fricke, Ron, 102n5
Fujiwara, Chris, 170n2
Fujiwara, Toshi, 3, 12, 159–70
*fūkei-ron*, 169
Fukushima, 48, 159–70

Gámez, Rúben, 8
Gandhi (Mohandas K.), 72, 76, 79
Gao, Shiqiang, 174, 187n8
gaze, 5, 28–9, 41, 42, 46, 58, 81, 82–6, 102n5, 109, 112, 167, 198–203, 214, 221
Gee, Grant, 3, 11, 12, 122–36
gender, 5, 8, 139, 140, 142, 143, 149–50, 151, 163, 176, 178, 187
*Genèse d'un repas*, 11, 94–6

genocide, 43, 135, 218, 223n4
gesture, 2, 26, 34, 49, 65, 110, 113, 138, 152, 164, 195, 217, 220, 223
Getino, Octavio, 7, 8, 79
ghost, 85, 109, 111–17, 120n5, 128, 130, 145–6, 168, 180–1, 185
Gitai, Amos, 3, 11, 93–5
Glawogger, Michael, 98–9
*Gleaners and I, The*, 82–3, 125
globalisation, 1, 3, 5, 7, 14, 22, 29, 56, 67n2, 92–102, 194, 197, 200, 202, 204, 207
Godard, Jean-Luc, 7, 25, 32, 43, 178
Godmilow, Jill, 63
Gorin, Jean-Pierre, 7, 25
Goya, Francisco, 223n6
Gramsci, Antonio, 146
*Grandmother's Flower*, 10, 56, 63
Greenhalgh, Cathy, 3, 10–11, 70–87
Grierson, John, 49, 97, 201, 202
*Grizzly Man*, 170n1
Guerín, José Luis, 3, 10, 36–50
*Guest*, 44
Gui, Shuzhong, 174
Güler, Ara, 126–7, 132
Guo, Ke, 187n7
Guo, Xiaolu, 187n13
Guzman, Patricio, 63, 64

Hamlet, 146
*Handsworth Songs*, 66
Hangzhou, 182
Harare, 139–40, 143–4, 147–8, 153
*Harat – A Journey Diary*, 63
Harris, Thomas Allen, 63
He, Yun, 174
Hebrew, 211–12, 214, 218, 220
*Hello, the Original Point*, 176
heritage, 7, 47, 71–2, 122, 135, 174, 177
Herzog, Werner, 170n1
heterotopia, 96
*Hiroshima, Mon Amour*, 170n6
history, 5, 11, 25–8, 33–4, 39, 41, 43, 45–7, 64–7, 72, 79, 86, 107, 112, 119, 120, 122–36, 176, 193–208, 211–23
Holanda, Francisco de, 39
Hollywood, 4, 25, 29, 65, 81, 98, 100, 140
Holmes, Odetta, 223n3
Holocaust, 47, 142, 214
home, 55, 62, 58–62, 90
*Home*, 10, 56

# INDEX

Homer, 59, 66
Homer, Winslow, 84–5
homosexuality, 152
Hong Kong, 26, 31, 179, 187n14
*Hong Kong: A Story of Space*, 31
*hongtuo see* juxtaposition
Hou, Hsiao-hsien, 120n9
*Hound of the Deep, The*, 199
*Hour of the Furnaces, The*, 7, 8
*House is Black, The*, 8
Hruza, Margareta, 10, 56, 63, 64
Hu, Xinyu, 174
*hüzün*, 131–6
humankind, 66, 180
humour, 76, 141, 150, 202, 211
*Hungarian Passport, A*, 10, 56, 63, 64
*Hunger*, 12, 162
Hungwe, Blessing, 146–7, 150
Hurley, Frank, 199, 201–2, 204, 208
Huxley, Aldous, 193

*I am Cuba/Soy Cuba*, 162
*I for India*, 63, 64
icon, 75, 82, 135, 146–7
identity, 4, 61, 64, 220, 221, 223n4
*Illusion, The*, 34
image, 4, 11, 14, 15, 33–5, 42, 49, 74, 80, 84, 89, 90–3, 96, 101, 115, 194, 220–1, 224n8
    ideographic, 12–13, 179, 187
    status of, 24–6, 30–1, 159–60, 163, 165–70, 176, 221–2, 223n6, 227
    –word dialectic, 7, 23, 37–8, 49, 60, 64, 66, 107–8, 120n2, 180, 195, 201, 204–5
'image writing', 81, 172–86
imagination, 23, 37, 49, 73, 113, 125, 198, 220, 223n6
immersive, 30, 73, 85, 173, 179
immigrant *see* migrant
*In the City of Sylvia*, 44
Iñárritu, Alejandro González, 102, 140
independent film practice, 3, 5, 13, 31, 43, 45, 63, 172, 173–4, 176, 186
indexical, 100, 124, 127, 128–33, 206–7
India, 8, 10, 63, 64, 66, 70–87
indicability, 99–101
Indigenous, 5, 13, 193–208
industrial, 65, 72, 79, 82, 86, 94, 175, 181, 184–6
inequality, 9, 205
*Inflation*, 120n3
injustice, 5, 142

*Innisfree*, 50n11
innocence, 133–4
*Innocence of Memories*, 11, 122–36
*Innocence of Objects, The*, 123, 125
insider, 26, 29
installation, 11, 21, 22, 27, 30, 34, 50, 108, 111, 113, 118, 119, 174, 179
interdisciplinary, 68n5, 72, 73
interpellation, 41, 50n7
intertextual, 5, 66, 130, 195, 199
intertitles, 59–60, 196, 199, 201–2, 205, 207
intimacy, 25, 80, 131
invisible, 5, 6, 11, 15n9, 89, 97–100, 162, 166, 170, 199, 217
irony, 117, 128, 142, 178, 182, 199–200, 203, 206, 208n10, 216
Israel, 13, 93, 211–24
Israeli cinema, 214
Istanbul, 3, 12, 122–36
*Istanbul: Memories and the City*, 125, 132
Ivens, Joris, 212

Japan, 4, 8, 23, 24, 39, 41, 43, 47, 48, 63, 82, 93, 159–70, 187n15
Jayasankar, K. P., 75–6, 86
*Jetée, La*, 114–15, 118
Jevtić, Mihajlo, 63
Jia, Zhang-ke, 120n9
*Jo Ha Kyu*, 24–5
journey, 10, 40, 41, 44, 46–8, 59–60, 63–4, 86, 100, 113, 116, 125, 143, 159–68, 180, 195–6, 214–23
*jugaad*, 79
juxtaposition, 13, 80, 128, 173, 178, 195, 205

Kafai, Tony-Leung, 26
Kafka, Franz, 23–4, 64, 68n8
Kahn, Albert, 90
Kalatozov, Mikhail, 162
Kang, He, 174, 176
Kaufman, Mikhail, 82
Kawase, Naomi, 36, 39, 41–2, 50n9, 118
Keiller, Patrick, 100, 125, 127, 201
Khanjian, Arsinée, 163, 170n4
Kiarostami, Abbas, 36, 42, 50, 117
Kim, So Yong, 36, 41–2
Kita-Kamakura, 43, 48
kite festival, 79
Kluge, Alexander, 7
knowledge, 3, 12, 32, 61, 68n5, 74, 79, 80–1, 89–92, 95, 101, 114, 119, 130,

133, 141, 144, 149, 177, 196, 198–9, 201, 205, 212, 218
Kogut, Sandra, 10, 56, 63, 64
Koretzky, Aya, 63, 64
Kracauer, Siegfried, 120n3
Kramer, Robert, 39

*Là-Bas*, 224n10
labour, 32, 58, 72, 75–7, 82, 85–6, 87, 94, 95, 98, 178, 181–5, 205
Lacuesta, Isaki, 36, 41–2, 50n9
Landrián, Nicolás Guillén, 34, 35
landscape, 12, 21, 25, 30, 43, 48, 64, 66, 73, 74–5, 92, 98, 100, 107, 109, 124–9, 132, 136, 159–70, 179–86, 212, 216–17
*Landscape Series No. 1*, 22
Lang, Fritz, 46
Langlois, Henri, 212
language, 6, 7, 11, 13, 15n8, 27, 31, 33, 37, 40, 62, 65, 72, 107, 142, 148, 163, 164–5, 172–3, 175, 177–8, 186, 187, 201–5, 208n11, 215, 217, 219, 221
Lebanon War, 216
Lehmann, Boris, 63
letter, 1, 10, 25, 28, 36–50, 78, 82, 86, 90, 99, 112, 130, 212, 214–15, 218, 220
*Letter from Siberia*, 6, 23, 37, 38, 120n1, 177
*Letter to Jane: An Investigation About a Still*, 25
*Letters from Panduranga*, 22–6
Li, Xianting, 186n4
Li, Xiaofeng, 174
Liang, Jianjun, 187n7
Liang, Qichao, 175
*Life in a Day*, 102n6
*Like Stone Lions at the Gateway Into Night*, 12
Lin, Xi, 174
Lisbon, 13, 43, 46, 213, 220
Lithuania, 39, 57, 58, 60, 61
Lledo, Jean Pierre, 63
local, 3, 4, 32, 76, 78, 85, 93, 102n4, 119, 120n5, 149, 160, 161–6, 178, 179, 185, 186n4, 212
Łódź, 11, 70, 71
London, 2, 3, 29, 33, 46, 72, 100
*London*, 100
looking *see* gaze
*Looking for my Birthplace*, 63

loom, 11, 70–87
*Loom, The*, 75
Lopate, Phillip, 38, 60
loss, 14–15n1, 62, 63, 66, 72, 81, 134, 136, 142, 145–8, 147, 204, 208, 219, 221
*Lost, Lost, Lost*, 46, 55, 56–63, 65, 67n3
*Lovers in Time or How We Didn't Get Arrested in Harare*, 12, 138–53
Lu, Pan, 30, 31
Lukács, Georg, 41, 42–3
Lumière Brothers, 44–5, 47
Lynch, David K., 117

Ma, Li, 174
MacDonald, Kevin, 102n6
McQueen, Steve, 12, 162
machine(ry), 65, 75–6, 79, 82, 85–6, 113–14, 115, 118, 180, 181, 184
Makuwe, Stanley, 153
*Man with a Movie Camera*, 7, 42, 82
Manchester(s), 11, 70–87
Mann, Thomas, 39
Mao, Chenyu, 174, 176
map(ping), 21, 72, 81, 86, 93–4, 97–101, 122, 124, 196, 199–200, 202, 207, 211
Marcuse, Herbert, 8
margin(al), 5, 9, 14, 196–8, 203–4
Marker, Chris, 6, 23–4, 28, 34, 37, 38, 82–3, 107, 114, 117–19, 120n1, 125, 164–5, 170n5, 172, 177, 178, 197, 201, 203
Marx(ist), 7, 8, 9, 67n2, 72, 85–6, 95, 146
*Masters in Forbidden City*, 187n7
material agency, 78, 80
Matisse, Henri, 44
Mazhetese, Anthony, 152
media, 3, 9, 199, 202, 204
 digital, 14, 46, 67, 129, 176, 226–7
*Megacities*, 98
Mekas, Jonas, 3, 8, 10, 36–50, 55, 56–62, 65, 67–8
melancholia, 145–6
Melitopoulos, Angela, 3, 56, 63, 64–5
*Melody of the World*, 89–90
*Memories of the Eichmann Trial*, 214
*Memories of Underdevelopment*, 34
memory, 4, 5, 11, 12, 13–14, 37–8, 63–4, 74, 77, 82, 85, 107, 119, 122–36, 138, 142, 146, 165, 168, 219, 221, 226
 as motor of images, 107–20

243

INDEX

meta-cinema, 50n7, 169
metaphor, 45, 46, 76, 83, 86, 94, 134, 143, 146–7, 160–1, 165–6, 168–70, 180, 182, 195
method, 14, 40, 46, 74, 78, 81, 119, 133, 136, 161–2, 169–70, 173, 178, 186, 208n7, 212
*Miasma, Plants, Export Painting*, 30
Michelangelo, 27–8, 39
migrant, 55–68, 111
migration, 10, 55–68, 72, 77
minimalism, 12
minority cinema, 65
minor literature, 65
mise-en-abyme, 76, 77, 78
mobility, 3, 31, 67, 72, 79, 134
modernity, 1, 10, 11, 14, 89, 98, 100, 133–6, 178, 180, 184
Modi, Narenda, 79
Mongolia, 12, 179–80, 184–5
Montaigne, Michel de, 6, 37, 38, 40, 41, 50n8, 55, 57, 60, 61, 144, 175
montage, 4, 5, 7, 25, 29, 80, 82, 84, 118, 119, 195, 199, 204, 206–7, 217, 219–20
Monteiro, Anjali, 75–6, 82, 86
*Motivos de Berta, Los*, 44
Moullet, Luc, 3, 11, 94–6, 101
mourning, 13, 41, 142, 146, 194, 204, 211, 220–4
Mugabe, Robert, 146, 153
Mun, Jeong-Hyun, 10, 56, 63
Murnau, F. W., 46, 109
Museum of Innocence, 122, 124, 125–6, 130, 132
*Museum of Innocence, The*, 11, 122, 125, 136
*My Family, One Person*, 42
*My Stills 1952–2002*, 214
*Mysterious Object at Noon*, 111
mythology, 66, 112, 120n1

*Nabua*, 113
*Nabua Song*, 113, 120n8
Naficy, Hamid, 10, 55, 56, 61, 63, 65, 74, 178
Nagib, Lúcia, 4, 40
name, 220–3
Nancy, Jean-Luc, 147
*Nanook of the North*, 47
narration, 30, 37, 46, 102n6, 122–8, 177, 182, 201, 212, 216, 219, 221
*Native Problem in Queensland, The* 205

Nehanda, Mbuya, 144, 146
New American Cinema, 8, 44
New York, 3, 27, 43, 46–8, 57–61, 220
Newie, Michaelangelo, 205–6
*News from Home*, 63
*News from Ideological Antiquity: Marx/Eisenstein/Capital*, 7
Nguyen, Trinh Thi, 3, 9, 21–7
Nietzsche, Friedrich, 66, 85
*Night and Fog*, 6
*Nihao Yuandian*, 176
*Nine Muses, The*, 10, 53, 63, 66–7
Njagu, Joe, 144, 148, 150–2
*No Man's Zone*, 12, 159–71
nomad, 40, 49, 50n5, 62, 76, 179–80, 184–5
non-western, 2, 4, 9–10, 22, 33, 172, 186
*Nostalgia for the Light*, 63
notebook, 12, 49, 60, 63, 178, 211, 219–20
*Nothing But Time*, 7
*Nouvelle Vague see* French New Wave
*Nuberu Bagu*, 8
nuclear disaster, 48, 159–70
nude, 180, 217

observational, 12, 23–4, 127, 139, 176, 198–9, 207
Ogawa, Shinsuke, 31
Opium Wars, 28
oppression, 5, 169, 178
O'Rourke, Dennis, 198, 208n8
Oshima, Nagisa, 8
'other', the, 118, 139, 141, 148, 149, 153, 194, 196, 207, 212
Ottoman Empire, 64, 132
outsider, 26, 29, 203
*Out-Takes from the Life of a Happy Man*, 50n10
Ozu, Yasujirō, 43, 44, 47, 48

*paibi see* parallelism
painting, 27, 72, 78, 83, 84, 85, 120n9, 166–7, 184, 212, 213, 216, 217
palimpsest, 5, 11, 122, 128–9
Pamuk, Orhan, 122–36
Panofsky, Erwin, 90
*Paper Airplane*, 179
Parallel Cinema, 8
parallelism, 13, 173, 178, 195
Paris, 3, 6, 7, 13, 45, 50n2, 150, 211, 213, 220
*Paris Belongs to Us*, 140

244

*Passing Drama*, 56, 63, 64–5
*Passion of Joan of Arc*, 217
*Patience (After Sebald)*, 124
*Patria*, 32–3
*Pauline at the Beach*, 140
*Pearls and Savages*, 199
Peirce, Charles Sanders, 129
Peleshian, Atavazad, 8
pensive *see* reflectivity
Perec, Georges, 223n3
performative, 1, 5, 12, 61, 72–3, 80–1, 86, 113, 120n8, 193, 194, 204
Perlov, Anna, 220–1
Perlov, David, 3, 211–24
Perlov, Mira, 212–13, 215, 220, 223n5
*Petition*, 179, 181
photograph, 46, 78, 84, 102n8, 113, 122, 125, 126, 127, 128–34, 198, 212, 216–18, 220–2, 224n8
photography, 12, 24, 27, 30, 71, 72, 76, 90, 99, 120, 169, 177, 195, 202
Piketty, Thomas, 9
*Pineapple*, 11, 93–5
*pinfa dianying see* poor cinema
Piotrowska, Agnieszka, 3, 12, 138–53
plot, 5, 74, 124, 139–40, 213
poetic(s), 24, 60, 61–2, 72–3, 87, 99, 107, 164, 180, 182–4, 193, 194, 201, 212
 spectrepoetics, 85–6
point-of-view, 70, 78, 85, 94, 184, 199
Poland, 10, 43, 47, 70, 71, 73
Polley, Sarah, 148
polycentric, 4, 5–9, 40
polyphony, 73, 80, 129
polyvalent, 4, 21
poor cinema, 175–6, 179
portrait, 25, 59, 63, 127, 133, 159, 165, 185, 193, 197
Portuguese, 39, 218–20, 223n1
postcard, 30, 37–8, 40–1, 198, 212, 216–17
power relations, 31, 86, 147, 149, 153, 169, 174, 198, 199, 201–6, 208n11
practice-based research, 12, 72–3, 78, 87, 138–53
presence, 2, 25, 37–8, 40, 45, 59, 61, 75, 80, 93, 126, 144, 145, 162–5, 167–9, 177, 198, 203, 221, 224n7
*Primitive* project, 111–17
*Promised Land, The*, 71
propaganda, 30, 205, 214
prostitution, 98–9
protest, 1, 65–6, 169; *see also* resistance

Provoke Era, 169
proximity, 24, 194
*Purgatorio, A Journey into the Heart of the Border*, 63

*Qatsi* trilogy, 102n5
Qiong, Jiongjiong, 174
quest *see* journey
*Quince Tree Sun, The*, 42

race, 5, 30, 139, 142, 143, 149–53, 205
radiation, 166, 170
Ramos, Graciliano, 219
Rancière, Jacques, 5, 11, 108, 118–19
Rascaroli, Laura, 1, 2, 7, 8, 9, 10, 12, 21–35, 40–1, 56, 59, 61, 83, 92, 123, 124–5, 133, 164, 177, 178, 193–4, 199, 204, 208n1
Rashomon effect, 198
Ray, Satyajit, 8
Reading conference, 2, 143
real, the, 11, 37, 92, 109, 115, 117, 119, 127, 221, 223n2, 226–7
realism, 129, 199, 207–8
reality, 4–5, 6, 9, 25, 27, 30, 34, 37, 46–7, 48–9, 57, 90, 93–4, 97, 101, 108, 118–19, 120n1, 123–4, 129–30, 134, 147, 159, 172–3, 175–6, 178, 213
*Reassemblage*, 13, 194, 226–37
reconciliation, 146–7
reflectivity, 10, 11, 12, 14n1, 21, 22, 24, 25, 28, 32, 36–50, 57, 60, 66, 67, 68n3, 70, 73, 74–5, 92, 100, 108, 123, 126–9, 134, 136, 138–9, 164, 204, 206, 221
reflexivity, 11, 38, 59, 87, 139, 159, 170, 193–5, 201–7
refugee, 9, 26, 64, 76
Reggio, Godfrey, 102n5
reincarnation, 110–12
remediation, 202, 209
*Reminiscences of a Journey to Lithuania*, 58
*Reminiszenzen aus Deutschland*, 50n10
Renoir, Jean, 44
Renov, Michael, 37, 41, 46, 56–7
repatriation, 13, 194
representation, 38, 42, 67, 74, 81, 89–93, 97–101, 102n2, 111–12, 118, 159, 161, 169, 178, 184, 197–9, 203–4, 206, 208
resistance, 1–2, 5, 8, 14n1, 113, 120n8, 196, 199

Resnais, Alain, 6, 23, 117–19, 170n6, 172
responsibility, 2, 92, 176
Reyes, Rodrigo, 63
Richter, Hans, 107, 120n3, 193
Rio de Janeiro, 3, 13, 213, 218, 220, 223n1
ritual, 5, 73, 91, 142
*Rive Gauche see* French New Wave
Rivette, Jacques, 140
*Robinson in Ruins*, 125
*Robinson in Space*, 100, 125
Rocha, Glauber, 8
Rohmer, Éric, 140
Rosales, Jaime, 36, 41
Rosenchan, Nancy, 218
Rotha, Paul, 91–4, 101n3
*Rückenfigur*, 167
Rue de l'Aqueduc, 222
Ruiz, Raul, 62
Russia(n), 7, 98, 107, 162, 218
Ruttmann, Walter, 7, 89–90, 100

Saibai Islander, 198
Saksena, S. B., 75
*Salles, Walter*, 2
*Samsara*, 102n5
*sankhâra*, 114
*Sans Soleil*, 24, 29, 38, 82, 125, 127, 164, 165, 170n5, 197
*sanwen*, 172–88
São Paulo, 13, 213–14, 220
Sauper, Hubert, 98
Schiller, Friedrich, 108
*Secret Formula, The*, 8
Sekula, Allan, 3, 9, 11, 96–7, 102n8
Sekuru, Kaguvi, 146
Serra, Albert, 36, 42, 50n9
sexuality, 133–4, 152
Sha, Qing, 176
Shah, Haku, 71
Shah, Parthiv, 76
Shakespeare, William, 66
Shoah *see* Holocaust
shot, 10, 46, 59–60, 74, 76, 78, 84, 96, 109–11, 116–18, 126, 130, 160–3, 165, 170n2, 180, 184–5, 195–6, 198–200, 202, 204–5, 207, 212, 216–17, 226
Shub, Esfir, 7
Shuji, Terayama, 39
Shuntaro, Tanikawa, 39
silence, 65, 143, 153, 164, 179–86, 227
silent film, 84–5, 199, 201–2

slowness, 2, 12, 14, 41, 66, 75, 77–8, 81, 109–11, 117–18, 160, 166, 180, 184, 227
Soderbergh, Steven, 102n9
Sokurov, Alexandr, 167
Solanas, Fernando, 7, 8
*Sorrow*, 217
sound, 8, 11, 23, 27, 30, 49, 58–9, 60, 64, 66, 78–81, 83, 109–10, 116, 118, 141, 179, 180–1, 194–5, 202, 205, 215–16, 218, 227
space, 2, 23, 30–1, 32, 34, 49, 67, 74, 76, 78, 89, 91, 97, 99–100, 107–8, 109, 112, 113–15, 120n8, 122–36, 147–8, 168, 175–7, 179, 180, 184, 186, 187, 197, 203, 205, 213, 217, 223n4
'third space', 12, 100–1, 199–200, 207, 226
*Stalker, The*, 167
state, 10, 12, 25, 35, 62, 67, 71, 72, 73, 79, 113–14, 132, 142, 145, 162, 164, 167–70, 174, 176, 186, 211, 213, 215, 216–17
State of Queensland, 196, 200, 208n3
*Statues Also Die*, 23
*Statues meurent aussi, Les*, 23
Steyerl, Hito, 9
*Still Life*, 12, 162
*Stone Time Touch*, 63
*Stories We Tell*, 148
storytelling, 4, 72, 86, 94, 136, 148–9, 163
*Stranger Here*, 223n3
stream-of-consciousness, 216–17
Su, Shi, 182
subjectivity, 10, 25, 27, 29, 32, 37, 56, 57, 61, 65, 67, 81–2, 83, 92, 123, 125, 127, 139, 149, 159, 162, 170, 173, 174–5, 177, 186, 193, 197, 199, 202, 204, 205–6, 207, 208n2
suffering, 48, 114, 142, 145, 159
*suibi*, 175, 176
*Sunless see Sans Soleil*
*sunnata*, 120n4
supply chain, 11, 97, 98
Suri, Sandhya, 63, 64
*Surname Viet Given Name Nam*, 63, 178
survivor, 13, 161, 168, 187n7, 213, 221, 226
*sutradhar*, 86
Svilova, Elizaveta, 82
*Syndromes and a Century*, 12, 118, 162

Tagore, Rabindranath, 66
Takeuchi, Kota, 164–5, 170
*Talking Broken*, 13, 193–208
Tarkovsky, Andrei, 34, 167
Tarr, Béla, 117
Tel Aviv, 13, 211–24
temporality, 5, 13, 74, 129, 134, 227
TEPCO, 161–2
territory, 40, 46, 124, 133
testimony, 125, 127, 129, 223n4
texture, 11, 74, 75, 79, 80, 81, 86, 141, 166
*That's My Face*, 63
theatre, 5, 39, 86, 108, 111–18, 141, 143–9, 165, 176, 185, 195, 223n2
theory, 6, 7, 8, 9, 14, 22–3, 32, 55, 61, 73, 138, 141, 142, 145, 169
   montage theory *see* montage
*There is No Ithaka*, 68n4
Third Cinema, 8, 119
Thomas, Dylan, 66
Thoreau, Henry David, 47, 49, 58
*Todas las cartas see Complete Letters*
*Together*, 188n16
Tokyo, 3, 24, 48, 64, 161
tomb, 185, 218, 220–1
*Tombstone Opening, The*, 13, 194
Torossian, Gariné, 63
Torres Strait Islander, 193–208
totality, 11, 89–92, 97, 100, 160
touch, 78–9, 80, 131, 147–8
tourism, 198, 202
traceability, 89–101
*Train of Shadows*, 44
transformation, 11, 30, 35, 100, 110, 112, 115, 119, 123, 125, 126–36, 147, 175
translation, 90, 132, 173, 178, 218
transmedial, 11, 12, 107–8, 111
transnational, 3, 5, 6–7, 10, 14, 15n6, 40, 55–6, 63–7, 72, 78, 81, 101, 133, 169, 173, 178, 196, 227
trauma, 5, 11, 12, 48, 65, 67, 142–7, 148–9, 153, 159, 168, 170n6, 213, 217, 221–3, 226
   eco-trauma cinema, 160, 165, 170n1
*Tren de sombras*, 44
Trinh, Minh-ha T., 3, 23, 13–14, 62, 63, 153, 178, 194, 226–37
trope, 13, 72, 74, 78, 101, 134, 166, 194–6, 199–202, 205, 207
*Tropical Malady*, 109
Truffaut, François, 6

truth, 29, 32, 34, 90, 129, 165, 195
Tsai, Ming-liang, 118
Tsuchiya, Yutaka, 39
tsunami, 159–70
*Twenty Two*, 187n7

*Uncle Boonmee Who Can Recall His Past Lives*, 109–11, 117
*Updated Diaries 1990–1999*, 13, 214, 221
*Uttarayan*, 79

Van der Keuken, Johan, 34
Van Gogh, Vincent, 217
Varda, Agnès, 82–3, 125, 172, 178
vernacular, 5, 175, 177, 179, 187n10
Vernant, Jean-Pierre, 221
Vertov, Dziga, 7, 42, 45, 82
Vietnam, 1, 9, 13, 22, 25–7, 178, 226–37
*Vietnam the Movie*, 25–6
Vigo, Jean, 7
visible, 5–6, 7, 11, 13, 15n9, 23, 25, 45, 80, 89–101, 108, 118, 160, 162, 184, 216–17, 222
voice, 3, 5, 7, 9, 11, 22, 26, 29, 30, 31, 46, 58–9, 61–2, 72, 78, 81, 83, 85, 86–7, 108, 115, 125, 139, 142, 147, 162–4, 168–9, 170n5, 173–8, 181, 194, 199, 201–4, 214, 220, 221
voice-over, 25, 28–9, 30–1, 37–8, 45–6, 49, 59–60, 86, 96, 112, 113, 115, 124–36, 163–4, 166, 170n3, 181–2

Wajda, Andrzej, 71
*Walden: Diaries, Notes and Sketches*, 8, 44
*Walk*, 170n3
Wang, Bo, 3, 10, 27–31, 187n13
Wang, Nanfu, 187n13
Warburg, Aby, 217, 223n6
*We*, 8
Weerasethakul, Apichatpong, 3, 11, 12, 107–19, 120, 162, 170n3, 178
*Weltanschauung*, 3
*Where Is the Friend's Home?*, 42
*Whores' Glory*, 98
Wilde, Oscar, 89, 100
Wills, Adrian, 196
windows, 46, 109, 112, 212, 213–14, 222, 224n10
Wiseman, Frederick, 31

247

witness, 1, 56, 58, 98, 129, 141, 162, 214, 220, 223n3
*Workingman's Death*, 98
world cinema, 1–9, 14, 15, 39–40, 56, 70, 73, 74–5, 80, 89, 93, 101, 172, 195–6
*World of Plenty*, 93–4
*World Without End*, 92
Wright, Basil, 92
Wu, Wenguang, 174, 176

Xi, Jinping, 173
*xiaoping*, 175
*xinwenti*, 175

Yiddish, 214–15, 218
*yingxiang xiezuo see* 'image writing'
Yom Kippur, 213, 214, 224n9
*Yungbogi's Diary*, 8

Zaatari, Akram, 9
Zeughauskino, 2
Zhang, Xianmin, 187n5
Zhangke, Jia, 12, 162
Zhao, Liang, 3, 12, 172, 173, 179–88
Zimbabwe, 139, 141–3, 146–7
Žižek, Slavoj, 9
Zuchuat, Oliver, 12

EU representative:
Easy Access System Europe
Mustamäe tee 50, 10621 Tallinn, Estonia
Gpsr.requests@easproject.com